Cyprus—War and Adaptation

A Psychoanalytic History of Two Ethnic
Groups in Conflict

Cyprus—War and Adaptation

A Psychoanalytic History of Two Ethnic
Groups in Conflict

Vamık D. Volkan, M.D.
Professor of Psychiatry
University of Virginia Medical Center

University Press of Virginia
Charlottesville

THE UNIVERSITY PRESS OF VIRGINIA
Copyright © 1979 by the Rector and Visitors
of the University of Virginia

Foreword copyright © 1979 by John
    E. Mack, M.D.

First published 1979
Reprinted 1980

Library of Congress Cataloging in Publication Data
Volkan, Vamık.
    Cyprus—war and adaptation.
    Includes bibliographical references and indexes.
    1. Turks in Cyprus—Psychology. 2. Cyprus—History—Cyprus crisis, 1974–
3. Cyprus—Social conditions. 4. Social conflict—Case studies. I. Title.
DS54.9.V64   301.45′1095645   78-57512
ISBN 0-8139-0775-6

Printed in the United States of America

In memory of my father,
whose love for walking in the
fields of Cyprus was restricted
in his last years of life, when
he became one of the "caged birds
of Cyprus"

Contents

Foreword

It may be argued that there is no psychohistory, but only history. The noted historian Jacques Barzun has warned students against expecting from psychology or any other allied discipline easier answers to history's complex questions. The study of history cannot, he writes, be anything "except the old familiar search for documents and the play of imagination and judgment upon them."[1]

Yet historians have always appreciated the power of human will and emotion to influence events. The ambition and fear, the pain and desire of individual human beings have been recognized since ancient times as important agencies in the determination of historical change. "It is evident" Barzun wrote, "that all the studies which deal with man's activities are branches of psychology" (p. 22). Less well appreciated, perhaps, and surely not as well understood, have been the ways in which the psychology of large groups may influence historical events.

Among such groups none are more important for history than those who are united by language, custom, racial characteristics, and an intense attachment to a particular geographic land area, to make up a distinct nationality. But until recently insights about the role of individual and collective psychological forces in the study of history have been offered to a large degree haphazardly, according to the interest, availability of materials, suitability of subject matter, and psychological gifts and orientation of particular historians. Whereas a historian might willingly acknowledge his concentration or expertise in the economic or military aspects of history, he would be unlikely to claim that he was a psychologi-

---

1. Jacques Barzun, *Clio and the Doctors: Psycho-history, Quanto-history, and History* (Chicago: University of Chicago Press, 1974), p. 4.

cally minded, much less a "psycho"-historian, however much he might base his interpretation of events upon the motives of this or that leader or the national characteristics of a particular people.

This is changing now, especially since the work of Erik Erikson. Among historians there are quite a number who recognize not only that psychological factors are important for history but that special training and study are necessary to use psychological data accurately and effectively. Similarly, psychiatrists, psychoanalysts, and psychologists who seek to study biographical and other historical subjects are recognizing increasingly the importance of the political and cultural context and the cautions and restraints which must be applied to the use of psychological evidence obtained from both documents and interviews.

Nations, even more than individuals, have difficulty accepting responsibility for aggression, and prefer to stress the pain of their histories, the provocations which gave rise to warlike acts, their experience as victims, and the resulting justifications for their hostile behavior. Rarely does a people acknowledge, for example, the aggression which must lie behind the establishment of itself as a new nation or its expansion to fulfill the collective myth of its territorial destiny. Yet such achievements can hardly be accomplished except at the expense, even the destruction, of another people.

In this book Vamık Volkan reviews psychoanalytic contributions to the study of international conflict and shows that such contributions as do exist are not based on actual studies of conflict situations. The case study approach, as employed by Freud and his followers, which has yielded such monumental contributions to the understanding of individual psychology, has rarely been applied to actual instances of intergroup conflict, and hardly ever to problems of inter-nation strife.

Volkan's study is a unique, pioneering exception. Advantageously suited for this work by virtue of his Turkish and Cypriot background, Dr. Volkan is, in addition, a gifted psychoanalytic clinical practitioner and theorist, who has already made significant contributions to the psychoanalytic theory of human relationships. He has familiarized himself fully with the political and cultural history of Cyprus in its Greek as well as its Turkish dimension. This work is, therefore, without precedent as a study in depth of the psychology of two ethnic groups engaged in a historical conflict. There is to my knowledge no study of the collective psychology of war that is anything like it.

Freud wrote like an early discoverer, identifying vast regions, as yet unexplored, to which the science he developed might someday make a contribution. The problem of conflict between ethnic groups was one such region. In *Civilization and Its Discontents*, published in 1930, Freud wrote: "it is precisely communities with adjoining territories, and related to each other in other ways as well, who are engaged in constant feuds and in ridiculing each other—like the Spaniards and Portuguese, for instance, the North Germans and South Germans, the English and Scotch, and so on. I gave this phenomenon the name of 'the narcissism of minor differences,' a name which does not do much to explain it."[2] One could readily add to such a list, English and Irish, Indians and Pakistani, Arabs and Jews, and Turks and Greeks, especially on the island of Cyprus where their proximity has been so close.

Freud's passing attention to the problem of conflict between national groups suggested that its psychological aspect belongs, broadly speaking, in the area of narcissism. By this is meant that the hostility which so readily erupts between such groups derives from the effect over time that the proximity of one group has had upon the way the members of another group feel about themselves, individually and collectively. Hostility, as the contemporary psychoanalyst Gregory Rochlin has written, arises in defense of the self.[3] Another individual or a group is likely to be perceived as an enemy when that person or group, rightly or wrongly, is seen as threatening the worth or the survival of the self.

In his study of the historical conflict between Greeks and Turks on the island of Cyprus, Dr. Volkan confronts many aspects of the

2. Sigmund Freud, "Civilization and Its Discontents" (1930), in *The Standard Edition of the Complete Psychological Works of Sigmund Freud*, 21 (London: Hogarth Press, 1961): 114.

3. Gregory Rochlin, *Man's Aggression: The Defense of the Self* (Boston: Gambit, 1973).

narcissism of inter-nation conflict. Some of these areas he has been able to explore fully. Where his material has not permitted a full examination, he has indicated the directions in which future work must go. No work in this field from now on can, I believe, afford to ignore his contribution. I shall attempt here to list the principal aspects of conflict between ethnic groups, as set forth or suggested in this study, upon which psychoanalytic understanding may shed light.

1. *The identity of self and nation.* The emotional relationship between the individual and the nation—or the idea of the nation—overrides all of the dimensions of interethnic conflict.[4] The individual human being derives much of his sense of self and self worth from identification with a nation, with its people, language, and customs, and, above all, with a land defined by definite borders. Boundaries, walls, enclaves, and cages, as this study shows, take on powerful meanings if they come to be related to the continuity and dimensions of the self.

The self-esteem of a people rises and falls with the fate of its nation. A people who define themselves as comprising a nation, or an emerging one, but who cannot give it geographic actuality, live in a constant condition of injured self-regard and inner rage. The nation and the idea of the self are in many ways fused. A political leader may intensify and cement this attachment, this identity of self and nation, if he can effectively represent to the people nationalistic ideals with which they can identify at a personal, emotional level.

Primitive meanings (not pathological) of motherhood and fatherhood are contained in the idea of the country or nation. The nation serves fundamental caring, protective, and guiding needs which relate to the basic security of the individual and the governance of the self. Any political thinker who seeks a fellowship of all mankind beyond allegiances to nation states must recognize the psychological meaning of the identity of the self with the nation. Failure to do so will limit such concepts as the "brotherhood of man" to philosophical and utopian visions and imaginings.

4. Group for the Advancement of Psychiatry, the Committee on International Relations, Report: "Self Involvement in the Middle East Conflict" (in press).

2. *The problem of historical grievances.* As Dr. Volkan shows in this book, the Greeks and Turks on Cyprus have a history of strife, which has grown out of their proximity to each other. In their case the history is relatively short—only four centuries—but it is a period filled with tragedy and conflict, with conquest, war, and victimization. The contemporary conflict on Cyprus, as in any similar struggle between two ethnic groups, must be seen in the context of the accumulated memories and historical hurts which each people has experienced at the hands of the other. As in the case of the individual, the memories of actual hurt have mingled for a whole people with fantasies of injury at the hands of the other. Each nation has monuments, living and dead (see Chapter VII), which not only embody the losses of the war just fought, or the hurts just suffered, but represent the accrued griefs of the centuries. Furthermore, where the suffering has been as intense as it has on Cyprus, and the injuries sustained so profound, the other side readily becomes the object of blame for tragedies and hurts for which it cannot be altogether responsible.

Thus, in the case of conflict between ethnic groups, there is a history of *real* hurts and atrocities for which ample evidence is easily found—the archives of documents (especially photographs) and memory—to which a people may convincingly point to justify the perpetuation of an attitude of hostility toward the other people. Scholarly historical works when written by members of one ethnic group or the other, even when they are of the highest quality, are rarely of value in clarifying the "facts" or "realities" of the conflict. For such studies are very likely to reflect the effort, often unconscious, of each historian to construct the conflict, to tell his country's story, in a fashion which will place blame on the other people and redound to the credit of his own. In such works, the superiority and innocence of one's own people and the inferiority and aggressive intransigence of the other are likely, however subtly, to emerge.

3. *The intergenerational transmission of attitudes toward the "other."* Mothers, fathers, older siblings, and other relatives begin from infancy to transmit through what they tell their children, by verbal nuance and through a variety of nonverbal gestures and

other cues, attitudes toward the other ethnic group which is gradually, but inevitably, incorporated into the thinking of the next generation of children. Later, teachers, media personalities, politicians, and other adults will underscore and contribute to these
early attitudes. Dr. Volkan describes how a Turkish mother "is apt
to sanction the anxiety of her child about a Greek visitor who had
been a target of her own externalization of the unwanted parts of
herself and her internalized world." If admiration toward another
ethnic group is conveyed, it is likely to be mixed with jealousy and
hostility. Children are thus consciously and unconsciously drawn
into the process of inter-nation conflict by adults and older children.
Because children constitute the richest resource that a society
possesses for the conduct of its future wars, governments may
be reluctant to permit the systematic study of the mechanisms
whereby their country's young people incorporate the elements of
national identity, especially political attitudes, into their emerging
self-concepts.

4. *Splitting, externalizing, and mirroring: the demonization of
the "other."* An Israeli journalist said recently: "We aren't fighting
each other. We fight masks of the devil that each side has painted
on the other." There is a human tendency to displace onto others,
to split away and externalize the negative aspects of oneself, the
dimensions one wishes not to acknowledge, or for which one will
not or cannot take responsibility. Disacknowledged aspects of the
self may be reflected or mirrored by the other. Volkan writes,
"Cypriot Turks make Cypriot Greeks the target of their externalization of 'all bad' self- and object representations." Virtue is the
possession of oneself or one's group. Evil resides in the other. At
a one-to-one level individuals whom one knows only slightly if at
all are the most convenient objects of externalization, especially
if there has been some real or imagined suffering at that person's
hands. In one-to-one relationships actual contact in a constructive
atmosphere may undercut such externalization or scapegoating.

In the case of large groups, especially national groups which
have lived in close proximity, there are several factors that favor
the unrestrained use of the other for splitting and externalization.
Ambiguities of good and evil are difficult to see. The recognition

of shared blame becomes virtually impossible. *First*, there is, generally, support and encouragement on the part of political leaders, the mass media, and other opinion makers for the negative or devalued view of the other people as a group. When the devaluation of an ethnic group becomes a matter of national policy, especially when directed by a demagogic leader, mass murder and genocide are likely to eventuate. *Second*, historically enforced and reinforced isolation of national groups from each other prevents the modification of the perception of the other which reality and reason might provide. Their confinement in enclaves fostered for Turkish Cypriots perceptions of the Greeks outside which supported a secure world view and bolstered the self-esteem of Turks, but which subjected them to later shocks. Once freed from the enclaves, as Dr. Volkan points out, "this world has now gone, and its inhabitants were faced with the humiliating recognition that a prosperous Greek life-style confronted them on every hand." *Third*, there is no equivalent at a group or collective level to the superego restraints which can operate at an individual level to curb hostile or violent impulses. *Fourth*, the history of inter-nation warfare, suffering, and actual mutual victimization provides a nearly endless supply of justification to confirm the view of the other people as vicious and barbaric, or otherwise hateful and less than human. *Finally*, the continuing existence of conflicting interests, such as disputes over land and boundaries, or the perpetuation of actual threats to national security which each side represents to the other fosters psychological regression and the emergence of splitting, externalization, and other primitive collective psychological mechanisms. All of the above factors, which promote the hateful devaluing of one people by another, may result more readily if aspects of child-rearing or of a society's family life foster externalization of the superego or of authority in general. However, this need not be the case. For it would appear that the collective forces favoring the mechanisms of devaluation between peoples who have a traditional and historical enmity are often so powerful as to obliterate, or vastly reduce, the relative importance of individual psychological factors in the maintenance of the hostile relationship.

A final element which favors the externalization and demonization of another people is difficult to categorize. This concerns the role of collective myths of good and evil, which develop over decades and centuries. The myth of the Jews as devils was developed by Christian Europe in the Middle Ages over a period of more than a thousand years and resulted in extensive persecutions. A similar fantasy/myth of cults of unmitigatedly evil witches grew up in the late Middle Ages in central Europe. Its origins may be traced back to ancient times. Volkan discusses some of the pagan and monotheistic elements in the history of the Greek and Turkish peoples on Cyprus which may have favored the mythic demonization of these peoples by each other. Historical myths which are adhered to explicitly, or remain latent within a society, furnish at the same time both a repository of primitive hostility and a collective sanction for externalization which has the coherent authority of history and the apparent sanction of God. They exert a powerful regressive influence on the minds of a people.

5. *The egoism of victimization.* It is remarkable how little empathy is felt by national groups for the suffering of their traditional enemies, even if the victimization on the other side is palpably evident and comparable to or greater than one's own. Certainly there are exceptions, but these stand out poignantly and are sometimes recorded because they are so noteworthy, or are ennobled in works of literature. The lack of empathy, the inability to identify with the anguish experienced by the members of a national group toward whom one bears hostile feelings, removes one of the central deterrents to the waging of war.

Not all of the reasons for this lack of empathy are well understood. Certainly the feeling of justification for hatred because of past grievances buttresses the hostility among individuals within the group and for the group collectively. The experience of traumatization has an additional effect which I would call *the egoism of victimization.* This is the tendency, which severe hurt and grief seem inevitably to bring about, to direct all investment, all empathy and love, toward those of one's immediate circle of fellow sufferers, defined generally in no broader terms than oneself and one's own afflicted people. Conversely any investment of caring in the other side is withdrawn. There is, as Alexander and Margarete Mitscherlich have noted in their study of postwar Germany, "an isolated regret for only one's own losses."[5] The value of one's own group is thus enhanced; the value of the other is reduced. The egoism of victimization thus has two fundamental interrelated aspects: the justification of continuing hostility on the grounds of having been victimized by the other, and the narcissistic focusing of empathy upon one's own people with the consequent inability to identify with the suffering of the other group.

Fear that one's people will once more be attacked by the other, will once again become victims, perpetuates a hostile vigilance and an unwillingness to take risks.[6] It is for this reason that intervention of third-party groups, whose members are able to appreciate the ambiguities of the situation and the humanity and worth on both sides, may be essential if the cycle of repeated wars between two ethnic groups caught in a web of hostility is to be interrupted. Third-party nations may, of course, exploit the conflict for their own national purposes, a phenomenon which is readily observed in many parts of the world today.

6. *War as Therapy*. Churchill's famous remark that there is nothing so exhilarating as to be fired upon without result captures the hearty enthusiasm with which men may engage in war despite all the horrors which they bring about. "The only time members of my family have ever been happy, brave, successful, was in time of war," declares the contemporary southern grail-seeker in Walker Percy's novel, *Lancelot*.[7] Dr. Volkan provides a detailed discussion of the curative value which the 1974 war had for the Turks on Cyprus, and he also reviews similar phenomena in the literature dealing with the psychology of warfare. War converts passivity and victimization into aggression and mastery. Worthless losers become glorious victors. Group purpose, a higher sense of one's collective and national cohesion, is achieved. The war leader be-

5. Alexander Mitscherlich and Margarete Mitscherlich, *The Inability to Mourn: Principles of Collective Behavior* (New York: Grove Press, 1975), p. 41.

6. Alexander Mitscherlich, "Psychoanalysts and the Aggression of Large Groups," *Int. J. Psychoanal.* 52 (1971):165.

7. Walker Percy, *Lancelot* (New York: Avon, 1978), p. 146.

comes elevated as a symbolic national hero (Ecevit, for example). There are indeed few national heroes who are not war heroes. The Egyptian newspapers heralded the 1973 Arab-Israeli war as a great victory, although it was a bloody affair that was in reality a tragedy for both peoples. When I was in Egypt in January 1978, our group was told that the 1973 war was a political success for Egypt as it restored the sense of national self-regard that had been so damaged in previous wars against Israel. There is much still to be learned of the purgative value of war, and of the relationship between success or failure in battle and the self-esteem of individuals and nations.

7. *Aggression and the inability to mourn.* As noted earlier the self-esteem of individuals is deeply affected by identification with the valued, cohesive entity of a nation-group and its collective purposes. Such elevation of self-worth is particularly intense if the nation is led by a charismatic leader who is seen as embodying in his words and deeds the most cherished values of the people and their country. The nation's military victories, as well as its defeats, inevitably create losses which must be mourned.

As Dr. Volkan writes of so movingly in this book, the losses with which the survivors of war must contend are not only of one's own people. The evidences of the enemy dead or vanquished must be confronted as well. The Turkish victors in northern Cyprus were faced with the inescapable physical evidence of the Greeks who had been killed in the 1974 war or had been forced to abandon their homes and places of work. Some mourning by the Turkish population for these victims among their enemies seems to have occurred in the three years following the war, which may bode well for future relations between these peoples. For mourning requires the acknowledgment of the humanness of the enemy, the realization that he possesses some worth. It means an assumption of responsibility for the painful fact that whether the acts of aggression were justified or not, other people have been destroyed or injured as a result of one's own aggression.

But there are instances—perhaps this is the commoner situation—where little or no mourning for the victims of one's own people's aggression against another ethnic group can take place.

This is likely to be the case where the aggressions committed have been so barbaric that to take responsibility for them would deeply damage a nation's view of itself, would be so shattering to the nation's self-regard as to produce a collective melancholia. Such has been the case in postwar Germany, as discussed by Alexander and Margarete Mitscherlich in their book *The Inability to Mourn.* Mourning for the victims among one's enemies is also defended against when a situation of continuing hostility and fear of attack persists and perpetuates distrust. The mobilization of self-justifying mechanisms is then employed to devalue the purposes and humanity of the other side.

I shall conclude with a word about the challenges and pitfalls that face investigators who undertake to write of the psychological dimensions of international conflict, indeed who choose to work in virtually any aspect of this field. There is to begin with the difficult methodological problem of finding a sound conceptual balance among the relevant insights of individual and group psychology in a field where realities are multilayered and compelling. But beyond this there are profound personal issues which are raised for the psychiatrist or psychologist who involves himself in the field of international relations.

He or she is not likely to become meaningfully involved unless there is some affinity with one or more of the ethnic groups involved in the conflict, unless the conflict *matters* personally at some level. Indeed membership in (or immediate descent from) one of the groups can facilitate an understanding of the psychology of that group and of its history and culture which it is not possible for someone outside of the culture to duplicate.

Searching challenges to one's personal identity are inevitably encountered in doing this work. "Who are you?" and "where do you stand?" are questions frequently encountered from those one meets in the course of an investigation in a foreign culture. These questions become much more than the clichés they often can be in a social or even a clinical context. Profound questions arise concerning the legitimacy of one's motives for being "involved." Old uncertainties about one's origins and historical being are evoked that invite a great deal of personal self-examination or reexamination. Too deep an identification with the sufferings and nationalistic aspirations of one party in a conflict may make it extremely difficult for the psychologist to retain the objectivity and detachment necessary for this work. The investigator becomes in some sense like the German sociologist George Simmel's "stranger," the marginal man, "at once near and remote, both at home and ill at ease in 'his' community," hence possessing "that rare quality, objectivity, a quality that those who really belong in a group are too deeply engaged to develop."[8] It is certainly advantageous for the investigator who is a member or descendant of one of the protagonists to have achieved some distance from the conflict, to have lived for sufficient time in another culture to have obtained considerable objectivity and perspective.

Dr. Volkan, as a psychiatrist and psychoanalyst of Turkish-Cypriot origins, who has lived and worked in the United States since 1957, is ideally suited for this work. Yet Dr. Volkan describes candidly in this book the profound questions of personal identity which he had to confront in the course of his investigations. I shall not anticipate for the reader what he tells of so candidly in the pages that follow. Dr. Volkan writes of the kinds of struggles that any investigator must confront who exposes himself to the psychological forces that dominate the conflicts between ethnic groups.

Finally, there is a problem, which may be unique to the psychology of political conflict, especially of international conflict, that deserves to be mentioned. One is dealing here with critical matters that involve the lives of great numbers of people. The psychologist's role, however modest—and it is vital that he recognize the limits of that role—may expose him to issues of great moment. He may, as was necessary for Dr. Volkan in this work, to have discussions with world leaders or other decision makers. This type of activity can easily threaten the balance or orientation of the investigator, who may be unaccustomed in his usual clinical or administrative work to functioning in the midst of such heady matters. Personal psychoanalysis or other efforts at deep self-knowledge

8. Peter Gay, *Freud, Jews, and Other Germans: Masters and Victims in Modernist Culture* (New York: Oxford University Press, 1978), p. 123.

do not generally provide by themselves sufficient awareness or mastery of the areas of narcissism or unconscious grandiosity which may be stimulated by work in the field of international relations. Dr. Volkan's evident grace, the tact and humility with which he moves from a discussion of meetings with Cypriot and Turkish leaders to a detached application of psychoanalytic theoretical concepts, makes this exacting work seem much easier than it really is. I know of no clinical work in which the injunction to know oneself is so compelling.

JOHN E. MACK, M.D.
Professor of Psychiatry
Harvard Medical School at
The Cambridge Hospital

Preface

It is ironic that the Mediterranean island of Cyprus has been the setting for so many bloody and brutal dramas throughout its long history, for it was once known as the birthplace of Aphrodite, the goddess of love. After falling under the sway of one conqueror after another over the centuries it became at last an independent republic in 1960, and it might have been supposed that the final goal of a colorful and complicated evolutionary course had at last been attained, and, with it, peace.

During the last four hundred years two ethnic groups have lived side by side on the island, the majority being Greeks and the minority, Turks. The establishment by law of the Republic of Cyprus did not, however, bring them together. No Cypriot nation resulted because each group adhered to an allegiance to its mother country on the mainland. The historical events that make the background of this book took place between Christmas 1963, when interethnic hostilities broke out on the island, until early 1978, three-and-a-half years after Turkish forces from the mainland took over the northern part of Cyprus.

In the summer of 1968 I returned to Cyprus for a visit after a dozen years spent in the United States. At that time the Turkish population of the island had been living for five years confined within crowded enclaves under the protection of troops assigned by the United Nations. On my arrival in the airport at Nicosia I was whisked to the enclave in that city where my relatives were living. To my surprise I found that parakeets were being raised everywhere, hundreds of them being watched over in their cages by owners preoccupied with their well-being and fecundity. They were in homes, coffee shops, and even grocery stores. A guest, surrounded by cages even in the dining room, would be struck by the way in which the people seemed to have "merged" with their birds, and with the sound of constant chirping and birdsong mingled with human voices. Although this phenomenon seemed extraordinary to my wife and me, everyone else seemed to take it for granted. It put me in mind of the Turkish saying that the fish who live in the sea do not know what a sea is.

I came to realize that the birds represented a needy aspect of the people imprisoned in their enclaves, and this needy part had been externalized onto the busy little caged creatures. People psychologically and geographically limited were gratified to feel themselves omnipotent caretakers of a miniature population. As long as the birds were happy and fertile, the people could deny the hopelessness imposed on them by historical reality. It was this observation that led to my examination of an ethnic group's self-concept and its concept of the opposing group, as such patterns took form under different political and historical circumstances. Cyprus is, after all, only about 160 miles long and 40 wide, so its occupation by two strongly antagonistic groups makes it a laboratory for the study of those psychological processes that accompany and sometimes influence historical processes. Here I apply the psychoanalyst's clinical knowledge to the Cyprus problem, having found that recent developments in the theory of internalized object relations shed light on the interaction between opposing groups on Cyprus.

The plan to write this book evolved slowly after my 1968 visit, stimulated by the observations I made then. My enrollment in 1970 as a member of the American Psychiatric Association's Task Force on Psychiatry and Foreign Affairs encouraged me to focus more sharply on the interethnic group conflicts and processes on display in Cyprus. This task force, although heeding several other interests, gave considerable attention to Cyprus during the seven years of my membership prior to its termination, and I enjoyed many opportunities to discuss with fellow members my ideas about my homeland, which I visited again in 1973 and twice in 1974–75 while on sabbatical leave from the University of Virginia. My assumption then of a one-year visiting professorship at the University of Ankara took me back into that part of the world only a month after the Turkish intervention on the island. On the mainland I was able to interview Cypriot Turks who had come there, and when it became possible to go to Cyprus myself, I could study the mourning of those who had been through the war and their initial adaptation to all the conflict had involved. My first return to northern Cyprus was made as soon as feasible after the occupation; my second, six months later, coincided with the first anniversary of the Turkish intervention. In the summer of 1977 I went once again to the Turkish part of the island to observe adaptation three years after the war. As it happened, I was there at the time Makarios, a key figure in the history of contemporary Cyprus, died, and I observed the reactions of Cypriot Turks to this event.

After summarizing the history of the present Cyprus problem, I examine the way in which each of the two ethnic groups on Cyprus persists in seeing the other as a mirror image of itself, so that each becomes the recipient of the other's split-off and externalized, aggressively determined "bad" image. One can understand this by noting the child-rearing practices within the (modified) extended family pattern common to both cultures. This kind of relatedness between two groups demands the maintenance of psychological distance between them. Certain taboos fostered this separation and helped keep the surface of this complicated relationship smooth and group interaction relatively bland in spite of the close physical proximity in which Greeks and Turks lived in a small land. I suggest that the establishment of the Republic of Cyprus threatened to defeat the customary distancing maneuvers and led to feverish new attempts to externalize the "badness" of one group onto the other in a way that made it impossible for the two to meld. Although my attention is directed specifically to Cyprus here, I feel that conclusions drawn from the situation there can be usefully applied elsewhere where neighbors remain hostile in spite of sharing Lebensraum over time.

Life within the Turkish enclaves after the turbulence of 1963–64 exemplified "group narcissism" developed as a defensive adaptation to conceal the low self-esteem inflicted on the group by a struggle that had gone against them. The "walls" of such enclaves were psychologically significant props to the cohesion of the grandiose image shared by those confined within them. Each group had to adjust to a new upheaval with the Turkish occupation of the northern

part of the island in 1974. I point in this connection to the importance of the mourning process to all human adaptation, individual
or collective; and in the final chapter I discuss the impact on
my own self-concept of my involvement with the restless forces
in my birthplace.

I want to thank here the many people in many different countries
who have been helpful to me in various ways in the preparation of
this book.

In the United States: Although I am solely responsible for the
contents of this book, I acknowledge with gratitude the contribution
made to my store of knowledge and the shaping of my view by discussions of the Cyprus problems that took place in meetings of the
American Psychiatric Association's Task Force on Psychiatry and
Foreign Affairs and in its collaborative sessions with the Institute of
Psychiatry and Foreign Affairs, the Middle East Institute, the
Brookings Institution, and Princeton University's Near Eastern
group. Members of the task force all or part of the time from 1970
to 1977 were: Dr. William D. Davidson of Washington, D.C., presi-
dent of the Institute of Psychiatry and Foreign Affairs; Dr. Rita
Rogers, clinical professor of psychiatry at the University of California
in Los Angeles; Dr. Jerome Frank, professor of psychiatry at
Johns Hopkins University; Dr. James Tenzel, former assistant professor of psychiatry at the University of California in San Diego;
Dr. John Racy, associate professor of psychiatry at the University of
Rochester School of Medicine and Dentistry; Dr. John Mack,
professor of psychiatry and chief of psychiatry at Cambridge Hospital
in Cambridge, Massachusetts; Dr. Demetrios A. Julius, Medical
Officer of the National Institute of Drug Abuse, now temporarily
located in Iran.

I learned much also from Parker T. Hart, former Assistant Secretary of State for Near Eastern Affairs and former United States
Ambassador to Turkey, and from Dr. Kemal H. Elbirlik, a col-
league of mine at the University of Virginia Medical Center and
former Medical Director of Sişli French Hospital in Istanbul. Dr.
William Niederland of New York generously corresponded with me
on issues related to my study, particularly about manifestations of
the survivor syndrome. And I gratefully acknowledge the suggestions

of Norman Itzkowitz, professor of Near Eastern studies at Princeton University, who read the first draft of my manuscript.

In Turkey: I thank Süleyman Demirel, who was the prime minister of Turkey, for granting me an interview in his home in September 1975 and for sharing with me his views on the Cyprus problem. I am also grateful to Dr. Oğuz Aygün, who was at the time of my visit in 1975 a congressman from the district of Ankara, for making it possible for me to talk with some of Turkey's key statesmen.

Special gratitude goes to Dr. Abdülkadir Özbek, professor of psychiatry at the University of Ankara, who generously gave me time throughout my stay in Ankara, discussing at length the psychology of the Turkish people. Dr. Gıyas Ünsal, the chairman of the same department, was very kind in seeing that I could spend the necessary time collecting data on the situation in Cyprus. Drs. Cemal Elmas, Ergün Münir, Hasan Niyazi, Rifat Siber, and Celâl Tatlıcıoğlu—now young physicians but at the time of my studies medical students at the University of Ankara—not only made themselves available for personal interviews about their recollections of the days of conflict on the island but gave me much practical help in both Turkey and Cyprus as I carried out my study. Professor and Mrs. Cahit Örgen did much to make my sabbatical year in Turkey a most pleasant one.

I also gratefully acknowledge consultation with James McHenry of the University of Kansas, who during my stay in Turkey was a Fulbright Scholar in the political science department of the University of Ankara and actively engaged in collecting data about the life of Cypriot Turks under the British rule.

In England: I learned much from Ahmet Cemal Gazioğlu, who has written at some length about Cyprus, and from Kerim M. Kuzey, a medical student from Cyprus.

In Cyprus: I acknowledge with warm gratitude the kindness of Rauf R. Denktaş, the President of the Turkish Federated State of Cyprus, who granted me a long interview in March 1975 and who met with me again on three different occasions in the summer of 1977; he allowed me to conduct studies in the refugee resettlement areas of northern Cyprus during the spring and summer of 1975 and helped arrange for my return to the same area in 1977. Very special thanks go also to Ahmet N. Savalas, a high school classmate of mine who became one of the senior officials in the Denktaş administration. He helped me to visit Turkish-held areas of Cyprus where I could observe refugees beginning their new life. Without his official guidance I could not have conducted systematic interviews nor could I have found all of those I wanted to interview. Hasan Fehmi, a senior official in Mr. Denktaş's office and an interpreter, helped me to talk to the Cypriot Greeks who found themselves under Turkish rule in 1975. Dr. Kenan Atakol, Minister of Education and Cultural Affairs for the Turkish section, whom I first met when he was at the University of Virginia, was also very helpful.

Dr. Sezai Sezgin, another high school classmate, Director of the Turkish Mental Hospital in Nicosia, deserves special recognition. He was extremely generous in consulting with me, and I greatly value his professional help in understanding the psychological processes of the people. He also permitted me to interview those patients in his hospital whose emotional problems he felt had been triggered by psychohistorical events. Mr. and Mrs. İsmet V. Güney and Mr. and Mrs. Mehmet Münir made their homes available to me; I was able to work in great comfort there on my notes, and for this I am most grateful.

In Virginia: I also thank Dr. Norman Knorr, a psychiatrist and the Dean of the University of Virginia Medical School, for his kind assistance in the publication of this book. Larry Merkel, my medical student assistant with an anthropological background, was also helpful. Virginia Kennan, editorial assistant for the department of psychiatry at the University of Virginia, deserves credit not only for polishing my English and editing my manuscript, but also for making the work on it gratifying for me because of our most pleasant working alliance.

Lastly, I want to say that historical outcomes are, of course, influenced by many factors altogether beyond the purview of the psychoanalyst. My purpose is a limited one—to demonstrate how psychological processes accompany historical processes, intertwining with them and demanding our attention if we are to understand our fellow human beings and thus understand ourselves as we identify ourselves with others in our own groups and become involved in historical events whether we want such involvement or not.

Cyprus—War and Adaptation

A Psychoanalytic History of Two Ethnic
Groups in Conflict

Aphrodite's Island as a Troubled Place

The Dream of Seven Layers of Oriental Rugs

When I underwent personal analysis in the course of my psycho-analytic training many years ago, I learned—or, to be more exact, relearned—what it meant to be a Turkish child growing up on the Mediterranean island of Cyprus.

One seldom recalls long after his analysis a dream initiated by the reactivation of real and fantasied childhood experiences within the psychoanalytic situation, but I do remember such a dream. I feel sure it came at a turning point in my analysis, although I cannot now remember what it meant to me at the time or how my analyst interpreted it. In it a small, frightened representation of myself was caught among seven layers of Oriental rugs. I suspect that it had, above and beyond its other possible meanings, much to do with my revisiting by means of regression the fragmented child-hood images of myself and others important to me as a child.

The rugs probably represented—as rugs usually do in dreams—the images of women remembered from childhood. The Oriental rugs were for me, then, images of women in the modified extended family into which I was born. The number seven has a mystic meaning among Turks, one going back to the Hittites, Sumerians, and Egyptians, all of whom contributed to the culture of Cyprus. The stories told to children there—at least to youngsters who were Turkish—spoke of the seven layers of the sky and the seven layers of the earth (Eyüboğlu, 1974). To rise to the seventh layer on high was to achieve omnipotence. In a psychoanalytic sense it might mean merger with the image of the "all good" mother, that entity that represents in the dawning awareness of the infant total dedication to his wishes. To sink to the seventh layer of the earth was to "hit bottom" and become helpless under the domination of an image neither gratifying nor soothing. The progression of the seven layers in either direction struck awe in the heart of one who knew that in reality he had to learn to deal with these good or bad images and all of the images of himself that corresponded to them and from such material build an integrated inner world and a sense of integrated identity. The manifest content of this dream, however, can be used to illustrate what it was like to grow up in Cyprus, not only from the point of view of the child's real or fantasied interaction with other family members but also from the point of view of the child's finding himself in a unique cultural and historical setting.

If one were to assign ethnic identity to those bits and pieces, generated in the course of internalizing one's interaction with others in the environment, that compose the mosaic of one's psychic structures, it would be necessary in my case to ascribe them to many different ethnic orders; in my homeland divers ethnic groups live side by side in a country smaller than the state of Connecticut (3,572 square miles). Although each influences the other, each remains rigidly differentiated by historical, cultural, and social peculiarities. In my self-concept my awareness of being Turkish prevailed over the other pieces of my psychic mosaic to the point where I was able to deny or repress their very existence in a defensive and adaptive enhancement of my cohesive identity as a Turk. In identifying early with my mother and father and other important Turks, I assimilated their way of stereotyping other groups on Cyprus. Stereotyped views of other groups sharing so small an island are put to the test of reality, but such reality testing paradoxically strengthens the stereotypes for defensive purposes. As he grows up, the Cypriot child's primitive fragmentation of the humankind around him according to ethnic differences mends very little. Parental attitudes support such stereotyping, and, later, the child's own superego (or "conscience")[1] tolerates it. Just as the natives of the Kilimanjaro

1. Throughout this book terms that approximate technical psychoanalytic terminology are offered to the general reader. The psychoanalyst who regrets the failure to refine such terminology further in closer accord with precise psychoanalytic understanding will not require such elucidation; his indulgence on behalf of the general reader is asked.

region in Africa provide names for each of the many nearby mountain peaks but none for the mountain range as a whole (Werner,
1948), so do the Cypriots fail to synthesize the ethnic elements of
their country (Greek, Turkish, Armenian, etc.) into any "Cypriot"
whole. When the Cypriot Turk as an adult must accommodate to
life experience that requires a less parochial outlook, he feels anxiety
over this inner change (Searles, 1961) and paradoxically clings to his
one mountain peak, his Turkishness, with increased tenacity, in-
dulging in stereotyping with more conviction than ever. It never becomes clear to him that his is but one peak in a whole range of
mountains. The culture supports this primitive mode of mental
functioning beneath a considerably higher level of functioning in
respect to other issues. Such incongruity is seen not as psychopathology but as a cultural adaptation.

A Greek family lived next to mine during my years of latency,[2]
and I played with the daughter of this family until we reached
puberty, when accepted cultural patterns made her taboo, and
whatever I had learned from her about real "Greekness" was thus
denied the more strongly. My violin teacher was Armenian, and I
practiced in an Armenian church. My pleasure in the musical aura
of this church was accompanied by a strong sense that since I was
not a Christian there must be something bad about this place of
worship. I needed to distance myself psychologically from its "bad"
priests, who wore brown robes belted with knotted rope; the stereotyped myth held that each knot represented a child strangled by
the wearer. The priests were representations of "bad" phallic
mothers (the mother seen not as nurturing but as threatening). Thus
my good and bad images of the Armenian church could be put on
one or the other side of the Oriental rugs of my dream, among the
"good" seven layers reaching for the sky or the "bad" ones that belonged toward the bottom of the dark earth.

A greatly admired teacher of my sister's took pride in declaring
herself a direct descendant of Phoenicians of the eighth century
B.C., and I remember comparing her features with those of the
Phoenician portraits in our history books. As a boy I played among

2. *Latency:* from the ages of 5–6 to 11–13, a period during which there is relative inactivity of the sexual drive.

historical ruins that had been under the dominion of Sargon II, Alexander the Great, Evagoras of Salamis, the emperors of Byzantium, Richard Coeur de Lion, Guy de Lusignan, Selim II, and other great conquerors who for me were not only great figures in history but magical beings. As children we dug for old pottery and ancient coins, and it was only much later, in school, that we found the past systematized into schema for the attention of secondary processes (the "intellect"). Since the island's administrators at the time were British, I added Britishness to my self-concept, which was otherwise dominated by the idealism of Kemalist Turkey.

The History of Cyprus

We learned in school that Cyprus was well populated during the late Neolithic (or New Stone) Age (4,000 to 3,000 B.C.). The Bronze and Iron Ages were well represented, and during the former period Mycenaean settlers arrived. Although historians are uncertain whether they came to colonize or to trade, wealth did pour into the island, and copper mining reached its peak; the word *copper* is said to be derived from the name *Cyprus*. During the early Iron Age (1050–950 B.C.) Cypriot, Mycenaean, and Anatolian elements fused. Phoenician penetration came during the eighth century B.C., and the year 709 B.C. marks submission to the Assyrian king Sargon. A hundred years of independence followed the end of Assyrian domination. Arriving about 560 B.C., the Egyptians allowed the Cypriot kings and kingdoms to continue. When Egypt was annexed to Persia, the island fell under Persian domination, in 520 B.C., only to come under Macedonia in 332 B.C. after the victory of Alexander the Great. It passed at his death to the Egypt of the Ptolemies, and in 58 B.C. it was annexed by Rome.

Cyprus underwent a dramatic religious conversion as a province of the Roman Empire, and Christianity replaced the many religious cults. In 395 A.D. the division of the Roman Empire made Cyprus part of the Byzantine (Eastern Roman) Empire, and for eight centuries Byzantine rule was unchallenged save for intermittent invasions by the Arabs. A resurgence of Hellenic influence in the Eastern Roman Empire appeared at the height of Byzantium.

Greek became the official language, and the culture of Byzantium penetrated every aspect of Cypriot life. The emperor Zeno made the Cypriot ecclesiastical province "autocephalous"—that is, he exempted it from direct jurisdictional, though not spiritual, dependence on the Patriarch of Constantinople.

In 1191 Richard Coeur de Lion of England seized Cyprus after hostility had been shown there to English crusaders. He then gave it to Guy de Lusignan, who had been dispossessed as king of Jerusalem. He founded a feudal monarchy under a court French in language and culture, and this lasted into the Middle Ages. With the growing maritime supremacy of the Italians, particularly the Genoese and Venetians, Cyprus, so crucial to Mediterranean trade, became part of the Venetian Empire in the fifteenth century and so remained until its conquest by Ottoman Turks in 1570–71, which introduced a cohesive and strong religious and cultural influence alongside the Hellenic survival. (See Chapter III for an account of the settling of Anatolian Turks on the island.) During the Venetian period the Greek Orthodox church was suppressed on Cyprus and attempts were made to impose Roman Catholicism on the people there. In taking over the island, the Turks restored the Greek Orthodox church to its former status by recognizing it as the only official non-Moslem religious body on the island.

The Turkish administration lasted for three hundred years until 1878, when Great Britain took Cyprus "in trust" by treaty with the sultan, who was assured of protection against Russia in return. Although it remained nominally Ottoman territory during this period, it was formally annexed by the British in 1914 at the start of World War I, in which Turkey allied itself with Imperial Germany. Turkey formally recognized British rule in Cyprus under the Treaty of Lausanne in 1923, and Cyprus became a crown colony in the following year. When the Republic of Cyprus was declared in 1960, the population of the new ministate approached 600,000, of which 79 percent were Cypriot Greeks, 18 percent Cypriot Turks, and the rest Armenians, Maronites, and others.

The Cypriot child's awareness of bonds to the past made the island a symbolic arena in which he lived out his internal dramas, put them to the test of reality, and attempted to integrate the meaning of

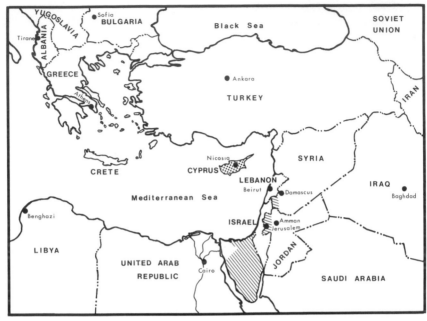

Map 1. Cyprus and the Eastern Mediterranean area

personal experiences. The impact of the twentieth century on Cyprus failed to obliterate the ancient past in a land where small farmers, as recently as during my childhood, could still be seen threshing wheat with stones set in a wooden platform, recalling the Stone Age within sight of the finest modern agricultural machinery.

Some degree of order was necessary in a small island in which populations and cultures left behind by a myriad of conquerors attempted to fuse, only to separate again like water and oil shaken in a bottle. Greek, Phoenician, Roman, Arabic, French, Venetian, Turkish, British, and other contributions were fused and separated until reality testing on a high level became possible, as it did for most Cypriots in the long run, but not without the persistence of a nucleus of lower-level fragmentation and confusion.

The Interaction of the Self with Its Physical Environment

A look at childhood development will contribute to an understanding of how the historical fragmentation of his country and his emotional investment in it provided an arena in which the Cypriot child could play out the trial and error of his search for a cohesive identity for himself as a person and for a realistic view of other people. What is particularly germane here is the development of an integrated concept of the self and of others seen as objects of the self's attention.

The term *self* in common use refers to the total person—the body and its parts, as well as the psychic organization of the individual and its components. In psychoanalysis we use the terms *self-image* and *self-representation*, the first referring to the image of the self which appears to the ego at any given time.[3] The ego uses perceptions, sensations, emotions, and thoughts to construct the self-image, similarly constructing the images of whatever is external to the self—the object. From a multitude of realistic or distorted images, the ego forms representations of the self and objects that are basic for the individual and that depend on some consistent continuity of collected images. Psychoanalytic investigation has made it possible to chart a schema to account for the development and integration of our self- and object images (Jacobson, 1964; Mahler, 1968; Kernberg, 1966, 1972; Volkan, 1975a, 1976).[4] The subject of absolute reality is one for philosophical consideration, but certain it is that each of us constructs a world view of our own and a self to cope with it. In the early interaction with the mother (or other chief caretaker), the infant first comes to know that some experiences are delightful (being fed, for example) whereas others are painful (being refused food when hungry, being handled roughly, etc.). An undifferentiated self-object constellation is built up under the influence of the pleasurable and gratifying experiences of the in-

3. As life begins, the ego and the id are undifferentiated, and the human organism has no images of the self or the object, but their precursors are generated in the infant's memory traces of pleasurable or unwelcome emotional experience.

4. For a searching psychoanalytic examination of this schema see Kernberg (1976) and Volkan (1976). This schema is discussed under the umbrella of the theory of internalized object relations.

fant with his mother. Simultaneously another undifferentiated primary self-object representation is formed, this one reflecting a consolidation of frustrating and painful experiences. We refer technically to the first constellation as "all good" and the second as "all bad."[5] This causes the building up of bipolar representations of self-object images and representations that reflect the original infant-mother relationship. As time goes on, the infant as he progresses into childhood gains the ability to differentiate the representation of self from that of the object, but the bipolarity persists. At about the third year of life, he begins to integrate "all good" and "all bad" self-representations and to integrate his bipolar object representations as well. He thus achieves an integrated self-identity and integrated representations of others, all being subject to modification by subsequent experience in life. The term *primitive splitting* is used to describe the division caused by the bipolarity I have explained. Primitive splitting disappears,[6] is mended as it were, when "all good" and "all bad" self-representations are integrated and the opposing object representations are also integrated.

My thesis here is that we initially treat our emotion-laden physical surroundings as though they were extensions of our self- and object images. As we undergo periodic change toward the achievement of an integrated self-concept and representational world of objects, we also develop a more realistic view of the physical environment of our childhood.[7] Before the sights and sounds of the neighborhood

5. See how Kernberg (1966, 1967) suggests the investment of the "all good" units with libido and the "all bad" units with the aggressive drive.

The first "all good" self-object representation becomes the nucleus of the differentiated ego (Kernberg, 1976).

6. This type of splitting occurs at first simply because the primitive ego lacks integrative ability, but it is then used actively to defend the "all good" self- and object representations that reflect a gratifying relationship with the mother from contamination by their "all bad" counterparts. Such splitting gradually lessens as normal development progresses, but it will increase under pathological conditions such as an overloading of the "all bad" constellations with aggressive drive. Adults with borderline personality organization (Kernberg, 1967) often use primitive splitting as a major mechanism of defense.

7. This formulation is in agreement with the findings of Searles (1960), who has studied perhaps more deeply than any other investigator the meaning of the nonhuman environment from a psychoanalytic point of view. He suggested that

in which the child lives, originally connected with his own pleasure and "unpleasure" within the child/mother interaction, can coalesce into realistic representations relatively free from distortion, they tend to polarize in his mind. Some remain "all good" and some "all bad," and evoke feelings appropriate in either case. With its dazzling cultural diversity and its ethnic fragmentation, Cyprus is a place likely to foster the continuation of childhood primitive splitting on one level, even when it may appear to be mended, for all practical purposes, on a higher level. The splitting of self- and object representations in early childhood is echoed in views of the physical environment which become so ingrained that they appear in one generation after another, just as behavior patterns do, and offer sanctuary in which childhood splitting can continue.[8]

---

the nonhuman aspects of his environment are of singular importance to the normal child, later (1963) revising this view to indicate that the nonhuman environment represents by displacement some increment of the child's feelings of love and dependence originally directed toward his mother. To these feelings I would add hate. In 1965 Searles noted that every child is confronted to some degree with a struggle to differentiate the human components of his life from the non-human, and the animate from the inanimate. The mother must help her child to make such differentiation; in fact, she must initially make it for him. If this process is not accomplished, the child will be unable to achieve and maintain full human individuality.

8. In normal development the mending of primitive splitting is followed by the appearance of *repression* as the ego's major defensive mechanism. Because aspects of the Cypriot child's primitive splitting are approved by his culture, total integration fails to occur, and when he enters the period in which repression predominates, unintegrated images may be repressed. In spite of this repression, however, they continue, along with their affective dispositions, to influence behavior.

See Kernberg (1976) for a parallel view and support of this idea, as well as for further psychoanalytic discussion of how the predominance of repression over earlier defenses organized around primitive splitting consolidates the id as "containing the sum of those internalized object relations which are unacceptable because of the dangerous, anxiety- and guilt-producing experiences involved in the respective intrapsychic and interpersonal interactions. . . . Primitive, unrealistic self- and object-representations remain relatively unchanged in the id, and so do their correspondingly primitive, overwhelming affect dispositions (p. 70)." Kernberg further states, in agreement with van der Waals (1952) that the repressed portion of the id is not pure id, but an ego id, and this portion contains repressed object relations.

In Chapter III, I will examine the child-rearing practices of the
Cypriot Turks and Greeks and show how certain peculiarities
occur in the development of self- and object representations within
the extended (or modified extended) family, which has more than
one mothering person. The protocol of such families helps maintain
primitive splitting, which then finds its way into sociocultural behavior patterns. I will, however, limit myself in this chapter to
examples of the ways in which Cypriot Turks and Cypriot Greeks
react to aspects of the country and the landmarks they have in
common. My thesis is that each group reacts to aspects of the physical environment as to "part-objects," to borrow a term from Klein
(1946) which means that whatever is perceived as either "all good"
or "all bad" is, in fact, seen only in part. Cypriot Turks tinge certain
landmarks, such as an Ottoman monument, with Turkishness, regarding them as extensions of their "all good" self- and object images
and representations. The Greeks are equally proprietary about
landmarks that seem "all good" to them. It is natural for all people
to have differing degrees of emotional investment in different features of the environment in which they conduct their lives, but in
a "part-object" relationship the object is either all black or all white,
never gray; the inability to comprehend "grayness" is a legacy from
an unfinished childhood task.[9]

A Cypriot Turk might, for example, be lost in wonder and admiration at the sight of a Byzantine church while traveling in Eastern
Europe; buildings in the Byzantine style often are breathtaking.
But the same Cypriot Turk would be likely to scorn a comparable
church in a Cypriot Greek village since his adult judgment is still
influenced by his childhood investment of the "all bad" in any Greek

9. It might shed light on this inability were we to compare the "part-object"
relationship with the ambivalent one. Ambivalence in its technical sense develops
when one relates to an object—a person, for example—with both love and hate but
nevertheless perceives him in toto, loving and hating him alternately or simultaneously according to his behavior at the time, or according to what one expects
of him at the moment. Although on the clinical level a highly ambivalent relationship resembles part-object relationship, in the latter the subject approaches the
object as though it actually were two entities, one loved (good) and one hated
(bad). When the object is seen as "all good," the subject's enthusiasm denies that
it ever has been, or ever could be, "all bad."

encroachment on the land of his origin. The reasons for his failing to stop and admire the beautiful edifice are unconscious but cogent. He perceives it as "bad" or, defensively, as so valueless that for him it does not exist. He might manage a brief visit and intellectual assent that it was beautiful, if circumstances required, but on a lower level he would long to escape from its contamination.

Any integration of opposing attitudes seems to threaten "all good" elements, treasured as emphatically as "all bad" ones are rejected. It is perhaps paradoxical that part-object relationships are intense, demanding close and continued emotional attention and betraying lurking anxiety. For example, although children are almost invariably drawn to farm animals, a Turkish Cypriot child would hurry away from a pig, however he might momentarily respond to a particularly engaging piglet. He would regard it with intense and unneutralized emotion since pork is forbidden to Moslems. It would be for him the repository of those "all bad" representations of those parts of himself and others that he must avoid and from which he must maintain psychological distance.

The magical "seven levels" of unintegrated history that the landmarks of Cyprus recall remain in the psychic structure of the Cypriot Turk. The primitive splitting begun years earlier in child/mother interaction, when it was natural to invest anything symbolically Turkish with libido and anything symbolically Greek with aggression, continues into adult life as ethnically weighted response. The Turkish Cypriot child condenses a considerable degree of idealism into his ethnically congenial percepts and keeps at a psychological distance those he regards as "all bad" in order to avoid contamination. In doing so he devalues the "all bad" to the point of denying its existence.

I feel sure that the mind of the Cypriot Greek unconsciously unfolds in much the same way. Each ethnic group has always understood on an intellectual level that the other owns part of the island, but although Turks are in a numerical minority and held only 35 percent of the land until the recent upheavals, they denied, on a lower than intellectual level, that the Greeks owned any part of it. To them the claim of the Greeks was "all bad"—so valueless that it should be rejected out of hand. In the fall of 1975, a year after

Turkish control was established in the northern part of the island, a high Greek official in the Cypriot Embassy in the United States told me that before the recent events some Greek friends of his who lived on Cyprus were astonished by the effrontery of the Turkish claim to any portion of it! I am afraid that I rather smirked at his comment until I suddenly realized that my childhood feelings, above and beyond my secondary process (intellectual thought), had been equally scornful and unrealistic regarding any Greek claim to the ownership of Cyprus. The dynamics of this attitude resemble those of narcissistic transference in psychoanalysis; the narcissistic analysand "blots out" his analyst when he finds him unwilling to adore him. I had felt that the island was totally Turkish since its Greek sectors lacked emotional value for me.

Psychogeography

As a child I felt not only that Cyprus was altogether Turkish but that it was part of Anatolia, a literal translation of whose name, *Anadolu,* is "full of mother." Symbolically, Turkey was the motherland and Cyprus was its child. Psychoanalytic writings unfortunately make little reference to what Niederland (1977) calls "psychogeography." He studied the symbolism of a river (1956, 1957, 1959) and that of the naming of America (1971a) and California (1971b). [10] He tells us that both were seen in fantasy as islands of Paradise full of eternal bliss; early maps separated them, surrounding each with water, and early descriptions were fanciful and euphoric in the extreme. It is interesting that the name *America,* although derived from the first name of Amerigo Vespucius, is feminine and that the belief in America's bounty drew countless immigrants who had fantasies of a great good mother taking them into her embrace.

Some of my own childhood memories may shed light on how Cypriot Turkish children symbolized a connection between the island of Cyprus and Turkey. Parents often spoke of Turkey and passed along to their children a sense of identity with the mainland country, which seemed a land of promise, much as America did to

10. See also Sterba (1965) for his study of symbolism in the river and jungle and Ferenczi (1921, 1922) on the symbolism of bridges.

the immigrants to this country Niederland describes. The map of
Cyprus made the connection concrete, since on maps the Karpasia
peninsula of the island looks like an arm stretching toward Anatolia's
(the mother's) Gulf of Alexandretta. I can still hear what we learned
in elementary school on Cyprus: "Cyprus was once connected with
Anatolia, but it sank into the sea. It rose, only to sink again. When
it rose for the third time after its third submersion, it was, alas, no
longer connected with Anatolia." This account reflects eons of
geological change, and to this day I do not know how close it comes
to the truth; but I do remember visualizing the island's being swal-
lowed up by the sea, and the picture of this event, along with the
fantasy of the island's rebirth, was very much before me up to my
teens, especially when the island shook with the earthquakes we
sometimes had.

In retrospect I can see that Cyprus represented myself in my
own process of separation-individuation from my mother (Mahler,
1963, 1968; Mahler and Furer, 1963). The sequence of the island's
submersion, reappearance, and ultimate separation from the
motherland suggests a symbolic enactment of the trials and difficulties I underwent in the process of psychologically separating
from my mother. As a small child I felt that another earthquake
might reunite the two lands, and the yearning for reunion of what
had been sundered persisted. I have no conscious memory of having
made a symbolic connection out of the phallic pointing of the
island's landmass into a Turkish gulf.

The part-object relationship with the land that obviates the need
to use reality testing about it makes his country's mythology and
folklore compelling to the mind of a child. As he grows, aspects of
the land which are for him laden with emotion take on a magical
quality, and although he becomes capable of reality testing, the
childhood magic continues sufficiently strong to influence his behavior. Near the town of Polis, which was once inhabited by both
Cypriot Greeks and Cypriot Turks, is a little cave in which a shallow
pool is fed by water dripping from the roof. Because the air is always
moist, a miniature rainbow appears at the mouth of the cave when
the sun shines directly upon it. Legend has it that Aphrodite bathed
in this cave and anyone who drinks the water from it will surely

fall in love with the first suitable person he or she may meet. Although this is clearly a myth, one almost believes it when in the grip of intense psychological pressure—when postpubertal hormones are making themselves felt, for example! There are, of course, places invested with less fanciful authority, and Cypriot Greeks and Cypriot Turks alike recognize the mystique of certain places toward which they turn when threatened.

Even the well-educated Turkish Cypriot adult is influenced in his reality testing by one legendary landmark, for example. The story goes that the aunt of the prophet Mohammed came to Cyprus with invading Arabs and is buried on the shore of a salt lake near Larnaca. A mosque was erected on the spot. Since *hala* means "aunt," it is known as Hala Sultan. It is said that after her burial a slab of stone rose in the air over her grave to shield her from the sun, and today there is a huge rock hanging in midair over the tomb, apparently without support. The whole affair is draped in velvet, which hides the supports that are necessarily there, but I can myself recall visiting the tomb as a teenager and hoping that the rock really did defy gravity, although I knew full well that there were hidden supports. I can only assume that for Cypriots who regress under the stress of intercommunal conflict, the line between longing for the return of infantile omnipotence[11] and actually experiencing it may be very thin indeed.

The Present "Cyprus Problem" and the Republic of Cyprus

This, then, is a small country into which the soul and blood of one conquering nation after another has seeped over the centuries, and in which men without the bonds of natural kinship live side by side. The part-object relationship with the physical environment seems more and more evident, characterizing particularly responses to political stress. Child-rearing practices in this part of the world

11. The apparently paradoxical designation of "infantile omnipotence" is used in psychoanalysis to indicate that the infant, entirely without any conscious awareness of the existence of others in the world, is obliged by default, as it were, to feel himself merged with all else as the cause and end of being—hence omnipotent.

(see Chapter III) encourage the inhabitants to view their surroundings, in which they have invested so much emotion, as either "all good" or "all bad." Until the recent troubles, Greeks and Turks lived all over the island; some villages were mixed and some were predominantly of one ethnic group or the other, and both groups mingled in the six cities. (See the statistical data in Chapter IV.) A demographic map of Cyprus showing its ethnic distribution would have looked like a tabletop covered with pepper (the Greeks) into which a small pinch of salt (the Turks) had been dropped in a random way.

Although the Cypriot Greek movement for *Enosis* (union with Greece) goes back a hundred years or so,[12] it can be said that the present "Cyprus problem" began in 1931 when the residence of the British governor was burned by some Greek Cypriots devoted to Enosis. In spite of Britain's reacting to this event with stern punitive measures, once World War II was over agitation for Enosis was resumed. Makarios, the archbishop of the Orthodox Church of Cyprus, who was born in 1913, became the leader of the struggle. The campaign for Enosis gained ground and was greatly resented in Turkey. British, Greek, and Turkish foreign ministers, meeting at

12. In fact, both Turkish and Greek writers find the origin of the wish for Enosis in the Greeks' "Great Idea." Markides (1977), a Cypriot-born Greek sociologist in the United States, who wrote on the "rise and fall" of the Cyprus Republic, describes the Greeks' "Great Idea" as "a dream shared by Greeks that someday the Byzantine Empire would be restored and all the Greek lands would once again be united into a Greater Greece" (p. 10). This Pan-Hellenic ideology arose in 1453 when Istanbul—then Constantinople—fell to the Turks. Markides continues: "The 'Great Idea' found expression in . . . parts of the Greek world, such as Crete and the Ionian islands. One could argue that the 'Great Idea' had an internal logic, pressing for realization in every part of the Greek world which continued to be under foreign rule. Because the Greeks of Cyprus have considered themselves historically and culturally to be Greeks, the 'Great Idea' has had an intense appeal. Thus, when the church fathers called on the Cypriots to fight for union with Greece, it did not require much effort to heat up emotions. . . . Enosis did not originate in the church but in the minds of intellectuals in their attempt to revive Greek-Byzantine civilization. However, being the most central and powerful of institutions, the church contributed immensely to its development. The church embraced the movement and for all practical purposes became its guiding nucleus" (pp. 10, 11).

the London Conference in September 1955, failed to agree on a solution of the problem, while on the island itself tension mounted. The British governor introduced emergency measures. Negotiations with Makarios broke down because he not only insisted on Cypriot self-determination, which would have led to Enosis since Greeks were in the majority, but wanted a commitment to it by a specified time. When the British government refused, Makarios was deported to the Seychelles in March 1956. Terrorism prevailed on the island, and a number of British nationals were slain. The Cypriot Greek guerrilla organization EOKA (Ethniki Organosis Kyprion Agoniston)—the National Organization of Cypriot Fighters, created in 1955 and headed by Colonel George Grivas—offered to suspend terrorist activity if Makarios was released from exile. Makarios was duly released and given freedom to go anywhere he liked except to Cyprus. Although his release led to improvement in British-Greek relations, the archbishop did not abandon his claim for the self-determination of Cyprus. The Turks insisted that *Taksim*, the partition of the island between Turks and Greeks, was the only acceptable solution to the unrest.

Negotiations between the Greek and Turkish premiers in Zurich brought agreement, incorporated in a resolution to establish a republic. This was signed by Britain, Greece, and Turkey in February 1959 in London. It provided for an independent state to be set up within a year, with a Greek president and Turkish vice-president, each elected for a five-year term. A cabinet was to be formed, composed of seven Greek and three Turkish members, and the same 70–30 ratio was to be maintained in Parliament and in all branches of the civil service. A series of compromise safeguards for guaranteeing the rights of the two major communities in Cyprus was established and spelled out in great detail in the new republic's constitution. Separate Greek and Turkish communal chambers were to deal with religious, educational, and other concerns of each group. It was agreed to approve British retention of two military bases that totaled 99 square miles of land. Britain, Greece, and Turkey made a treaty guaranteeing the new arrangements in Cyprus, and Greece was authorized to station 950 military men on the island, Turkey being allowed 650. The Cypriot army was to limit itself to 2,000 men in a 60–40 ratio of Greeks and Turks. The Republic of Cyprus was officially born in August 1960. Grivas denounced it, claiming that he had been tricked by Makarios and would continue the struggle for Enosis.

Problems of interpretation and application of the constitution arose immediately. Xydis (1973) called the new republic a "reluctant" one, and Adams (1966), in a review of its constitution, called it "unworkable," explaining: "The story of the first constitution of Cyprus—which has been likened to a masterfully jewelled watch—is one of the finely drawn compromise, a fascinating account of sincere though unrealistic legalism or how not to bring an anxious colony into statehood" (p. 475).

I will speak later of the psychological implications of bringing Cypriot Greeks and Cypriot Turks "together" under a single flag, the flag of Cyprus, which, although it did replace the Union Jack on a few government buildings, never supplanted the Greek and Turkish flags that still flew over the strongholds of Greek and Turkish sympathizers. The focus here will be on the events that set the stage for the subsequent explosion.

The constitution of the Republic of Cyprus takes both communities into account. It is long and complex, with 199 articles and 6 appendixes. As might have been expected, the Turks and the Greeks on the island disputed its interpretation. It seems to have been the emotional attitudes of the two groups in Cyprus that made its constitution unworkable. Sporadic outbursts of hostility between them occurred during the first three years of the Republic's existence.

One of the spots on Cyprus in which the Turks had made a heavy emotional investment is called the place of *Bayraktar,* the "flag bearer." This "all good" place, on which stands the mausoleum of the first Turkish soldier to fall during the Turkish conquest of Nicosia in 1570, is in a sense the center of Turkish libidinal investment—a treasured shrine. The Cypriot Greeks not surprisingly bombed the mausoleum in 1962, and again in 1963, as a blow struck straight to the heart of Turkish nationalism. Not only was considerable damage done to the walls, but the minaret topping it was cleared away altogether after it had suffered some structural ruin.

One cannot know whether the Greeks who made the building look as though the minaret—that phallic symbol—had been struck off by a castrating knife had any conscious awareness of the injury this act was bound to inflict on the Turks, but we can safely assume that, unconsciously at least, they were castrators. At any rate, the narcissistic blow (humiliation) was so widely felt that even in Turkey crowds gathered in protest. What had begun as hurt and passive helplessness in the face of this outrage became something more active as aggressive feelings were discharged. Tension on the island was high enough to keep each community there busy training irregular forces since the regularly established soldiery was unable to prevent the outbursts.

In 1962 serious friction was evident concerning the status of municipalities on Cyprus. According to the constitution, the Turks living alongside the Greeks in six major cities there could continue for four years to have separate Turkish municipalities. The Greeks insisted that after this time this arrangement be discontinued, but the Turks wanted it kept, and each side claimed the other was violating the constitution by its plans. Discussions betweeen the Greek president Makarios and the Turkish vice-president Fazıl Küçük broke down in May 1963, and in November of the same year Makarios outlined a thirteen-point amendment to the constitution in a memorandum entitled "Suggested Measures to Facilitate the Smooth Functioning of the State and Remove Certain Causes of Inter-communal Friction." This revision demanded that the president and vice-president be deprived of veto power and that majority rule be honored, with representation based on proportionate populations. Fearing that this amendment would restrict the rights of Cypriot Turks and lead to the Enosis that most Cypriot Greek leaders openly supported, the Turkish government in Ankara challenged it, and on December 21, 1963, violence erupted in Nicosia. Two Turks were killed and five wounded. Turks called this outbreak and the events of the following days "the bloody Christmas massacre." The psychological processes of Cypriot Turks on which I focus in this book manifested themselves strikingly from 1963 until 1978, three years after the intervention of the Turkish army which divided the island into two sectors, the northern one becoming Turkish and the southern Greek.

Greek and Turkish writers naturally disagree over the cause of the origin at Christmastime in 1963, which signaled the beginning of a series of bloody events. American observers (Keefe et al., 1971) asserted that "it was neither a carefully planned Turkish rebellion, as the Greeks maintained, nor a systematic attempt to exterminate the Turkish population, as some of the Turkish spokesmen alleged" (p. 211). Nevertheless, the average Turk did feel that this was the beginning of extermination, and I suspect that the average Greek felt that the Turks had started systematic rebellion.

By December 23, 1963, Nicosia, the capital of Cyprus, had become a battleground. Each side took hostages and brought charges of atrocity against the other. Since it was physically impossible for Turkish Cypriot ministers and members of the House of Representatives to attend meetings of the Parliament, which met in the Greek sector, they were effectively excluded. None wanted to risk their lives to attend, whatever their views. Thus control of the legal government of the Republic of Cyprus fell into the hands of Cypriot Greeks only, which was considered unlawful by the Turks. Since that time there has been no cooperation of any kind in the government and the polarization of the two groups has become increasingly fixed.

In the face of continuing hostilities, the United Nations Security Council authorized in March 1964 the provision of an international peacekeeping force in Cyprus, and United Nations troops took command before the end of that month. During March and April, however, more heavy fighting took place. Since only Cypriot Greek members of the House of Representatives were functioning in the government, there was no difficulty in getting a bill passed for the establishment of a National Guard composed of Greeks. Grivas, who was out of the country, returned to Cyprus in June 1964 to assume its command. At this time a large number of Greek regular troops from Greece were clandestinely infiltrating the island. Since these developments put the Cypriot Turks in great danger, the Turkish government on the mainland undertook military preparations to intervene. The United States, under President Lyndon Johnson, intervened in the crisis,[13] which was exacerbated for

13. In a letter to the late İnönü, then head of the Turkish government, President Johnson warned against any Turkish military operation on the island.

three days in August 1964 when the air force of the Turkish mainland government bombed Greek Cypriot positions in support of Turkish Cypriots who were under attack and faced with the possibility of extermination. The bombing brought the "hot" phase of the conflict to a temporary halt.

Twenty-five thousand Cypriot Turks became refugees between December 1963 and the summer of 1964, and the report prepared by Ortega, the United Nations expert, showed damage to Turkish properties in forty-four villages, as well as heavy damage to the Turkish sectors of the large cities. Before December 1963 the Turks on Cyprus, a minority of the total population of the island, were interspersed among the Greek majority as I have described, but by the end of 1964 the Greeks occupied 97 percent of the land; 18 percent of the population was thus confined in enclaves controlled by the Turks and surrounded by United Nations troops, with an outer circle of Greek soldiers. Chapter IV examines in detail the psychological processes at work among Cypriot Turks crowded for eleven years into enclaves occupying only 3 percent of the landmass.

No political solution was found, and tension persisted. The AKEL, the almost entirely Greek Communist party, was considerably less interested than the controlling Greek government in Enosis.[14] During the winter of 1966–67 the shipping lanes were crowded with craft bringing arms to the Greek Cypriots from Czechoslovakia, and a battle between the Greek Cypriot National Guard and Cypriot Turks broke out in April 1967, after which further attempts were made to find a political solution of the differences at issue.

The letter specifically stated that the use of American arms in such an operation would violate bilateral agreements between Washington and Ankara. It also stated that a Turkish military action "would unleash the furies" and that it "could not be sufficiently effective to prevent the wholesale destruction of many of those whom you are trying to protect."

This letter was written in a crude and brutal tone without regard to standard diplomatic communication, and when its content was made public in Turkey it generated general anti-American feeling there. I later met a former American ambassador to a country in the Near East who boasted to me that he had ghost-written this letter for the president.

14. See Adams's (1971) account of the role of AKEL in influencing negotiations.

During the same year a coup in Athens brought a Greek junta into power.

On the last day of October 1967, Rauf Denktaş, the first president of the Turkish Communal Chamber, exiled since January 1964, returned secretly to Cyprus, only to fall into Greek hands. His capture precipitated another crisis, but political pressure from mainland Turkey brought about his release, and he left the island. In retaliation Grivas's men attacked a Turkish village and killed twenty-six villagers. [15] By November 1967 Turkey was again ready to step in unless certain conditions were met. These included the removal of Grivas, now a general, from Cyprus; the withdrawal of illegally introduced Greek troops; indemnity for the death of Turkish Cypriots killed in the village attacked by Grivas's men; and disbandment of the Greek National Guard. Grivas left the island within two days of the publication of this ultimatum and resigned his position as commander of Cypriot Greek forces. Greece agreed also to the withdrawal of all forces in excess of the 950 allowed by the original treaty, and between December 8, 1967, and January 16 of the following year an estimated 15,000 Greek soldiers left the island they had entered clandestinely. Turkey in turn dismantled the arrangements for military intervention. Cyrus Vance, President Johnson's envoy at the time, played an active part in these negotiations. As it turned out, however, the dispersal of the Greek National Guard was postponed and never ultimately effected, and Greece left behind nearly 2,000 officers; these or their replacements were to plan the final coup against Makarios later.

In December 1967 the Cypriot Turks set up a Turkish provisional administration to care for their own community affairs "until the provisions of the 1960 Constitution were fully implemented." Küçük, vice-president of the Makarios government, became president of this adminstration. In April 1968 Rauf Denktaş was allowed to return to the island, and he was later elected head of the Turkish administration, replacing Küçük.

In June 1968 representatives of the Cypriot Greeks and Turks

15. Denktaş told me in an interview (1977) that at the time of his capture these attacks were scheduled, but that his capture postponed them since Grivas did not want to have two crises occur at the same time.

started talks in Nicosia to find a solution to their differences. When these talks failed in 1972 after three years of negotiation, the United Nations intervened and reactivated them, this time with representation from Greece and Turkey and with the participation of the United Nations itself. This five-party parley did not seem effective, however.

In 1969 terrorist groups in support of Enosis surfaced again. Despite Makarios's continuing speeches in support of Enosis, the followers of the mainland Greek junta tried to assassinate him in 1970. Grivas returned secretly to Cyprus during the following year after "escaping" from house arrest and organized EOKA B for a new fight for Enosis. There was violent friction between EOKA B and Makarios's followers, and although Grivas died in his hideout on Cyprus in January 1974, EOKA B continued its activities in full force.

The New Reality

Flirting with Russia, Makarios was supported by the 40,000 members of AKEL, the Cypriot Communist party. By 1974 anti-Makarios sentiment peaked in Greece; the junta, regarding him as a "Red" and also as an obstacle to Enosis, feared that he would open Cyprus to the Soviet navy and ordered a coup against him. An attempt was made by the EOKA B, with the support of the junta, to kill him on Cyprus in the summer of 1974. While Greek fought Greek on Cyprus, Makarios fled. Cypriot Greeks in sympathy with the junta declared Nikos Sampson their president.[16] Sampson, thirty-nine

16. Stern (1977) describes how Nikos Dimitriu, the Cypriot Greek ambassador to Washington, was received by Henry Kissinger on the day of the coup against Makarios. Dimitriu, asked by Kissinger to identify Sampson, stated that he was "an egomaniac." Kissinger's response—that he himself had been so described—surprised the ambassador, coming as it did at a critical moment. Although Stern is responsible for the first reporting of this exchange in print, I have since confirmed it independently from a prime source. I learned further that Dimitriu's brother, who had joined the Sampson government in Cyprus, called the ambassador in Washington and relieved him of his post when he did not want to go along with the coup. Dimitriu tried to tell his brother by telephone that this time the Turks might intervene, but met with a refusal to consider any such possibility.

years old, was a known murderer who bragged openly of killing at least a dozen men and had been sentenced to death for the EOKA murder of seventeen British soldiers before the Republic of Cyprus was founded. A general amnesty declared in 1959 just before the recognition of the independence of Cyprus had spared him.

A reporter become the editor-publisher of a rightist newspaper, Sampson was remembered by one senior British army officer to have been often the first reported on the scene of some bloody event. As this officer noted in an interview given to *Time* magazine (July 29, 1970), his timely presence was not due to any prescient alertness; he himself had done the killings. Believed to take sadistic pleasure from inflicting pain, Sampson was a powerful warlord who maintained a small private army to attack the Turkish enclaves. On several occasions he had his photograph taken with one foot resting on the corpse of a fallen Turk as though he were a hunter who had just killed a deer. His ascendancy to the presidency seemed to be the first step toward Enosis, and the Turks felt sure they would be exterminated within a few days; but Denktaş refused to recognize his takeover. The emotional reaction of the Turks was such that when Turkish Prime Minister Bülent Ecevit flew to London to seek a peaceful solution, the Turkish Parliament openly fretted. Turkey demanded that independence be restored to Cyprus and that the Greek officers serving as agents be withdrawn. Ecevit, in his negotiations with Harold Wilson, James Callaghan, and Henry Kissinger's envoy Joseph Sisco, held that Turkey would be only exercising its treaty rights if it moved into Cyprus. The original Treaty of Guarantee drawn up at the birth of the Republic of Cyprus established the right of guarantor powers, whether Britain, Turkey, or Greece, to intervene unilaterally should territorial integrity

---

Stern's book gives details of the American involvement in the Cyprus crisis, and the book's title, *The Wrong Horse,* suggests openly that he is critical of American policy under Kissinger as it related to support of the junta in Greece and American inability to prevent Turkey's military intervention. I feel, however, that Stern falls into the same condemnation he has for others—that he makes assumptions from the American frame of reference and treats these assumptions as facts. He holds that political events in other nations can be controlled almost solely by the United States, although in the case of Cyprus, American "mismanagement" resulted in the same kind of situation that he deplores.

be breached, as it would be by the union of Cyprus with Greece. Since Turkey had threatened to intervene militarily twice before, it was widely believed that Ecevit was bluffing, but this was not the case. As a senior official of the State Department in Washington told me, the situation created on the island by the junta was an invitation to Turkey to act. He went on to say that the Greek action was so unbelievable it would do credit to a scenario planned by the CIA.

The degree to which the Cypriot Greek government—and the average Greek citizen of Cyprus—remained blind to rising Turkish passions is interesting. The Cypriot Greeks saw their Turkish neighbors in an increasingly stereotyped way and expressed contempt for Turkish soldiers, scoffing at the idea that they would do anything if they did move in. Even Cypriot Turks, recalling two earlier threats of intervention that had failed to materialize, doubted that Turkish troops would actually come to their aid. But the intervention did come, early in the morning of July 20, 1974, when Cypriots awakened to the sound of Turkish aircraft and saw Turkish paratroopers land on the plateau between Nicosia and the Kyrenia Range. A frenzied euphoria swept over Nicosia's Turkish section. Patients in the Turkish mental hospital there embraced their doctors, and all began to dance about spontaneously. Doctor Sezai Sezgin (1975), the hospital's director, told me later that the excitement was so compelling that even chronic schizophrenics were caught up in it and for a while showed no evidence of mental illness, but one must remember that Sezgin himself was at the time gripped by intense emotion and may have been less than objective.

The air attacks and the troop landings from the sea near Kyrenia secured a corridor between Nicosia and Kyrenia within three days. The fighting was brutal in the extreme. Subsequent activity of Turkish troops in August secured the northern 37 percent of the island within two days. Markides (1977) gives Greek losses during the war as 6,000 dead and 3,000 missing, but Turkish sources insist that if these numbers are to be considered accurate, one must include in them the Greeks who died during the EOKA B movement against Makarios and his followers before the Turkish action took place. Denktaş (1977) gave Turkish losses as 1,500 dead and

2,000 wounded. As a result of the Turkish military intervention, Sampson gave up the presidency, and the Greek junta fell. Democratic government was reestablished in Greece after many years, and Makarios returned to Cyprus. Sampson was arrested by the Makarios government in 1975 after an agitation and is now serving a twenty-year sentence.

The Turkish military intervention cut the island in two. Ecevit declared a cease-fire and announced that "we are now in a situation where the foundations have been laid for the new Federal State of Cyprus." There was an inevitable sequel of social turmoil, and a new series of tragic events. About 160,000 Cypriot Greeks became refugees, fleeing toward the south from the Turks; and about 65,000 Cypriot Turks began a slow trek toward the north. EOKA B fanatics, angered at the failure of the United States to prevent the Turkish intervention, assassinated the American ambassador to Cyprus. The organization was also linked to an attempt on the life of Ecevit when he visited the United States in 1976. He was at the time no longer the prime minister of Turkey, having lost his position some months after the war to Süleyman Demirel, who headed a coalition government. He was, however, to return to power some years later.

The establishment of Turkish control in the northern part of Cyprus unified the approximately three million persons of Greek descent in the United States, who until then had been bitterly divided over the dictatorial junta in Athens. United, Greek-Americans provided a powerful and influential lobby,[17] and their demands resulted in an American embargo on military aid to Turkey. Ankara retaliated by closing American military bases in Turkey, exempting only those involved in the NATO joint defense system. When the situation became less acute, negotiations were again undertaken in an effort to find solutions to "the Cyprus problem." This small Mediterranean island was an object of interest to the whole world!

In February 1975 the Turkish Cypriot administration decided to change the status of the island's government and unilaterally proclaimed a Federal Republic in anticipation of the union of a Turkish Federal State with the Greek Cypriot community within the frame-

17. See *Time* magazine, July 14, 1975, for a detailed account of this lobby.

work of a federation based on two geographical regions. The Greeks refused to accept such a plan. By the autumn of 1975 virtually all of the Turks from southern Cyprus had relocated in the north, where no more than a few thousand Greeks still remained. In January 1977 Denktaş and Makarios met under the auspices of the United Nations, facing each other for the first time in fourteen years and raising the hope of fresh negotiation, which did not materialize. Makarios died of a heart attack in the summer of 1977. In January 1978 Spyros Kyprianou became the new president of Cyprus, but he is not recognized by the Cypriot Turks as their president. Ecevit having become prime minister of Turkey once again, it was generally believed that he might be the only Turkish leader who could realistically negotiate a solution of the Cyprus problem. In January not only did Kurt Waldheim, secretary general of the United Nations, bring Denktaş and Kyprianou together for luncheon on Cyprus,[18] but Cyrus Vance, President Carter's secretary of state, flew to Ankara and Athens. Ecevit's government publicly declared the Turkish desire to work alone and without outside interference toward a solution of its problems with the Greeks. When he suggested a meeting between himself and Constantine Karamanlis, the prime minister of Greece, he received a favorable reply to his invitation.

For all practical purposes the island remains divided in two, awaiting political settlement. As far as the Turks are concerned, return to the old status of Cyprus is impossible, and any settlement would have to include separate sectors for Cypriot Turks and Cypriot Greeks. In the meantime the island continues to be a psycho-social laboratory.

18. According to one guest, the luncheon meeting was rather cold, and neither leader made any effort to break the ice.

II Cyprus as a Psychosocial Laboratory of Politically Induced Stress

A Task Force on Psychiatry and Foreign Affairs

Couloumbis and Georgiades (1973) called the island of Cyprus a "treasure house" for the social scientist. They note that it is a small place manageable in terms of research and add that the almost universal use of English there, because of the long period of British government, reduces problems of communication. Its rich accrual of one cultural influence after another over time, as it was conquered by one foreign power only to be eventually ceded to another, offers much to the historian, providing fascinating examples of different styles and governmental structures for comparison. The cultural anthropologist can embark on research to account for the remarkable persistence of Hellenic culture throughout the island's long and turbulent history, and there is a wealth of fascinating folklore. For the student of international relations Couloumbis and Georgiades declare the island to be "a living and continuous illustration of the effects of geopolitics and the 'balance of power' on the international system and subsystems." The conflicts between the great powers, between Turkey and Greece, and between the Cypriot Turks and the Cypriot Greeks present overlapping circles of interaction, so that the island has become a data-compact region for the study of the management and resolution of conflict and the processes that go into the building of a nation. These writers go so far as to suggest that Cyprus is an ideal location for an international or regional academy in which "citizens of the world" might study historical and contemporary issues and observe them operating in a microcosm. Writing before the Turkish military intervention, Stephens (1966) contemplated the possibility that Cyprus might become the training center and base for the United Nations' peacekeeping operations in all of this highly volatile region of the world.

In spite of all that seems obviously attractive to the investigator now, Cyprus was until recently a "virgin field" (Peristiany, 1976) for studies in social science. In 1969, however, a Social Research Center was established with the aid of UNESCO. This was purely a Cypriot Greek enterprise inasmuch as Cypriot Turks were not asked to contribute to it, nor did they do so. It was under the direction of a social scientist from mainland Greece and was staffed by Greek sociologists who considered the island "part of the Greek world" in terms of culture (Peristiany, 1976, p. 344). It did not—indeed, could not—study intercommunal problems since its establishment came at a time of great turbulence and aggression. It did collaborate, however, with Tenzel and Gerst (Tenzel, 1971; Tenzel and Gerst, 1972; Gerst and Tenzel, 1972) in their study of the cross-cultural, cross-national conflict on the island.[1] Their study was the only serious psychiatric-psychological study of the most crucial issues on the island, and I will refer to it at some length. They regarded Cyprus as a laboratory for the observation of psychological processes rather than a treasure house from the past, but both points of view are inevitably intertwined in any consideration of the present problems of Cyprus.

The Tenzel and Gerst study was conducted under the auspices of the American Psychiatric Association's Task Force on Psychiatry and Foreign Affairs, which spent its first few years studying the Cyprus situation, continuing to do so off and on even after addressing itself to the psychological components of Arab-Israeli and Pakistan-India differences; during the three years between the Turkish military intervention on Cyprus and the termination of the task force in 1977, it again gave full attention to Cyprus. Those who originally planned the task force felt: "Our basic shared interest was the psychological and cultural factors involved in international relations and, in particular, the problems resulting from the breakdown of communication and perception between nations. . . . The psychiatrist has a unique professional experience and training which helps

1. This center also offered Markides (1977) help in carrying out sociological research there. Markides, who was on the island during the Turkish intervention, wrote a book on the "fall" of the Cyprus Republic and examined the reasons for it from a Greek sociologist's point of view.

him to understand the problems faced by the policy analyst and foreign service officer" (Davidson, 1968). The establishment of this
task force under the auspices of the national psychiatric organization marked a big step toward the expansion of psychiatry to apply
to world problems. Such a departure from the concept of psychiatry
as a traditional medical specialty was regarded by many psychiatrists with dismay, and the task force has been considered rather
controversial, to say the least.

In 1949, twenty years before the establishment of the task force,
the American Psychiatric Association made a statement declaring
that "unusual psychological factors" were contributing to the
international tensions then being felt. The Association was careful
to offer this document not as a political criticism of any nation but
"as an objective medical document" for the attention of the public
and, more particularly, for national leaders. It explained: "The
American Psychiatric Association makes this statement because
psychiatrists are expected to understand the psychological causes
of difficult and faulty interpersonal relationships, and should be
able to offer some advice on their improvement. Such knowledge
and advice should be applicable whether the adjustment difficulties are between individuals or groups of individuals, even
national groups of individuals." This document referred to war as
a plague, a public health problem, and suggested that it could be
eliminated only by "rigid self-scrutiny of national motives, by re-
fusals to accept or give spurious rationalizations for unfriendly
behavior, and by conscious achievement of sublimation of leaders'
personal aggressive hostility, which is present to some extent in
everyone." In spite of the acknowledgment of "unusual psychological factors" that underlay contemporary international tensions,
no serious and searching study in this area was carried out. The
threat of nuclear war led, however, to the publication in 1958 of a
report from the Group for the Advancement of Psychiatry, which
concerned itself with the psychiatric aspects of the prevention of
nuclear war but left many crucial questions unanswered.

I believe that the importance of the emotional component in the
conduct of politics and wars hit home for Americans during the
Vietnam conflict. Halberstam (1972) relates how, during the ad-

ministrations of Kennedy and Johnson, "the best and brightest" and the most well-meaning of men were gathered in the White House. They had the kind of superior intelligence that can understand and control irrational concerns, and they had modern technology at their command. As architects of the Vietnam War, they had been ordered to build "the greatest house in the world . . . but had by mistake overlooked one little thing; the site chosen was in a bog." Halberstam identifies many factors that affected policy in foreign affairs and that affect the historical process in general, but it became clear that there was a misreading of the emotional processes involved—those of the Vietnamese people or those of the Western world, in our own country and elsewhere. Faced with Vietnam, not only mental health professionals but also policy makers within the government sought more seriously than before to bring the issues of psychiatry and politics together. Interest in psychopolitical and psychohistorical studies grew, and what was published as a result of this heightened interest was felt to break new ground in psychiatry.[2] Wedge (1968) called for training in a psychiatry of international relations. It was in this favorable climate that the Task Force on Psychiatry and Foreign Affairs was organized. One of its members (Frank, 1967, 1969) had already published studies of the psychological aspects of war and peace and of international negotiations.

I hasten here to express my personal belief that those psychiatrists who are trained to understand the psychological processes at work when one national group opposes another should not be expected to attempt the solution of conflictual problems on the international level; this would be not only presumptuous but absurd. No psychiatrist has the training to deal with the infinite number of variables in any specific instance of international tension. All psychiatry is able to contribute is to make available to the experts in policy matters its insights into psychological processes. Even then, it must be remembered that understanding a problem may help one solve it, but understanding per se provides no solution. Berger (1951), a critic of the notion that an understanding of the differences between one national group and another can help prevent conflict between them, noted that understanding "only gives one greater power to choose

2. See Sinofsky et al. (1975) for a systematization of collections of such papers.

among several courses of action." Even in the case of an individual's problems, an understanding of them may promote unwanted side effects—perhaps diminished observation in certain areas and diminished reactivity. For example, a medical student whose interview with a patient I had observed complained bitterly to me about how aggressive the patient had been toward him. Although retaining his professional stance, the student clearly thought the patient obnoxious and felt an angry need to protect himself from his verbal assaults. During consultation with me the student came to "understand" that the unacceptable behavior had not been directed toward him personally, that he was only a symbolic target of the patient's "transferred" emotions, and that the trouble lay altogether within the patient's own psychological conflicts. During the next interview, the patient behaved as outrageously as he had before, but this time the student was armed with the "understanding" that he was not the true target of the attack and felt no need to defend himself. But when the interview was over, the student stated flatly that the patient had not been angry during their interaction; his "understanding" had simply distorted his judgment without contributing to a solution.

It would seem well, then, that the question of whether psychiatrists can contribute to the solution of conflictual process brought into play by political differences remain a matter of speculation. It will take time to determine whether psychiatrists can become expert in helping avert international conflict, and whether a mutually beneficial exchange between psychiatrists and policy makers can be established. Meanwhile, those who made up the task force hoped for such beneficial exchanges, feeling that at least the notion of establishing a bridge between psychiatry and foreign affairs was sufficiently important to warrant serious effort and study. The original proposal for the task force (Davidson, 1968) noted how often the psychiatrist has to function as an intercessor and interpreter and how often he helps others clarify and interpret confused communication and perception through his insights into differences of personality type and cultural framework. He is also accustomed to confrontations that occur in situations of conflict and is trained to observe the unconscious processes that become cogent forces in personal and social interaction.

It is safe to assume that those who make up and lead one national group are likely to perceive the contemporary situation and history of their people in ways unique to them and often at odds with the views other nations entertain. Each group is fired by unconscious as well as conscious aims, and each is strongly influenced by deeply ingrained value systems. National groups differ from one another also in their way of communicating expectations, as well as in their anticipation of how well they will be understood, particularly in emotionally charged issues.

When the United States embargo on arms to Turkey was declared after the Turks intervened in Cyprus, Demirel (1975), then the Turkish prime minister, remarked to me that it would be amazing if Americans could understand the emotional component of the Turkish position on Cyprus or grasp how "Turkish hearts beat as one" on the Cyprus issue, from the little villages near the Russian border to the cosmopolitan sections of Istanbul. Demirel had observed while living in America how remote from the emotional attitude of a Kansas farmer is that of an American living in the Bronx. He also felt that the American people lack the kind of enduring common voice one hears in Turkey—that they tend instead to echo whatever is currently offered by political leaders.

One of the concerns of the task force was to learn how Cypriot Greeks and Cypriot Turks perceived one another and what peculiarities they might have in intergroup communication. It is difficult if not impossible to study the human factors in any situation in which intergroup conflicts are boiling over because they are so involved with the emotions of the people and their leaders. The Cyprus problem smoldered like a volcano, with periodic eruptions. During all of the cool periods the possibility of eruption was always present, and the memories of past violence were never forgotten. Many psychological phenomena of interest could be seen at work even during times of "peace." In the beginning of 1970 an attempt was made under the sponsorship of the task force "to conduct a 'psychological ethnography' of the Cypriot Greeks and Turks with a focus on the psychological and cultural factors related to the present conflict." Then the task force met with others at the Brookings Institution on October 4–6, 1971, for a seminar on Cyprus. This meeting was attended by psychiatrists, psychologists, and political scientists, as well as by career policy makers. It was at this seminar that Tenzel and Gerst, psychiatrist and psychologist respectively, presented for the first time the results of their Cyprus study, which had been supported by the task force.

Mirror Images?

Using Cyprus as a psychopolitical laboratory, as it were, Tenzel and Gerst attempted to explore the cultural and psychological dimensions of the continuous cross-cultural conflict in Cyprus by examining the beliefs, values, and stereotypical cognitive structuring of each of the two ethnic groups involved. Naturalistic observations, structured interviews, and psychological tests were used with a stratified cohort of adults in both the Cypriot Greek and the Cypriot Turkish communities. By these means some salient features of each group as compared with the other were identified, although "it should be emphasized that these descriptions are given in terms that relate one culture to another and should not be viewed as absolute."

These investigators found the Turkish group on the island to be hierarchal, patriarchal, and authoritarian, with a society in which roles are clearly defined. Respect and formality are valued as fostering ways in which the society is bound together by a reaffirmation of the relationship of each individual within it to the whole. The Cypriot Turk describes himself in terms that reveal an emphasis on communal values and a willingness to forgo any individuality beyond what attaches to the clear-cut role assigned to him by society. In one interview question Turks ranked "community service" first as a goal, with "wealth" last, and responded affirmatively to being described as "conventional, dependent, obliging, self-denying, and thorough."

Tenzel and Gerst found a contrast in the Cypriot Greek society, which they describe as "horizontal, competitive and individualistic." Conversation in the staccato Greek speech is louder than Turkish talk, and Greeks are respected for striving to improve their socioeconomic status. The investigators noted that among the Greeks on Cyprus a competitive spirit is encouraged at an early age and self-esteem is high. Likewise pride in the cultural heritage is instilled early and self-esteem is linked in part to the maintenance of a bond with the classical Greek period. The present desire for Enosis does not seem to be based on social, political, or economic realities but rather on an identification with a common and heroic past. The Greek Cypriot openly believes in his cultural superiority over the Turkish community. A public comment to one of these investigators that this cross-cultural study was invalid because "it compared the biggest of cultures to no culture at all," while extreme, is nevertheless indicative of feelings held by a large segment of the population even though only occasionally expressed. [Tenzel and Gerst, 1972]

At the same time these investigators, who conducted their study when the Turks were confined to their own enclaves, suggested that beneath the exterior calm of the Cypriot Turks "there resides a sensitivity and self doubt of a people whose minority culture has been the subject of criticism and negative stereotyping."

Seeing the Cypriot Turk as "more quiet, reserved and unemotional" and the Cypriot Greek as "more emotional and flighty," these investigators proposed a formulation to apply to the problems involved in political negotiation between them. "The Greeks would see the Turks as being cautious and overly suspicious and less inclined to be trustworthy, while the Turks would see the Greeks' actions as being facile and manipulative and thus also untrustworthy. It is not difficult to imagine what the outcome would be in, for example, a political negotiation where the level of suspicion and vigilance is already extremely high" (Tenzel and Gerst, 1972).

The difficulty with descriptive studies is, of course, their limitations in respect to any probing of the unconscious forces that determine—or strongly influence—behavior patterns. One basic problem with studies summarizing what was said or done on a conscious level is that they are likely to be interpreted by shapers of foreign policy according to "common sense" rather than with the insights available to students of intrapsychic process. Of course, even when psychological background is given to people unsophisticated in psychodynamic formulation, they may fail to grasp its implications; but they will at least know that matters are more complicated than they seem on the surface to be. The presentation made by Tenzel and Gerst at the Brookings Institution exemplifies this situation, particularly in respect to the concept of so-called mirror images.

Gerst and Tenzel (1972) postulated that (a) each subculture on Cyprus perceives the personality characteristics and values of its own group very similarly; (b) each subculture perceives the other group's characteristics in related but negative terms, using the same dimensional frame of reference but applying the negative side of each dimension to the other group; (c) within these frames of similar autostereotypes and reciprocally negative heterostereotypes there exist differences which reinforce the negative judgments of each other. To test these hypotheses, the investigators used four different instruments in addition to an interview structured to yield demographic, educational, and attitudinal data. These included the Harrison-Gough Adjective Check List (Gough and Heildrun, 1965), the Osgood Semantic Differential Test (Osgood, Suci, and Tannenbaum, 1957), the measure of social distance developed by Bogardus (1928), and the scale of optimism and pessimism described by Cantril (1965). They tested 216 Greek and 62 Turkish adults, with as even as possible representation of each sex and of urban and rural residents.

When they presented the results of their survey at Brookings in 1971 and, later, at the 1972 Annual Meeting of the American Psychiatric Association, they warned that any conclusions drawn from their study should be considered tentative since "the state of cross-cultural research in general is still in a primitive stage." Nevertheless, their data consistently represented the personality styles of each group in bipolar terms, with each located at an end of the spectrum. "Each seems to share the same common cultural reference which magnifies small areas of difference such that they become the main criteria for the establishment of trust or its reciprocal in the relationship between each group. It is tempting to conclude that the pattern of similarities and differences we have found [has] contributed to the periodic outbreak of conflict on Cyprus, and [continues] to maintain tension at an unacceptably high level" (Gerst and Tenzel, 1972).

One of the basic difficulties in conducting a meeting attended

by people from different professional backgrounds, like the one at
Brookings, is that of finding a "common language." Unless this can
be done, as is sometimes possible when the group is small and
meets long and regularly enough to reduce competition among the
members and the systems they represent, there is likely to be insufficient mutuality to keep the exchange from becoming political
in tone or esoteric.

The Tenzel and Gerst data were "interpreted" to show that
Cypriot Greeks and Cypriot Turks are, after all, very much alike.
Each group seemed to value similar qualities, but each claimed
them and denied their possession by their opposite numbers. They
were, nonetheless, sufficiently alike to be mirror images one of
the other. It was proposed that all that was necessary was to show
them how very much alike they are. This proposal was supported
by research data collected from the English high school in Cyprus.
Gerst and Tenzel (1972) obtained their data from two small samples
drawn from a population of Cypriot Greek urban high school students. One of the samples attended the English school, and the other
the Greek gymnasium. Most of the teachers in the latter had been
educated in Greece and placed strong emphasis in the classroom on
the classical period of their homeland. The spirit of Greek nationalism was far less dominant in the teaching of history and social
relations in the English school, which was attended by a number
of children neither Greek nor Turkish, children of foreign diplomats.
Almost all of the island's schools, even during the days of British
government, were ethnically segregated; the English school was
one of the few high schools that both Cypriot Greek and Cypriot
Turkish young people had been able to attend together before the
upheaval. It seems that when Tenzel and Gerst conducted their
study this school had no Turkish students, but the past, during which
the student body had been mixed, must have remained in memory
since in this more polyglot institution Greek students saw Cypriot
Turks in a far more positive light than did students attending the
gymnasium. "Greekness" and "Turkishness" were more nearly re-
conciled in the English school.

The United States has been successful in the degree to which it
has melded a diverse population in spite of the continuing ties with

"the old country" its ethnic components may have preserved; so it is not surprising that Tenzel and Gerst, like the Americans at the Brookings conference, used the American model in their thinking and, almost desperately it seemed to me, tried to identify clues for its successful application to the situation under study—to the creation of an integrated country that could be known simply as "Cyprus." I recall the outburst of a career statesman at the Brookings conference when he demanded: "What is wrong with those people who cannot *get together* and be a single nation the way we have in America?" It is interesting to speculate what the emotional tone of the participants might have been had the meeting taken place in Switzerland, for example, instead of in the United States. Would the group have expected Cypriot Turks and Cypriot Greeks to dilute their ethnicity in the service of a common state?

The "cure" suggested for the Cyprus problem was the use of public television in Cyprus to convey in subtle ways to each group how greatly it resembles the other, in the hope of overcoming the polarization. The surface manifestations of the Tenzel and Gerst study were thus considered to yield clues for practical actions that might be undertaken to resolve the conflict. Although surface manifestations are important, generated as they are by powerful buried forces, it is never enough to manipulate them as though they are by themselves the root causes of disturbance.

In the following chapter I will try to shed light on the Tenzel-Gerst material by examining the child-rearing practices of Cypriot Turks and Cypriot Greeks and providing evidence that the externalizations of Turkish and Greek children are perpetuated in their adult life. The incomplete but important offering of these two researchers—surface observation of the bipolarity of mirror images—may very well be a reflection of deep-rooted psychic mechanisms that both groups share.

Further Notes from the Brookings Meeting

During the Brookings Institution Seminar on Cyprus, I became aware that Americans tend, perhaps unwittingly, to compare the Turkish minority in Cyprus with the black minority in the United

States. However intellectually aware we may be of the inappro-
priateness of comparison, we tend unconsciously to view any social
situation in the light of those with which we are familiar, particularly those with which we became familiar when our psychic structure was being laid down in childhood. The blacks in America were
at no time masters and rulers of the country to which they came,
as the Turks were on Cyprus. On the contrary, they came as slaves,
with the self-concept of slavery forced upon them. This self-concept
and the defensive-adaptive responses it evoked, as well as the humiliation of holding only second-class citizenship, tragically stamped
their psychological being (Erikson, 1963). They fought back with
the reactive statement that "black is beautiful," uttered over and
over again during the struggle for civil rights. The Turks on Cyprus
had for centuries owned the most desirable land on the island and
had Greeks work for them. Although with the arrival of the British
the Greeks gained economic superiority, the Turks clung to their
self-concept of lordliness and mastery pending the slow test of time
and the impingement of reality. At no time were they without
roots and lively connection with the homeland. There remained
long-standing family ties, and, indeed, island Turks voluntarily
embraced the cultural revolution launched in Turkey by Atatürk
in the 1920s and continued into the 1930s. Moreover, there was
little physical difference between the two groups on Cyprus, and
certainly none of the problems inherent in the psychological reaction to black skin color.[3]

3. The black color of the minority group in the United States may not seem
per se to be a major cause of social attitudes so strongly felt here in the past (and
still to some degree evident), since the psychic representation of the historical
fact of a master/slave relationship is clearly dominant. However, psychoanalytic
insight indicates that the color difference itself was an unconsciously significant
obstacle to racial integration. The symbolism (in its widest sense) invested in the
color black (Thass-Thienemann, 1968; West, 1969) had become an arena for unconscious projections and for the externalization by the white majority of whatever
was bad and unwanted. "True symbolism" in the psychoanalytic sense (Jones,
1949), which is a result of intrapsychic conflict and evidence of something repressed, makes black contain anal components (Erikson, 1963; Kubie, 1965),
consistent with Hamilton's (1966) paradigm of "up-breast-milk-white-God-heaven-
good" related to the color white, and "down-toilet-feces-black-Devil-hell-bad"
to the color black.

In Cyprus the fascinating diversity of cultural influences, the legacies of one conquering power after another, resulted, in the end, in social bipolarity. The bipolar stance of Cypriot Greeks and Cypriot Turks persisted even after the island was placed under a single flag, that of the Republic of Cyprus. Writing before the events of 1974, and noting how hugely difficult it was to strike a balance between the rights of the majority and minority groups in the island population, Couloumbis and Georgiades (1973) suggested that in some respects the situation was like that in French Quebec or Catholic Ulster, or that the uneasy population was like that of blacks in the United States, the Muslims in India, the Hindus in Pakistan, or the Palestinians in Israel. There are, however, important differences from the situation in other countries, as I indicated in pointing out how the mental self-representation of a black American differs from that of a Turk in Cyprus.

Writing about the formation of new states such as that attempted in Cyprus, Geertz (1973), an anthropologist, suggests that they are abnormally susceptible to serious disaffection arising from primordial ties (Shils, 1957). Such a tie is "one that stems from the 'givens'—or, more precisely, as culture is inevitably involved in such matters, the assumed 'givens'—of social existence: immediate contiguity and kin connection mainly, but beyond them the givenness that stems from being born into a particular religious community, speaking a particular language, or even a dialect of a

---

In a society dominated by white people, the symbolic "badness" of blackness was forced onto the psyche of those who were black until the civil rights movement was seriously under way. It was transmitted by black mothers to their children (Brody, 1963). It is thus not surprising that when I was a staff psychiatrist at a segregated state mental hospital in the South, I noticed that one of the most common delusions among my black patients was an openly or indirectly expressed wish to be white (Volkan, 1963, 1966a). This consuming desire of blacks to become white has been widely documented by many, including Armstrong and Gregor (1964), Brody (1961, 1963), Goodman (1952), Kennedy (1952), Lind (1914a, 1914b), Myers and Yochelson (1948), Teicher (1968), Vitols (1961), and Vitols, Walters, and Keeler (1963). It would be interesting to learn whether it has become less cogent or disappeared altogether among mentally ill blacks since the civil rights movement strengthened black self-esteem. I do not know of any study made on this subject.

language, and following particular social practices. These con-
gruities of blood, speech, custom, and so on, are seen to have an
ineffable, and at times overpowering, coerciveness in and of themselves" (Geertz, 1973, p. 259).

The network of primordial alliance is, in most cases, the product
of centuries of gradual crystallization. There are many foci about
which primordial attachments tend to crystallize; Geertz sees racial
difference as one of them, in addition to the common language,
religion, homeland, and customs shared over time. He also noted
another level of bonding among human beings, in which a more
superficial operational homogeneity based on class, political party,
or occupation brings people into groups. Although differences on
this operational level can pose a threat to the administration of
government, it is only when they are infused with primordial sentiment that they become strong enough to undermine the state itself,
and the population drawn together by operational ties alone seldom
becomes a nation on such grounds. Geertz declares: "Economic
or class or intellectual disaffection threatens revolution, but disaffection based on race, language, or culture threatens partition,
irredentism, or merger, a redrawing of the very limits of the state,
a new definition of its domain. Civil discontent finds its natural
outlet in the seizing, legally or illegally, of the state apparatus.
Primordial discontent strives more deeply and is satisfied less
easily" (p. 261).

Primordial sentiments in operation in the Cyprus conflict included
ethnicity, language, and religion. Although groups in conflict in
different parts of the world may have different primordial sentiments, careful examination of the problems in Cyprus may help to
uncover the reasons why people who have been close neighbors for
so long get along so poorly.

My Psychoanalytic Background

When I joined the Task Force on Psychiatry and Foreign Affairs I
was for some time the only psychoanalyst among the five psychiatrists in membership, but John Mack, another psychoanalyst, joined
us in 1975. I felt an initial hesitancy about trying to apply formula-

tions from my specialty to national or international political issues
that affected masses of people. I believe that any psychoanalyst
would have felt the same, in spite of being ready to address himself
to clinical issues concerned with politically induced stress. Psychological effects of the Nazi terror have been closely studied by
psychoanalysts, for example, as I will describe in Chapter IV. There
are many reasons for the psychoanalyst to refrain from any intrusion
on the territory of the political scientist. Although the tradition
of "applied psychoanalysis" began with Freud, his famous exchange
of letters with Albert Einstein served notice to his followers that
political problems should be left to statesmen (Freud, 1932a).[4] Also,
one needs to understand group processes in dealing with the political
aspects of groups whether they are in conflict or coexisting peace-
fully. Although Freud's (1921) group psychology linked individual
psychology with social process, he limited his discussion to "regressively formed groups" (Waelder, 1971) and the impact of their
leaders on them. Redl holds that "this is not enough" (reported
by Stanton, 1958, p. 123) and that there is a "glaring need for recon-
ceptualization of the psychoanalytic theory of group behavior."
In spite of the fact that the psychoanalytic literature continues to
provide more and more information about various aspects of group
process, I felt constrained in the task force from jumping too readily
from what I knew about the individual to an attempt to understand
different types of groups. Moreover, I had a nagging sense that
knowledge of unconscious psychological processes cannot be
"taught" to policy makers, recalling what Langer (1971) said
about how dubious historians are about gaining any benefit from the
teachings of modern psychology. "Those who have attempted to
utilize such teachings have for the most part been those who have
undergone analysis themselves and therefore have some comprehen-
sion of fundamental principles and procedures. Others, even when
interested, are reluctant because they feel the need for more systematic knowledge than can be acquired by independent reading"
(p. ix). Langer also looks at the other side of the coin when he states
that psychoanalysts, trained as they are to work with imaginative
material, with bits and pieces of human recollection, are apt to

4. See Chapter V for further discussion of this correspondence.

overlook the rigorous standards that historians have set themselves.

Mitscherlich's (1971) voice is perhaps unique in clearly urging psychoanalysts to participate in research into the collective behavior of groups and the political implications of such behavior. He writes: "If we, as analysts, persist in restricting ourselves to an exclusively medical and clinical position, the research into collective behavior, for instance research on the psychology of war, would proceed without our participation. Predictably, this would lead to a further plundering of analytic findings and theories without analysts having any effective share in the direction of the research, nor any means of protesting effectively. Moreover, one would have manoeuvred oneself into an isolation of one's own making" (p. 164). Mitscherlich urges that in doing this type of research the psychoanalyst be willing to collaborate with related scientific disciplines. I have mentioned the difficulty in finding a common language in such collaboration, and how it can be found when scientists from different disciplines meet regularly together over some period of time (Bateson, 1972).

When the United States became embroiled in the Vietnam crisis, Rangell (1974) expressed concern about "the crime of silence" in his presidential address to the twenty-eighth International Psycho-Analytic Congress. By this he meant the passivity of an individual who sees a street mugging and does nothing about it, or the indifference of a nation toward genocide or what he considered "an immoral war." In 1976 he wrote about Watergate. However, I sensed in him an almost apologetic attitude as though he were reluctant as a psychoanalyst to venture into any attempt to understand other human behavior than that manifested on the couch. He said: "It is a wide span from Watergate to psychoanalysis. But Richard Nixon closed the gap. His men invaded our space and brought Watergate in direct touch with the psychoanalysts' terrain. We might as well get something out of it. Nothing can be better than an advance in knowledge" (Rangell, 1976a, p. 60).

I was born in Cyprus, so the "Cyprus problem" invaded my space. My study of it will be limited, although it would be interesting to study Denktaş, Makarios, or Grivas and their influence on their followers, for example, and then to ask if the Turkish military intervention of the 1974 summer would have taken place had Turkey's prime minister been someone other than Bülent Ecevit.[5] This book will not raise such questions, but I will discuss the psychological makeup of the Cypriot Turk; ask why a "Cypriot nation" could not have been established; and describe the mass reaction of the Cypriot Turks to politically induced stress over an eleven-year period, and their mass reactions to war when it came.

The Background of My Data-Gathering

Since I grew up on Cyprus I have firsthand experience of Turkish child-rearing practices and the experiences Turkish children have in common. The young of any nation are exposed to child-rearing practices approved within that nation's culture, and since the events and the climate of childhood and adolescence play an important role in forming adult character, common early experiences are sure to mark the characterological makeup of any national group as a whole.[6] Roheim (1950a) warns against oversimplification, however, pointing to the fact that the unconscious life of all human beings is much alike, whatever the nationality; he sees the mores of a country as depending more on historical events than on the infantile situation. He stresses that the parent is the culture's surrogate only to a certain extent and, moreover, that the child reacts not to what his parents do but to their unconscious, which is beyond

5. There are descriptions in English of the lives and activities of both Makarios and Grivas. For example, see: Alastos (1960), Barker (1959), Grivas (1961, 1964), Mayes (1960), and Markides (1977). After the Turkish military intervention in northern Cyprus, the Turkish press was flooded with books on Ecevit with titles such as *The Making of a Prime Minister, Yesterday Atatürk, Today Ecevit,* and *Third Man* (in reference to the first man of modern Turkey being Atatürk; the second, İnönü; and the third, Ecevit himself). Sağlamer (1974), Selçuk (1974), and Yurdanur (1974) were among those writing about Ecevit, almost all of whom idealized him. Although I believe in the leader's influence on groups, I have insufficient data on these leaders to make sophisticated psychoanalytic formulations about them or their role in the Cyprus conflict. Thus this important area of investigation will be left for future study.

6. See Favazza (1974) for a critique of so-called child determinism in the importance of the childhood experience within a given culture to the determination of adult character.

the dictates of any culture. According to Roheim, what we are talking about in analyzing the "character" of any nation is the collective superego or ego-ideal (the upper strata.).[7]

The mother and important others enact socially sanctioned roles in their interactions with the child and induce his responses accord-

7. The theory of internalized object relations gives us a more systematic understanding of the integration of the superego and ego-ideal and their pre-oedipal precursors in "all bad" and "all good" self- and object representations. The superego is formed by the fusion of the superego proper and the ego-ideal (Lampl–de Groot, 1962; A. Reich, 1953). The ego-ideal serves wish fulfillment and is a gratifying agency. Nonetheless, in the course of normal development, both agencies unite into one substructure: "The ego ideal's content, 'I am like my parents,' can acquire an imperative compulsive character. 'I must be like my parents.' Later on high ideals in general may be experienced as demands." (Lampl–de Groot, p. 100). The superego will not be integrated if the individual arrives at the oedipal level with the primitive splitting of his self- and object representations still actively in operation. The "all good" units will foster the creation of an all-powerful ego-ideal, while the primitively split "all bad" self- and object image unit contributes to the qualities of the unintegrated superego. Thus there is a constant attempt to project the prohibitive aspects of such a superego in this situation. Since the superego proper and ego-ideal are located in dissociated camps, so to speak, it can be said that the superego is itself split. Instead of demanding that the ego itself remain in an integrated state, such a superego may tolerate contradictory ego states. The ego boundaries are stabilized when there is sufficient delineation between self- and object representation. When this occurs it permits a practical, immediate adaptation to the demands of reality; deeper internalization of the demands of reality, especially social reality, cannot be maintained when there is interference with the integration of those nonintegrated self- and object images with superego (Kernberg, 1967).

I believe that the theory of internalized object relations will help us to see group processes in general from a newer and clearer angle than would otherwise be possible. It contributes to our understanding of what sort of a concept of social system is internalized by the individual at different levels of early development, and how such a concept can be shared by people in the same group. Kernberg (1972) writes: "As the self-concept develops, role integration and differentiation of the self occur automatically with it; and as the child develops differentiated relationships with both parents and his siblings, these role differentiations acquire a highly sophisticated organization embedding the developing personality in *the social system which it develops* [italics added]. . . . as the child grows up and assumes mothering, fathering, and sibling roles in relationship to other people, he "identifies" his self-concept with the internalized object representations that constitute his role model under such circumstances" (p. 244).

ing to their expectations, but the way in which this reciprocal process is internalized depends on the stage the child is in. After the
self-images are differentiated from the object images—but before
the primitive splitting is mended—images of the mother are internalized in bipolar fashion under the influence of libidinal and
aggressive drives respectively. When, between the age of six and
ten months, the child feels anxiety at meeting strangers (Spitz, 1965),
we can assume that such strangers are the targets of the externalization of the "all bad" self- and object images. Such anxiety
gradually lessens and ultimately disappears. How can this observation be applied to experiences shared by Cypriot Turkish children?
We can hypothesize an event to symbolize all events in which the
mother conveys her attitude to her child: During the period in
which a child normally experiences "stranger anxiety," a visitor
enters the Turkish family home and the child, as expected, feels
anxious. If the mother will not sanction such a response but per-
suades her child that there is nothing to fear, disclosing no anxiety
of her own, the child who at first externalized the "all bad" onto the
visitor "learns" that he has been mistaken. Not only has his externalization been challenged, but he has been marginally introduced
to the testing of social reality. In truth, however, the Turkish mother
is apt to sanction the anxiety of her child about a Greek visitor who
had been a target of her own externalization of the unwanted parts
of herself and her internalized world. Even if the Greek visitor is
courteously received and the social surface is unruffled, the mother
may nonverbally convey to her child that the visitor is "different"
from their kind. Of course, at this point the child is not able to
differentiate Greekness from Turkishness, but the precursor of
this differentiation is supplied by the mother.

As the child develops further and establishes a superego, this
superego takes no punitive measures as long as such socially sanctioned externalization is continued.[8] In fact, part of the superego

8. Lustman (1962) proposes a similar formulation in his paper, examining the
development of a character trait or a symptom in children. Both character trait
and symptom arise from the interplay of impulse, anxiety, conflict, and defense.
The adaptive value of the character trait is consistently related to reality. He says:
"the first ego syntonicity is not exclusively an intrapsychic ego syntonicity but
rather primarily a syntonicity with the parental ego. If the structural development

itself—the part that reflects bad and fearful object images—will be kept externalized on objects tinged with Greekness. The ego-ideal, on the other hand, enhances the child's self-perception of being uncontaminated with Greekness. Children raised alike share an object representation of an "all bad" kind resident in the opposite ethnic group on the island and share a corresponding idealized concept of their own group. I will return at greater length to the child-rearing practices of the Turks and show how certain shared cultural patterns themselves, i.e., the presence of multiple mothers in the (modified) extended family, make for the sharing of certain aspects of self- and object concepts within a group setting.

Shared childhood experiences examined from the point of view of the theory of internalized object relations will begin in the next chapter my formulations of the Cyprus problem and my interpretations of Tenzel and Gerst's (Tenzel, 1971; Tenzel and Gerst, 1972; Gerst and Tenzel, 1972) research findings. I collected my data by observing experiences the Turks shared, not in their period of childhood but as adults swept up by the events of the past fifteen years. I was on the island during the summer of 1968, soon after the Greeks permitted the Turks to move freely outside their enclaves for the first time in years. My next visit took place in the summer of 1973 during a time of "peace." My sabbatical year, which I spent in Turkey, began by coincidence a month after the Turkish military intervention on Cyprus. I visited Cyprus in the spring of 1975 and in the summer of the same year, during the first anniversary of the intervention, returning in the summer of 1977 during the third anniversary of the war. There I collected data about the reactions of Cypriot Turks to events that affected them all. I used a method like that described by Lifton (1972), which he appropriately called "the shared theme approach."

Lifton (1961, 1968, 1970) focused on three specific groups and

---

of the child—molding and being molded by the parental relationships—produces behavior which is consonant with the unconscious needs of the parents, the likelihood of a character trait is enhanced. . . . when behavior is alien to the superego demands of the parent, the likelihood is greater for crystallization as superego elements with corresponding tension and the possibility of symptom formation" (p. 236–237).

observed the psychohistorical themes the men and women in them shared as they underwent particular kinds of collective experience. In preparing his study of the psychological effects of the atomic bomb in Hiroshima, Lifton, having spent several years in Japan, interviewed seventy-five randomly selected survivors of the holocaust during the six months he spent in Hiroshima. He explained: "My focus has been upon themes, forms, and images, that are significant ways shared, rather than upon the life of a single person as such. The shared-themes approach is based upon a psychoanalytically derived stress on what goes on inside of people. But, as compared with Erikson's great-man paradigm it moves still further from classical analytic tradition. That is, it moves outward from the individual in the direction of collective historical experience" (Lifton, 1972, p. 363). Lifton suggests that the "shared-theme" approach requires considerable innovation in interview method. First of all, the people the investigator interviewed were selected by him and were not themselves seeking therapeutic help. Moreover, they were chosen according to their shared experience rather than according to any psychological sequelae. Thus Lifton found himself developing a freer style of interviewing than is usually considered appropriate for the psychiatrist—a probing style that encouraged the widest range of association, the disclosure of life stories, and the exploration of dreams; but one that at times closely approached an "open dialogue" about the experiences being reported. Lifton (1972) describes this method as being

partly empirical (in its stress upon specific data from interviews); partly phenomenological, or, as I prefer, formative (in its stress upon forms and images that are simultaneously individual and collective); and partly speculative (in its use of interview data, together with many other observations, to posit relationships between man and his history, and to suggest concepts that eliminate the artificial separation of the two). In this speculation, the investigator has the advantage of beginning from concrete information that is a product of his own direct perceptions. While I recognize that subjective distortion can render the advantage a mixed one, I think it can be said that exaggerated concerns with detached objectivity have too often caused us to undervalue what can be learned about history from our direct perceptions. [p. 364]

Shared psychohistorical themes can also be found in Keniston's (1965, 1968) studies of activist American students and in Coles's (1967) well-known work with children and adults caught up in this country's racial conflict.

My approach was similar as I attempted to understand the reaction of Cypriot Turks to the historical events they had experienced together. I developed with those I interviewed a relationship "neither that of a doctor and patient nor of ordinary friends, though at moments . . . [like] either." Each interview was an exploration of the subject's world with means that were simply humane as well as professional. In working at Hiroshima, Lifton moved out of his interviews with individual survivors into a relationship with the groups they belonged to and the leaders that had emerged from these groups. Similarly, in Cyprus I not only interviewed individuals but made careful observation of group processes, as when I studied those groups of Cypriot Turks from the south who went north in 1974 to relocate in the abandoned Greek villages; and I also talked to the leaders, particularly those in government. In Cyprus, I had long talks with Denktaş, and in Turkey I was given a special appointment with Demirel, the prime minister, to hear his views on the Turks as they related to the Cyprus problem.[9] Like Lifton in Hiroshima, I also sought out creative notables, writers and poets,

9. On November 28–30, 1977, the Middle East Institute and the Institute of Psychiatry and Foreign Affairs cosponsored a meeting in Washington on "The Psycho-Political Dynamics of the Cyprus Problem." Takis Evdokas, a Greek psychiatrist from Cyprus who had been actively involved in Cypriot Greek politics, and I were the principal speakers. This meeting, like the one at Brookings, brought together many political figures, personnel from the Departments of State and Defense, professionals from the CIA's Office of Regional and Political Analysis, and psychiatrists. The latter included Dr. Jack Weinberg, then president of the American Psychiatric Association; Dr. Melvin Sabshin, its medical director; Dr. William Davidson, president of the Institute of Psychiatry and Foreign Affairs; and Dr. Rita Rogers, former chairperson of the American Psychiatric Association's Task Force on Psychiatry and Foreign Affairs. This meeting gave me the opportunity to hear a serious analysis of events that had taken place on Cyprus. Leaders who, although neither Greek nor Turkish, had firsthand observations to report, included Lord Hugh Caradon, the last British governor of Cyprus; former Ambassadors Taylor G. Belcher and L. Dean Brown, who had represented the United States there, and Parker T. Hart, who had served in Turkey.

since a significant aspect of history is the creative struggle of the people involved to come to terms with what has happened to them. I also interviewed professional people, among them psychiatrists who had themselves shared the historical events under study but who had also been able to observe how the people reacted to them. In addition, I dealt therapeutically with four persons who asked my professional consultation for "emotional conditions" attributable to recent events of historical consequence.

My situation differed from Lifton's, however, since during the time I was collecting information I lived with relatives and friends who belonged to the ethnic group under study and shared their day-by-day experiences with me. I was able to watch children at play in their unguarded moments. Lifton demonstrated that an American with two years of past experience in Japan could, within six months, grasp the basic meaning of what the cataclysm meant to those who survived it—their immersion in death and their guilt at still being alive. Tenzel also prepared himself for his work by spending much time in Cyprus and acquiring both Greek and Turkish friends there. Nevertheless, although an analyst or psychiatrist who knows a country but has no family or social ties to it may profitably study its position in international conflict and become aware of its shared emotional problems, peculiar perceptual patterns, and subtleties of communication, he is likely to miss some significant clues that readily reveal themselves to the investigator reared in its culture from birth to adulthood. I was able as a participant observer to see much in addition to what I gathered in systematic interviews; examples of such unconscious disclosures are my noting in 1968 the myth of "the great weapon" and, in 1975, my observation of the "itching phenomenon" explained in a later chapter.

III The People

Who Are the Cypriot Turks?

Turkish history began in Central Asia. Turks were first mentioned during the sixth century A.D., appearing in the writings of Chinese and Byzantine historians. That they throve is indicated by inscriptions dating from the eighth century such as: "The poor I made rich, the few I made many" (Muller, 1961). They founded two large empires in Central Asia, in Turkestan. A westward migration began to fill with Turks the vacuum left by the collapse of the Arabic Empire, and about a thousand years ago Turks began settling in Anatolia, where conquerors and the conquered merged, bound together by common allegiance to Islam (Cahen, 1968), which the Turks adopted. The empire of the Selçuk Turks in Anatolia gave way gradually to domination by the Ottomans, who, as soon as they gained the ascendancy over rival Turkish dynasties, became the undisputed leaders of the Moslem world. After its capture by the Ottomans in 1453, Constantinople (now Istanbul) became the capital of the then powerful empire.

Turkish settlement on Cyprus goes back to September 2, 1572, when, after his forces took the island, the Ottoman sultan Selim II signed an imperial order that certain towns and cities in Anatolia send a specified number of Turkish families to colonize Cyprus.[1] This systematic emigration, the "exile method," had been used elsewhere by the Ottoman Turks to establish their ethnic group in territories newly conquered. It not only set the Turkish mark on such places but hastened the establishment of an effective economy and administration (İnalcık, 1974). The takeover of Cyprus by the Ottoman Turks came after Venetian domination of eighty-two

1. See Başbakanlık arşivi (Archives of the Office of the Prime Minister), Mühimme Defteri, 19:334.

years and required a war that lasted for a year, begining in the
summer of 1570. A number of geopolitical, economic, and religious reasons have been given to account for it (İnalcık, 1964;
Bedevi, 1965). The Turkish need for a shipping base between Istanbul and Alexandria added motivation, as did the rivalry between
the prime minister and an influential statesman to whom the support
of such conquest was a bid for recognition. To win Cyprus it was
necessary for the Ottoman Turks not only to overcome the Venetians, but to oppose also the combined forces of the Catholic states
with interests in the Mediterranean. As Turkish casualties mounted
into the tens of thousands, "it was a fact of history that they risked
the fate of the Empire" in order to conquer the island (İnalcık,
p. 26). The imperial order to colonize acknowledged the devastation
on the island but emphasized the suitability of the land for agricul-
ture.

Under the Venetians the island population had dwindled to little
more than 200,000. The imperial order called for certain towns in
Anatolia to send one family out of each ten engaged there in any
given trade. Tailors, shoemakers, cooks, candlemakers, carpenters,
stonemasons, jewelers, and so on were relocated. Those chosen to
resettle had to be strong. Unskilled workers, failed farmers, or those
unable to get title to their farms had to register if they wanted to
resettle, and await the decision of the authorities. Farmers chosen
to go carried their own farm implements and seed with them. The
settlers were guaranteed protection and forgiven their taxes for two
years. Only a third of those going to Cyprus went voluntarily, and
some of the reluctant tried to escape, although the sultan ordered
hanging for defectors. This "forced exile" method was taken so
seriously that the imperial order included a suggestion for recording
detailed descriptions of all ordered to Cyprus so that officials there
could make sure that all had complied; Moslems frowned on making any graphic representation of a human being, so identification
depended on written description.

Approximately 30,000 Turks had been settled in Cyprus by the
end of the seventeenth century, and this method of colonization
was used until the middle of the eighteenth century. The people
whose psychological history I am about to describe descended from

migrants who populated Cyprus as a result of this forced exile, and who took with them to the island their heritage of Turkish culture, their tradition of the extended family, and a tenacious adherence to their religion.

As conquerors of Cyprus the Ottoman Turks seem to have been welcomed at first by the island's indigenous population (Hill, 1940–42). In 1575, soon after the occupation, the Ottoman government liquidated the Latin church in Cyprus and restored the autocephalous Orthodox archbishopric, thus reestablishing the religious and political leadership of the Greek-speaking community and assuring its cultural autonomy. Cypriot Turks and Cypriot Greeks lived side by side for four hundred years. Traditions and customs developed in ways that effected a bipolarity of the population although Turks and Greeks were geographically scattered throughout Cyprus. Both groups considered interethnic marriage as taboo as incest. There was superficial friendliness, to be sure, but no possibility of any growing intimacy between Cypriot Turk and Cypriot Greek individuals, and hence no opportunity for one group to understand the other truly. Although both groups were interestingly alike in regarding natural phenomena with superstitious awe, each had its own belief system, basically dissociated from the other in spite of some areas of similarity. Certain holy places were revered by both groups, as was the case in other parts of the Ottoman Empire with mixed populations (Hasluck, 1929). For example, the same cave or significant rocky place would be visited by both groups with reverence; the Greeks might visit it on Sunday to remind themselves of their pre-Christian veneration of pagan gods, and the Turks might go on Friday to make offerings for which they expected to receive favor from the spirit of some "holy man" connected with the place.

Although the traditional dress of male villagers is seen less and less often on Cyprus, until recently Turkish and Greek men alike wore baggy trousers with a sash around the waist. Virtually the only way to tell a Cypriot Greek peasant from his Cypriot Turkish counterpart is by the color of his sash. Turks wear scarlet, and Greeks blue. Nevertheless, over the years no Cypriot nation came out of this mixed population. Neither group proselytized. From the records of the Ottoman period we learn that not more than two hundred Christians on the island became Moslem (Bedevi, 1965, p. 139) over three centuries of Turkish rule.[2] Until the recent outbreak of hostilities one could see Greeks and Turks working side by side in government offices on Cyprus, sometimes using the same shops and places of entertainment. No intimate cross-cultural friendships were ever sought, however, and the children of each group attended their own schools in which the mother tongue was spoken. The term "modern Cypriot culture" refers to the one in which, before the war, the two separate groups coexisted, divided by a psychological chasm and by certain customs, though not separated physically. The psychological determinants of this enduring separation merit study.

The Turkish Family Group

In order to illuminate with insight such surface material as that gathered by Tenzel and Gerst (see Chapter II), I must turn attention to the Turkish family and its child-rearing practices, peculiarities of which may give us clues to the failure of a Cypriot nation to evolve, and to the development of recognizable types of group process among Cypriot Turks under political stress. It must be acknowledged at the outset that with "the passing of the traditional society" (Lerner, 1962) in Cyprus, as well as in mainland Turkey "a single family type or a unique way of child training cannot be taken as the prototype of a typical Turkish family. One can only speak in terms of dynamic changes in Turkish families which correspond to cultural changes occurring in Turkey" (Sümer, 1970, p. 413). There remain some Turkish families dominated by tradition (Erdentuğ, 1959); but some others are "westernized," and still others function as "transitional" groups.

I will describe the traditional Turkish family in the belief that in

2. There are, however, contrary statements. Referring to wholly Turkish villages with Greek names in the Karpasia and Paphos areas of the island (before the present Cyprus problem erupted), the sociologist Markides (1977) suggests that during the Ottoman rule some Greek villages voluntarily Islamized to avoid the taxation required of Christian communities.

spite of change its impact still continues. The patriarchal, patrilocal, and patrilinear characteristics of the extended family were strengthened under Islam and are still evident, even in the modern segments of Cypriot Turkish society as well as in Turkey itself, although "a change toward a 'modified extended family' is occurring in that the family is not breaking down into modern families, but into a confederation of nuclear families with supporting lineal and collateral ties" (Öztürk and Volkan, 1971, p. 244).

Close relatives live under the same roof in the traditional family, which usually includes the father and mother, married sons and their families, and other kinsmen such as the father's younger brothers and their families and the father's unmarried sisters. The relationship that bonds such a family is usually through the paternal side of the house. Each family member is to some extent the psychological extension of all the others, and all feel dependence on the same interpersonal web for support and emotional nourishment, sharing emotional, social, and economic problems and presenting a unified front to the world. The need of the individual to assert himself is secondary to the mutual identification within the family. When a girl becomes engaged, sisters, brothers, aunts, and cousins, as well as her parents, are emotionally stirred. They all share the success of any member, as well as his or her misfortunes. Although its senior male member has authority over the family, it is the mother who is responsible for its emotional climate. A Turkish saying has it that Hell and Heaven lie at the feet of the mother, and certainly her affect-laden reactions are likely to determine the behavior of all in the home. It may rest with the father to approve his son's marriage to a certain girl, but his wife's attitude toward her will make up his mind for him. A new bride is timid when she enters her husband's family, but as time goes on and her husband dies, "a striking metamorphosis takes place from what she was . . . to what she becomes—a powerful, authoritarian old woman taking revenge for her early sufferings and treating the new bride as herself was once treated. The sinister figure of the old woman is well known in Turkish folklore where she appears as an omnipotent character who can do either good or harm, who gets involved as a go-between in the love affairs of the young, and who is to be feared, respected, and consulted in every difficult subject including illness" (Sümer, 1070, pp. 418–419). When either parent is removed from the supportive web woven by family relationships, an older brother or sister will take the place of the dead or incapacitated parent; so the fabric remains relatively intact.

The individual Turk can be viewed (Özbek and Volkan, 1976) as being within his family circle in a *satellite state* (Volkan and Corney, 1968) indicative of failure to complete entirely the process of separation-individuation (Mahler, 1963; Mahler and Furer, 1963). This term refers also to his establishment of a stable but malignant adaptation, his fixation in orbit around the central figure from the representation of which he failed to separate and achieve individuation—that of the mother. Anyone not liberated from his mother's representation by having become a freestanding person in his own right must stay near it, although since he is afraid of being altogether engulfed by it, he maintains some psychic distance. Since he can differentiate her representation from his own, he does not enter into symbiosis but is drawn toward the center when it represents the "good" mother and repelled when it is the "bad" one, flying in orbit like a moth irresistibly attracted by a flame (Volkan, 1976). Like the moth whose plight is so often described in traditional Ottoman poetry as well as in folk verse, he is suspended between two dangerous possibilities—being destroyed by flying into the flame or being lost in darkness by abandoning it. The typical Turk is in a similar satellite position around the family center. He is aware of his individuality and of being differentiated from the heads of his family, but some of the important ego functions he has developed operate to maintain his orbit, which protects him from either being burned to death or lost. In the family many moths orbit together around the candle, delicately keeping apart from one another. The small hit-and-run collisions that occur are, in human terms, psychological assertions of one's identity; the bickering, nagging, and sulking that take place within the family fold serve to reduce anxiety over the possibility of becoming genuinely symbiotic, but the family readily acts as one in response to outside influences, and its group self-concept prevails over the individual self-concept of any member.

Although the tight cohesiveness of the Turkish family is a culture-specific adaptation and should not be seen as pathologic in this context, it provides interesting clues to certain problems of Turkish behavior. A reflection of this developmental pattern can be seen in the way Turks handle their cars in traffic (Özbek and Volkan, 1976). The average Turk flouts traffic rules unless he actually sees an officer giving tickets to offenders; the outside authority represented by an officer stands for the external superego that people in the satellite state never fully internalize. The Turkish driver makes little distinction between red and green traffic lights, and the yellow signal does not exist for him. Disaster is nevertheless averted, if narrowly, by the uncanny awareness each driver seems to have of the mood of others and how they can be expected to move. Turkish traffic has a kind of choreography based on empathy. The busy streets become a playground for the discharge of aggressive feelings born of togetherness. Wherever driver education is taken seriously and traffic regulations are enforced, this intuitive driving style begins to change. The Turk driving in Western Europe, missing the synchrony he is accustomed to, becomes so perplexed over absolutes of traffic control that, as statistics show, Turks account for more motor accidents there than any other nationality.

In the world of business in Turkey a similar togetherness is accompanied by the belief that "someone out there" is either "good" or "bad" for one's enterprise. Although official transactions require an inordinate amount of red tape, negotiations are made largely on the basis of knowing the right people and being able to depend on them for protection. Such grapevine conduct of business may be a survival from the Ottoman period during which it was useful in engaging profitable prospects in the web of government. The Ottoman Empire included a number of different ethnic groups in its widespread holdings, and the complications of red tape enmeshed them all in bureaucratic procedures and kept them tied to the central authority. This apparently paradoxical obsession with making regulations customarily flouted is an example of the two-sided coin; those constantly involved in the affairs of other people must emphasize regulations if they are to maintain the limits and boundaries within the extended (or modified extended) family (Özbek and Volkan, 1976).

The ready availability to the Turkish child of more than one mothering figure accounts for certain typical psychological characteristics (Volkan, 1973a). In the extended family the upbringing of a child is not the exclusive prerogative of his mother; other women in the household feel entitled to mother him in their own way. Thus, until in adult life he becomes a satellite around the family center, he has many "mothers," the list often including, besides the natural mother, a grandmother, an aunt, an older sister, and perhaps a wet nurse, all competing. The classic child/mother unit must be stretched to include them, and under these circumstances the frustrations of the child struggling for separation-individuation are unlike those of the child constantly in a one-to-one encounter with the same woman.

Although one might see a superficial resemblance to the situation of the white child growing up in the "old South" of the United States under the devoted care of a black mammy, there is an important difference. The southern child's white natural mother was psychologically widely separated from the nursemaid or mammy, whereas the Turkish women who share interest in a child share their lives in general. Smith (1949) states that southern whites mothered by a white mother and a black mammy grew up to feel allegiance to the former and to her authority and culture but attached many feelings of pleasure to the black mammy. She observes that the psychological ramifications of this dual relationship "make the Oedipus complex seem by comparison almost a simple adjustment." Her meaning is clear, of course, but it should be added that when pregenital issues are not resolved by the time the child reaches the oedipal phase, that phase will also be complicated and difficult to resolve.[3] An examination of borderline per-

3. Cambor (1969) describes the influence of multiple mothering on the development of ego and superego and gives case histories in which the biologic mother was perceived by her children as relatively rejecting in comparison with the maternal surrogate. He says of the two mothers: "There is . . . a greater tendency for a delay in the establishment of stable object representations, and this delay may be re-enforced by interference with the process of fusion of good and bad maternal object representations. This interferes both with the process of separation-individuation and the progressive maturation of identification processes, and encourages the regressive wish for fusion with the idealized good

sonality organization (Kernberg, 1967) will help us appreciate the
family dynamics that support it and promote our understanding
of the reciprocal effects of child-rearing practices Turkish people
use, and their culture.

Borderline personality organization is accounted for by a specific
failure in ego development. The individual is fixated at (or regressed
to) the stage in which active defensive primitive splitting of "all
good" from "all bad" self-images and "all good" images of other
people from "all bad" ones of the same others (objects) occurs, along
with the corresponding splitting of their affective links. There is
adequate differentiation between the representations of the self
and the representations of the object, however, with concomitant
integrity of ego boundaries in most areas[4]—that is to say, the individual knows where he ends and the other person begins, and does
not confuse his personality with that of the other. Persistence of
primitive splitting seriously interferes with the integration of the
superego, as noted in the previous chapter. I have described in
detail the borderline personality organization as it appears in a
clinical setting (Volkan, 1975, 1976). Kernberg attributes the
failure to synthesize "all good" with "all bad" constellations to
such etiological factors as primary (constitutional) aggression;
aggression secondary to early frustrations; probable deficiencies

---

mother only. There is a prolongation of the period during which more primitive
identification prevails through the process of refusion of self- and object images"
(p. 91). Thus a split in the identifications pertaining to maternal object representations results in difficulties in establishing healthy ego and superego structures;
the ego cannot establish realistic object relations, and the superego reveals harsh-
ness and archaic strength. Such patients, then, have "a strong tendency to rely
unrealistically on the structure provided by external objects" (Cambor, 1969, p.
95). This suggests that the adult who has had many "mothers" as he grew up will
depend on others for stimulation and consolation.

The splitting according to opposite affects of object (mother) representations
and self-representations has been elucidated by Jacobson (1964), Kernberg (1966,
1967, 1975, 1976), and Volkan (1975a, 1976). The so-called British school of
psychoanalysis, using a different frame of reference, had previously directed our
attention to such splitting processes.

4. However, ego boundaries may be breached in those intimate areas in which
projective identification and fusion with idealized objects occur.

in the development of primary ego apparatus; and the inability to tolerate anxiety

The intense aggression that contaminates "all bad" self- and object constellations makes it necessary to keep them split and to externalize them in order to permit the "all good" ones that have been retained to be consolidated and protected. Kernberg (1972) holds that the role of the mother is crucial in facilitating the mending of split representations: "her tolerance of [the child's] anger and her continuing provision of love may crucially strengthen the infant's conviction in the strength of the good self and the good object, and decrease his fear over his own aggressive tendencies" (p. 241). This supports the belief that the child needs a "holding environment" (Winnicott, 1963, 1969; Modell, 1976) in which the mother withstands her child's instinctual assaults readily enough to reduce the intensity of his externalized "all bad" constellations. By an appropriate response she makes it possible for him to tame his externalized image when he repossesses it and to begin mending his antagonistic constellations.

Berkowitz et al. (1974), E. Shapiro et al. (1975, 1977), and Zinner and R. Shapiro (1972) have added to our knowledge of how a family contributes to the development of a borderline type of personality organization in its children. These investigators, working together, report on borderline adolescents in a series of families, demonstrating the defensive ways in which these young people split contradictory ego states one from another, and reveal contradictory representations of the self and object. These writers saw this as a group phenomenon by which these adolescents reacted to the challenge to become autonomous and separated from the family matrix; and they proposed a need for the family group to provide a "holding environment" to facilitate the child's integration of positive and negative constellations pertaining to the self and to others. They concluded further that the parents of the youngsters studied had themselves typically failed to loosen altogether their own symbiotic ties to their families of origin and that they lacked the ability to integrate positive and negative ego states adequately. Such parents chose their borderline child to participate with them by means of projective identification—a feeling of being identified with the other because one attributes his own qualities to the other—in a relationship that embodies the aggressively contaminated self-object representations they would deny. Such a family group has regressed to a preambivalent state wherein each family member seems single-minded in relation to the borderline child.

Shapiro et al. (1975) write:

We characterized various forms of family splitting in which attributes of "goodness" (loving, gratifying and providing) and "badness" (hating, punishing, depriving) were dissociated from each other and reinvested either in different family members or in the family and *the outside world* [italics added]. In the families presented, the predominant parental solution to conflicts over autonomy involved a denial of *autonomous* wishes and a projection of these wishes into the borderline adolescent. The parents were then observed to behave intolerantly towards the child's autonomous strivings. We inferred a shared unconscious fantasy in these families that the child's autonomous wishes represent a hostile condemnation of the family which would destroy the loved ("good") anaclitic object. This shared assumption, we suggested, created the defensive imperative for family members to split off and project these hostile self and object representations in order to preserve the paramount positive libidinal ties. [p. 401]

Such an explanation of family dynamics gone amiss in the American society makes it easier to grasp the genesis of the other-directedness "normal" in the Turkish culture.

The Turkish child growing up in a family considerably more ample than our usual nuclear group need not accept as final the refusal of one "mother" to grant a request; he can usually find another, more amenable "mother" to oblige and soothe him. Indeed, he may be able to carry his case to as many as three or four women until his wish is ultimately gratified. Satisfied, he can readily let bygones be bygones in respect to having been refused. He is spared the necessity of having to accommodate to "all bad" behavior of a principal figure in his life whom he recognizes as "all good" when it gratifies his needs and wishes. It remains true, nevertheless, that if the individual is to appreciate the independent reality of another person, that other person must be perceived as being on some occasions complementary to oneself and one's enterprises, but on others, antagonistic. Such natural inconsistency no longer conjures up in his mind the notion of two persons, one "good" and one "bad." With the ability to understand this comes a corresponding ability to see the negative and positive aspects of oneself. It is no longer necessary to entertain two self-representations. What has been split is mended.

The child with many mother figures learns little about how to tolerate frustration. Without this early learning an individual is easy prey to anxiety and responds exaggeratedly to frustrations considered normal by other people. The mother figures who reign together in the Turkish home are fused together in their common idealized role, but they are not immune to the need to have small collisions to prevent a total loss of individual identity. They work in concert to provide the child with images of himself and the world that the family as a group approves of, but they help at the same time to maintain his "primitive splitting" in other areas.

As in the families described by Shapiro et al. (1975), the autonomous wishes of children are seen as evidences of hostility and are disapproved except when they serve the purposes of one "mother" who wants to prevail for the moment over another. A longitudinal study of the stresses the Turkish individual faces in the course of his life (Öztürk and Volkan, 1971) shows the early presence of "inhibiting and restricting tendencies." It is customary in the traditional Turkish household to swaddle infants for the first six to nine months of life. Subsequent effects of this practice remain rather speculative in spite of some studies on the subject. Benedict (1959) and Öztürk and I feel that what swaddling does to children depends on the attitudes of their parents. What can be viewed as a practice designed protectively to continue the security of the womb may also contain a concomitant unconscious parental desire to restrict the infant's autonomy. We know that the traditional Turkish home prizes and rewards docile, imitative behavior in children and discourages activity, curiosity, and talkativeness.

Turkish boys are usually circumcised during the oedipal or latency years. Much has been written about the psychological effects of the Turkish rites of circumcision, which are performed without anesthesia (Cansever, 1965; Öztürk, 1963, 1973; Öztürk and Volkan, 1971). The ceremony offers the youngster being prepared for the knife many compensatory and counterphobic experiences since it involves the recognition of his becoming at last a man. The razor that cuts his foreskin in a more than symbolic castration also initiates him into manhood. Thus "this potentially traumatic operation becomes something strongly needed by the child—so much so that the lack of it may be severely traumatic" (Öztürk and Volkan, 1971, p. 249).

The psychologically minded reader of Baybars's (1970) account of childhood in Cyprus will recognize characteristic problems of the separation-individuation struggle of the growing child. Baybars was born and reared in Cyprus, made a name for himself as a Turkish poet, and subsequently received acclaim in England as a literary figure writing in English. His romanticized autobiography concludes with a poem on his circumcision, which took place just before puberty. Everything he says in his book may be associated with it.

> . . . Say I can't
> tell I am not afraid to who is stretching
> my legs still. Nothing wrong, he has, nothing
> he has done nothing wrong. Boy becomes a man
> and they know. Not through fear. Pain, not
> them, pain, my pain is fresh and bandaged,
> not through pain do I achieve this.
> . . . And in bed, my legs, yes, stretched
> apart, tenting my newfound wisdom. [p. 223]

With a poet's insight he sees his circumcision as a turning point in his life, one in which the boy became a man. "The paradise is lost. The rest of your life is an attempt to regain it. Some of us succeed, some of us do not" (Baybars, p. 223). Öztürk (1973) has shown that among Turkish children castration fears associated with circumcision are at least as common in latency as during the phallic stage. In the Turkish culture, he says, the latency stage—the period between the oedipal stage and puberty—is not characterized in either sex by relatively dormant sexual development as in Western cultures. Although there is no practice or public knowledge of female circumcision in Turkey, women and little girls hear about and discuss male circumcision and see the ceremony for which they help to prepare. Circumcision is too real and too concrete an event not to leave a scar. It provides a quick graft over the separation-individuation problems of the past. Having been pushed into manhood overnight, the child needs to reenforce his new manhood with the denial of everything "unmanly." (The Turkish girl is early made aware of differentials in sex role and identity by being introduced while very young to domestic responsibilities traditionally those of women.) The young boy's striving paradoxically continues the fear of castration he must deny. When he becomes an adult, he will threaten little boys with castration.

Such early sex-role differentiation—the awareness of what is considered manly and what is not, and what is womanly and what is not—is condensed with the "all good" and "all bad" self- and object constellations respectively. The multiple mothering of his early childhood and the quick establishment of role differentiation in latency allow the child to continue into his adolescence much of the primitive splitting he has been practicing; and when his character jells in this period (Gitelson, 1948; Blos, 1968), it includes adaptation to this type of psychic organization. The maneuver of primitive splitting is then carried over from the family circle into the larger arena of circumambient culture.

In adolescence, when regression in the service of developing a "second individuation" (Blos, 1967, 1968) becomes necessary, the conflictual constellations of childhood affect the more advanced ego. His growing awareness of the island's ethnical bipolarity encourages the Cypriot Turk's use of displacement. Cypriot Turks make Cypriot Greeks the target of their externalization of "all bad" self- and object representations. Such externalization permits the Turks to keep for their kind all of the "all good" constellations in a rather cohesive way. By way of displacement the Turkish child can distance himself psychologically from the Greeks so completely that he need not mend the split in his perception of external objects around him as being tinged with either Turkish or Greek reference.[5] The habit of externalization actually begins in the child's

5. See Chapter I for the ways in which aspects of the land itself become extensions of the primitively split self- and object representations.

first acquaintance with the Greek-scorning nursery rhymes his mothers teach him. It is reenforced by the common designation of Greeks as *gavurlar*—"unbelievers." Early awareness of the masculine role defines the Cypriot Greeks as castrated and "bad" beside sturdy Turkish manliness, but they are also paradoxically seen as a castrating people, as in the episode of the Bayraktar mosque described in Chapter I.

On one level the taboo on intermarriage strengthens the distancing between the two ethnic groups, and on another it helps repress actual incestuous strivings. The child-rearing practices I have described do not help resolve the individual's pregenital issues or promote a move toward total psychological freedom from the mother. When the child brings pregenital problems into the oedipal phase, "togetherness" with the mother heightens incestuous desires. The energy needed to repress such desires is taxed by the energy demands of a continuation of primitive splitting, and the displacement of the incest taboo onto the taboo on intermarriage provides relief. Thus the social customs of the island support the psychological distancing and primitive splitting that keep the two ethnic groups on the island from merging. And the interplay between established social custom and psychological modes of life is, of course, reciprocal.

Externalization as a Powerful Psychological Mechanism in Turkish and Greek Cultures

I will now examine externalization in the Cypriot Turks and Cypriot Greeks, and the idea that each of the two groups sees the other as a "mirror image" of itself as described in Chapter II. The point is that the kind of psychological set each possesses has over the four hundred years of this coexistence raised firm barriers against merger.[6]

6. Although Freud developed the concept of *projection* in 1895, modification of psychoanalytic theory since that time has added to the meaning of this process. Rapaport (1952) suggests that one might envision a continuum "extending from the externalization of a specific type of tension in paranoid projections, to that of any kind of tension in infantile projection, to that of a whole system of attitudes and tensions in transference phenomena, to where it imperceptibly shades into

Novick and Kelly (1970) explain how Freud subsumed under the general heading of *projection* five interrelated but differentiated applications. They use the term *externalization* as it pertains to *aspects of the self*, differentiating it from projection proper, which is motivated by the sequence of fantasied dangers that arise from drive expression. About the externalization of aspects of the self-representation they wrote:

> With the emergence of the self from the state of "primal confusion" the child faces the extremely difficult task of integrating the various dissonant components of the developing self. . . . The earliest conflicts confronting the child in his attempts at integration relate to the existence of dissonant, seemingly incompatible aspects of the self. These conflicts are intensified as some aspects become narcissistically valued through both the child's own pleasures and, more importantly, the parent's response to one or other aspect of himself. Those aspects which are not so valued may become dystonic. Their retention within the self representation will lead to a narcissistic pain such as humiliation. [p. 83]

They give as an example that of the toddler who falls repeatedly and who cries not only from physical pain but from the humiliation of seeing himself unable to walk. "One solution is to *externalize* that aspect of himself, for instance, to make the doll or the baby the one who is incapable of walking, thus avoiding the narcissistic humiliation. At this stage of development such externalization is both normal and adaptive" (p. 83). When the child's self-representation is stabilized at a higher level, he can integrate without threat many

---

the externalization in the form of a 'private world' defined by the organizing principles of one's personality " (p. 463).

D. S. Jaffe (1968) discussed the ambivalent mode of dealing with object relations involved in the mechanism of projection. This mechanism seeks on the one hand to effect the object's annihilation but on the other to preserve a tie with the object. Klein (1946) described a phenomenon which became known as "projective identification" as "a combination of splitting off parts of the self and projecting them onto another person" (p. 108). She later (1955) added to this description "the feeling of identification with the other people because one has attributed qualities or attributes of one's own to them" (p. 58). Zinner and E. Shapiro (1972) asked what "parts of the self" are, in fact, projected. They identified whole objects, part-objects, drive representations, ego-ideal, and superego elements as the elements of the personality that are projected.

aspects previously externalized; thus when he is fully able to walk he may allow himself to crawl without humiliation.[7]

I have been using the term *externalization* in the sense in which Novick and Kelly use it, but refinement of the theory of internalized object relations adds to their formulation. The bipolar development of self- and object images due to the primitive ego's lack of integration results in the primitive splitting of "all bad" from "all good" representations because of the pleasure principle, according to which the individual wants to keep "all good" units. As Kelly and Novick suggested, what is externalized is the dystonic "all bad" self-representations, and the "all bad" internalized object images as well.

Novick and Kelly also state that although transitory externalization is normal, its persistent and extreme use can have serious psychological effects; it may result in a constricted personality with a permanent splitting off of important aspects of the self and their consequent unavailability. There are important clinical and technical implications involved in refining the difference between externalization and projection proper, and the issue certainly has important implications in relation to the Cyprus problem. Novick and Kelly always see in projection "some degree of fit." What is projected always has a basis of reality somewhere, i.e., in child analysis the child hangs projection on some real event, a canceled session, for example; and the projection of hostile impulses will always touch upon a core of truth. "In contrast, there may be a very small, or even no degree of fit between an externalized dystonic self representation and the reality" (Novick and Kelly, 1970, p. 86). In

7. Novick and Kelly suggest that the term *projection* be used for a defense against a specific drive derivative directed against an object. It is possible to use projection at a later stage than externalization "at a stage, in fact, when the capacity to manipulate objects in fantasy has developed to the point where a drive derivative originally directed at an object can be subjectively allocated to that object, while the self is experienced as the object of that drive derivative. . . . In contrast to externalization of aspects of the self, which can effectively do away with painful affect, projection may leave the subject a constant prey to anxiety. . . . Externalization is more closely bound up with impairment in the integrative function, whereas projection relates to a weakness in the defense system vis-à-vis the drives" (pp. 84–85).

Cyprus, contamination with Greekness may be the necessary in-
gradient for the Turkish child to externalize his "all bad" self-representations onto an object neither hostile nor unpleasant for him *in
reality,* and I believe that the reverse of this situation is true for the
Greek child. Thus although the Turks and Greeks lived scattered
all over the island, they never came to know each other as they were
in reality, seeing one another always through a hazy aura.

Later, projections are on occasion condensed with these externalizations. Such externalizations and projections are supported by
cultural "habits" designed to separate the "all good" from the "all
bad" psychologically. It has been observed in clinical practice
(Giovacchini, 1967) that some patients with character disorders
make the environment compatible with their excessive use of externalization. The very environment they construct themselves is
frustrating in order that they may justify their defenses and maintain their total ego orientation. A similar situation occurs in Cyprus.
The Cypriot Turk, no matter what pleasant relationship he might
enjoy with one or more Greek individuals, has to maintain the idea
that the Cypriot "Greek world" is always frustrating to him and
that his expectation of something "bad" from such a world is valid
from a psychological point of view. This formulation does not, in
fact, apply to Cypriot Turks only, but to Turks in general. For example, a Turkish book (Sâlışık, 1968) on the relations between Turks
and Greeks throughout history tries to prove that Greeks exist to
frustrate Turks. Certain it is that whenever the two groups collided
throughout their common history, as they did many times, old hurts
and old passions were clearly reactivated.

Although those inhabiting the Greek world have jaundiced views
of those in the Turkish world—and vice versa—the individual of one
group is unlikely to feel "paranoid" about his opposite number in the
other; the suspicion and antagonism are directed toward the *collective out-group.* The situation nevertheless permits occasional devaluation of the other so complete as to constitute denial of his existence.
One side of the coin is an expected threat, but the other is blank;
and as the coin spins, the views alternate.

To return to externalization as a way of life employed by both
ethnic groups, I will offer some relevant observations from the lit-

erature and add to them some notions of my own. It is striking how sociologists and anthropologists, without referring to psychological apects of human development, identify what the psychoanalyst knows as "externalization." For example, McNall (1974, 1976) identified a set of dominant values common among Greek villagers, among them dependence on the extended family and distrust of those outside the immediate family unit, including distrust of public officials. He refers to the principle of limited good (Foster, 1965), i.e., that any scarcity or limitation of the supply of needed goods, prestige, or land sets up a situation in which one person or group can gain only at the expense of another person or group, and to the principle of amoral familism (Banfield, 1958), i.e., that each villager operates on the assumption that everyone operates to maximize the material advantages of his own family unit. He feels that these values explain the attitudes of the Greek villagers and that they indeed reflect what are to some extent universal peasant values that will change as the material situation changes. He fails to take into account the contribution to these characteristics made by the psychological forces at work in child-rearing or by interaction among the members of a family. Loizos (1976), a Greek anthropologist, suggests: "It may be fruitful to see the Cypriot and mainland Greek villages in the last century as units of defence and identification *roughly on the same level of functional importance as the large patrilineal groups found in Turkish and Arab villages.* The paradox of Greek culture is the *tension* between individualism and association. In my experience urban and rural Greeks are continually stressing the need to organize, to combine to pursue collectively goals that cannot be achieved by the individual alone" (p. 357; italics added). Greek students of human behavior (Vassiliou and Vassiliou, 1974) offer similar findings. They write:

Research clearly shows that in the Greek subjective culture, the individual perceives survival to be possible only with the support of his ingroup. Greeks define the ingroup as "people concerned with me, people with whom I can establish interdependencies." Within the context of his ingroup, the individual functions as a subsystem. In order to survive he has to maintain his interdependencies and interrelations with the other members of his ingroup. He is trained, therefore, to perceive self-actualization,

the fulfillment of his personal goals, as occurring in the context of his in-
group. He has learned to set his personal goals in a manner which is syntonic
with the group goals and which strengthens the ingroup system. [p. 56]

Although I could find no psychoanalytic study of the Greek family,
another report by Vassiliou and Vassiliou (1970) in which descriptive
material is reenforced by statistics suggests dynamics that interfere
with separation-individuation and result in the Greek's reliance
on his ingroup for "sheer survival"; "despite the quickly accelerating
socioeconomic and sociocultural developments described as 'modernization' in the Greek milieu, the in-group maintains almost fully
its operational potential" (p. 442). Vassiliou and Vassiliou are clear
in their description of how Greek children are raised by many
"mothers" rather than by only one, in spite of the fact that in the
big cities the Greek family, like the Turkish, is moving away from
the extended family toward the nuclear model. Their account of
Greek child-rearing thus resembles my observations on the Turkish.
They note: "Mothers are assigned and assume a primary role concerning child-rearing. It is not simply a matter of being assigned
this role. They seem to seek it out and compete with other potential
sources of child-rearing (father, grandparents, other relatives,
teachers, etc.) in order to perform it exclusively" (Vassiliou and
Vassiliou, 1970, p. 440). Moreover, as in the Turkish family, there
is little tolerance of the child's wishes for autonomy or of aggression
directed against a parent. Mothers function as mediators in transactions within the child's milieu. The child feels that he has been
"chosen" and that

a very special task (in exceptional cases a kind of mission) is bestowed on
him, and it is intimately related to his family's or his in-group and (through
it) his country's future . . . he is taught explicitly or implicitly that the kind
of linear and collateral relations he develops *depend on where the other
belongs* [italics added]. If he belongs to the in-group he is due unlimited
respect, concern, and loyalty, collaterally and, in addition obedience
linearly. . . . If he belongs to the out-group he is treated in ways that do
not fall into any fixed rules. Both collaterally and linearly he can be
antagonized, defied, cheated, misled, outmaneuvered. [Vassiliou and
Vassiliou, 1970, p. 442]

Skinner, a psychiatrist (1966) who spent a year in Greece, speaks of the Greek family and its components much as I describe the satellite Turkish. He found Greek society to be "other-directed" and noted that, contrary to popular opinion, the Greek individual

is not particularly independent. In social, political and personal life problems, he is quite dependent upon the "extended family unit" and upon the institutions to whom he has assigned responsibility. . . . The Greek feels himself to be a part of a large group, not only close to his family but also close to his neighbors. . . . He never feels alone in any crisis which may occur since he knows that a large number of people are immediately available to listen, to give advice and to offer their services. . . . As useful as this "extended family" security may be, it seems to, at the same time, represent a drain upon the energy and time of the society. [pp. 480–481]

Skinner describes how the Greek sees the source of disturbance in terms of black and white, and how he has traits of suspiciousness, a sharp awareness of intrigue, and a characteristic distrust, along with the notion that the world contains much evil. He sees these Greek characteristics as the end result of the long Turkish occupation, and it remains unclear whether he knew of the existence of similar belief systems among the Turks themselves. Their status as the conquering group did not make them immune to what Skinner attributed to the Greeks—"a tendency to feel as external all that is painful and to assign responsibility to forces outside of one's own self" (p. 482). It is more likely that the Greek characteristics described by Skinner are influenced by child-rearing practices as stated by Vassiliou and Vassiliou (1970), above and beyond the impact of the Ottoman occupation of Greece.

Skinner observes that the Greek tends to deal with external "evil," to which his own externalizations contribute, with active alertness. The Turk, however, responds to it with pervasive passivity and dependence (Öztürk and Volkan, 1971). It is interesting to speculate as to why Turks, especially those of the traditional rural kind, exhibit such passivity. Do Turkish childhood rites of circumcision push outward-directed aggression and curiosity beneath the surface? The quasi-religious Moslem belief in fate and passive surrender to it may direct instinctual expression. Thus on the surface, as Tenzel and Gerst (Gerst and Tenzel, 1972; Tenzel, 1971; Tenzel and Gerst,

1972) noted, Greeks as a group seem loud, but Turks seem serious
and, by comparison, subdued. In neither group is the use of externalization confined to any one segment of the population, nor does it
seem negatively correlated with socioeconomic success or intellectual sophistication (Skinner, 1966). For example, belief in the
evil eye is not in either ethnic group limited to the poor and ignorant,
although intellectual and social finesse may serve to conceal it.

People with blue eyes are thought to have the power of the evil
eye, to which sickness, particularly that of children, is attributed
(Öztürk, 1966; Öztürk and Volkan, 1971; Volkan, 1975b). Successful, healthy, and attractive people are considered particularly
vulnerable to its malign influence, and there are rituals to fend it off.
One may burn olive leaves and wave away the smoke with the hand
in order to exorcise its spell, or wear amulets for the same purpose.
Or, to bargain with and keep evil at a distance, the Cypriot Turk
may refuse to cut his fingernails at night or hasten to put in place a
shoe that has been accidentally overturned. The psychodynamics of
other rites of exorcism no longer used for this purpose remain within
the personality of many individuals.

Lewis (1971) describes other methods of exorcism in her book on
the everyday life of Ottoman Turkey. Blue beads with eyes painted
on them are offered to tourists today as typical Turkish souvenirs,
but they still hold magic for the native under stress who believes
they offer protection. Certain words and phrases are considered
efficacious against bad luck or a threatening influence. In Chapter
I, I spoke of the inclusion of certain landmarks in the externalized
good or bad self- and/or object images; one can still see in the
residential sections of Cyprus occupied by Turks the tombs of
babalar (fathers) or *dedeler* (grandfathers) laid away there so long
ago that neither their names nor the story of their lives is known,
and these exert an eerie spell on all passersby, however repressed
the response of the educated may be today. Even now one can see
people placing candles before such tombs or knotting rags around
the tombstones as a petition for help or a means of unburdening
aggressive feelings. The Greeks do this sort of thing, too, and have
their influential saints to turn to (Hasluck, 1929; Lewis, 1971).

It is interesting that in speaking of the dreams they have while asleep both Turks and Greeks imply that dreams have external existence. The Greek is apt to say, "I saw a dream," in spite of the availability in the Greek language of a beautiful word for *dreaming* (Skinner, 1966). The cogency of externalization, condensed with projections, is evident in their religious practices and their quasi-religious beliefs. Skinner (1966) suggests that the Greek Orthodox church encourages a believer to forget the past as rapidly as possible in order not to be overcome by feelings of guilt. He writes: "For the Greek, God does seem too heavy a burden to have inside one. There is a constant externalization of all that is felt to be painful and a continual assignment of responsibility to forces or individuals outside the limits of the individual's own self" (p. 480). A study of religious and quasi-religious beliefs among the Turks (Öztürk, 1966; Öztürk and Volkan, 1971; Volkan, 1973a) uncovers examples of externalization and the practices that support it. Externalized influences are separated into those that are "all bad" and those that are "all good." An attempt to reinternalize the latter is made, and psychological bargains are entered into to keep the former away. Laws and customs that arose from the roots of the religion became highly stylized and ritualized, regulating every detail of daily life (Lewis, 1971).

The great Islamic scholars of both the Turkish Selçuk and Ottoman periods were deeply involved with religion qua religion and its philosophical implications, and the government and social organizations relied on patterns derived from classical Islam, or what Itzkowitz (1972) refers to as "High Islam." But the average Turk received his religion modified by a system of quasi-religious beliefs and superstitions. These provided targets for externalization and at the same time reenforced externalization. Islam had in any case been introduced to the conquering Turks in a peculiar derivative form that fostered the proliferation of quasi-religious notions. Cahen (1968) writes that "it was not the Islam of the great scholars, but that of the itinerant popular monks, of merchants of varying degrees of culture and of frontier soldiers, and was compounded as much of various practices, words, and charms, as of true dogma" (p. 8).

Although the Koran discloses a consistent body of doctrine and obligation, it falls short of a full explanation of the Moslem belief and ritual (Gibb, 1949). It tells of Mohammed's purification of the concept of God from the elements of polytheism, and it proposes one omnipotent Being. Although the Moslem religion disapproves of magic, sorcery, and superstition, it includes concepts that can tolerate if not nourish a tendency toward magical thinking and magical practices. Angels and jinns, creatures resembling men, are acknowledged; angels are messengers of the God they worship and the recorders of man's performance.

Jinns are invisible, active, and usually aggressive creatures who live in ruins, rocks, deserted houses, and chimneys. They can seduce human beings and are traditionally blamed for any illness, particularly for mental illness (Lewis, 1971; Öztürk, 1966; Öztürk and Volkan, 1971). Öztürk reports having had many patients who claimed to have been frightened by jinns and who had in consequence free-floating anxiety or repeating anxiety dreams. It is now customary among Turks who live in the cities or on Cyprus to seek help from a medical doctor when they are ill. They have broken with tradition to this extent and now have available in Cyprus more than the usual number of professionally educated physicians. On a conscious level, the modern Turk on Cyprus would not consider turning first to the *efsuncu*, that religious or quasi-religious functionary who can exorcise bad spirits, and he would deprecate any resort to such practices. But if his grandmother or someone else still clinging to the notion of external forces suggests that he overcome his discouragement by the knowledge that no stone has been left unturned in his search for health, he may, in the long run, consult the *efsuncu* after all.[8]

Externalization in the Cypriot Republic

Since both Turks and Greeks employ daily the mechanism of externalization supported by projection within their cultural matrix, their coexistence within the narrow confines of the island leads

8. It is noteworthy that a Turkish book (Kutadgu-Bilig) written in the eleventh century by Yusuf Hacı Habib describes the practice of the medical man and of the efsuncu, and ranks the latter only slightly inferior.

each ethnic group to see the other as a mirror image of itself and to receive its split-off, externalized, and aggressively determined images. Such relatedness demands psychological distancing, and this need may very well be a significant factor in the failure of the two groups to meld into a true Cypriot nation. It was to be expected that the establishment of the Republic, which attempted to consolidate the population to a great extent without respect to ethnic origin, language, or religion—primordial sentiments (Geertz, 1973; Shils, 1957)—would threaten the continuation of psychological distancing and, by causing widespread anxiety on both sides, initiate renewed efforts to reestablish distancing. Everything we know about the psychological makeup of each group suggests that the establishment of the Republic paradoxically heightened the aggressive feelings each group held toward the other.

Although the former British government on Cyprus had used a religious classification of Turkish islanders rather than an ethnic one, calling them all "Moslems" rather than "Turks," these so-called Moslems voluntarily and enthusiastically adopted the reforms Atatürk instituted on the mainland, including his restriction of religion, which he saw as "bad."[9] Atatürk's generation of Turks on

9. In the 1920s and 1930s a cultural revolution took place in Turkey under the leadership of Mustafa Kemal Atatürk, the founder of modern Turkey and its first president. The Ottoman Empire collapsed after World War I, and from the ruins of this spacious, multinational, multireligious, and multilinginual empire a nation-state, considerably smaller but unitary, emerged. As the military hero who had saved most of what is now Turkey from the grasp of other nations in his war of independence, he was able to demand great change. He called for a revolutionary alteration of deeply entrenched Moslem cultural patterns along Western lines, proscribing all education based on the Koran and the laws of Islam and all their hitherto sacred values and symbols. He replaced them with the Swiss Civil Code, the Italian penal code, and German business law. He banned veils for women and within a few years gave them rights equal to men's. He also introduced Western dress for men and began to purge the Turkish language of its Arabic and Persian influences. Latin characters replaced the old Arabic ones.

Atatürk's revolution can be summarized as an attempted "purification" to purge Turkey and all that was Turkish of those aspects of religious or quasi-religious influences that he saw as "bad." He had been born into a house of death. His mother had been a child bride. She had three children before giving birth to Atatürk, and all three died before the age of seven. The father, a minor customs official, was forty when Atatürk was born, and his mother was half that age. The

the island resented being designated as Moslems. I recall the struggle of Cypriot Turks as they tried to change the name of the main Turkish high school in Nicosia from Nicosia Moslem Lycée to Nicosia Turkish Lycée, and the feeling of joy expressed by the students when the British permitted this change in the late 1940s.

Since the Cypriots had much readier contact with the West than did the Turks in Central Anatolia, they were quicker to become "westernized." Over the last few decades, even in the rural areas, change in family structure has been taking place, and the traditional extended family has been giving way to the "modified extended family" and even quite independent nuclear family units. When the Cyprus situation exploded, Cypriot Turks were confined to enclaves in which they lived crowded together. Such confinement returned them to the life of the extended family when it became necessary for those already living in the enclave area to offer shelter to many needy relatives who had to abandon their own homes. During this eleven-year period old familiar psychological maneuvers were reactivated.

---

birth came during a brief period of family prosperity, and the mother saw her fourth infant as a symbol of hope for the future, and the family's savior. The child was thus not only a living link to the dead children (Volkan, 1972b) but he was named Mustafa after an uncle accidentally killed in infancy by Mustafa's father (Kinross, 1965). One of the two siblings born after Mustafa's birth died while still a child, and the father died when Mustafa was seven. My (Volkan, 1978a) psychohistorical research on Atatürk enabled me to make the formulation that even as a small child he developed an inflated self-concept due to his mother's communication of her perception of him as a savior and, as a link to the dead, an immortal. The grieving mother of his early childhood turned for solace to religion, and since the boy perceived the grieving (religious) mother as "bad" and smothering, he tried to create a house of life in Turkey, one without what he saw as the fetters that had constrained his youth.

His cultural revolution came from the top down, propelled by his charismatic personality. The Turks saw him as a deity, and down to the present day act under his influence. Needless to say, however, as they moved toward a "Western" life-style the Turks did not overnight lose the psychological marks of certain of their old ways, such as their child-rearing methods.

IV Interim Survivors

The Meeting of Invisible and Visible Walls

Psychiatrists and psychoanalysts see many people who have built "invisible walls" around themselves. In everyday practice such walls are most often seen as the obsessional patient's "isolation" or "intellectualization" or in the "dissociation" of the hysteric. In neurosis such walls are used chiefly as protection against what is happening within the person's psychic structure, the experience of dangerous affects, for example; but other invisible walls may reflect fundamental disturbances of object relationships (Modell, 1976; Volkan, 1976) in narcissistic or psychotic patients. The latter assure their psychological survival by dealing with relationships to other people, which they find frightening, by walling themselves in. Some schizophrenics build such strong walls that they seem to have lost human contact, and anyone approaching them feels as though in doing so he is running into a concrete barrier. Some people with narcissistic personality organization adhere to long-standing fantasies of living alone in a glorified kingdom within a glass enclosure (Guntrip, 1968; Modell, 1968; Volkan, 1973b, 1976, 1978b). Such fantasies may be so actualized that the person behaves as though he were truly living in confinement and views those outside his enclosure as either contemptible or destined only to adore him from afar. Such invisible walls not only keep out all of the fearful things in the outer world but also make a boundary for the self-concept and help maintain its cohesion (Volkan, 1978b).

Throughout history man has built real walls around any domain he wanted to protect from real dangers in the environment. The Great Wall of China, the eighth wonder of the world, sends its mighty protective arm over 1,500 miles, and more modest walls have been built for protection around cities and castles everywhere

in all periods of time. It is more than likely that psychological
dangers have been condensed with the actual perils being guarded
against. In our time, the Berlin Wall, which in a sense protects the
cohesion of all that is included in East Berlin, has become a symbol
not only of a geographically divided city but of opposing and divided
ideologies. To the Western world it symbolizes a dagger thrust into
the heart of human freedom, and we have all heard of the many
people who put their lives at risk, and sometimes lost them, in their
effort to escape over it to West Berlin. Its symbolic meaning has
perhaps been condensed with the symbolic barriers existing within
ourselves.

Falk (1974) has written that borders between countries (and, I
may add, those between groups that prize separation from one
another for some reason) symbolize not only interpersonal barriers—
a man's crossing an international border may mean crossing the incest barrier into the mother—but it may symbolize internal boundaries also—the discharge of impulses from the id through the barrier
of the ego and the superego. Falk reports the analysis of a young
Israeli's dream of crossing the Israeli-Jordanian border into Jordan-
ian territory and points out that this dream exemplified both meanings of a border crossing. By seeing the meaning of the border or
wall from the standpoint of internalized object relations, I would
add that it may symbolize for the individual or his group the protection of what is included in the self- or group concept. What lies
outside may include "all good" or "all bad" image constellations
according to what the individual or group externalizes. I will return
to this point later in discussing life within the Turkish enclaves in
Cyprus, but here I will illustrate the condensation of invisible and
visible walls and their convergence. The analysis of a woman in her
late twenties who had a narcissistic personality organization revealed this phenomenon clearly.

A newly married and beautiful woman, she sought analysis after
being frightened by an aggressive act of her husband's. She wanted
to know why she should stay married to this man, and why she had
no desire for children. In my first hours with her I thought I was
dealing with someone with a hysterical personality and hysteria of
the dissociative type. Her father was a gynecologist. When intoxi-

cated he was frightening and aggressive. As an oedipal child she had heard the outcry of women being delivered in her father's clinic, which was next to the family home, and had supposed that her father was mutilating them. I initially felt that her fear of becoming pregnant came chiefly from fantasies on the oedipal level. Although her rather schizoid husband had occasional temper tantrums, he did not "bother" her sexually, and this eased her fear of sexual involvement. Soon, however, I saw in her a "grandiose self," to borrow a term from Kohut (1971), one developed pathologically as a defense against oral aggression. Her mother had been cold and distant, relating to her little girl as though the child were a doll on display, proof of the unusual beauty characteristic of the family. The mother was considered a great beauty and saw her daughter as an extension of herself. This patient came to my office during her first year in analysis dressed elaborately and lay on my couch for me to adore. When she felt I was not adoring her, she denied my presence in the room, inducing in me occasional boredom, the typical countertransference feeling elicited by a patient of this kind. She was continuing to be a doll in order to protect herself from an underlying self-image of a child deprived of mother love. During this year she became slowly aware, helped by the interpretation of her dreams, that she lived behind a sheet of glass and that this invisible wall stood between us. She behaved as though there were an actual glass bubble around her rather than one she fantasied. I readily perceived what she described, and sometimes felt that the words I spoke to her struck the glass and echoed back without entering her lonely but glorified kingdom at all.

Her wall occasionally cracked during the second year of her analysis, after much work on her narcissistic transference. The change was acknowledged in a repeating dream in which she saw a beautiful flower in a glass vase. At last the vase fell on the floor and broke, releasing the flower. Soon after dreaming of the broken vase she attended a horse auction where she bought a scrawny, neglected animal that represented by projective identification her deprived self split off from her grandiose self. She restored him to health and vitality. Later, on a higher level of her psychopathology, he represented her penis as she rode him. She gave up the

horse (penis) after a year, when she developed an open erotic transference toward the oedipal father/analyst. By then she could under
stand the oedipal fantasies condensed in her glass bubble, which
represented an externalized hymen. I refrain from further discussion
of this analytic process here in order to focus on the glass barrier.

By the termination phase of her analysis she had given up wearing
her elaborate costumes and the riding togs that had followed them.
Now she felt very womanly and motherly, and dressed accordingly.
She not only wanted to have children but wanted to raise many
kinds of animals—dogs, sheep, cattle, and horses. At her insistence
her husband began looking for a farm home, which he was well able
to afford. She fell in love at sight with one farm and told me about it
three weeks before the date set to terminate her analysis, musing
that she could not altogether understand the fascination the place
held for her. When she visited it again she spontaneously realized
what its unique appeal was—it was surrounded by a stone wall in
the New England manner, unlike most of the local farmhouses. She
had not seen in all her search another so walled in. She told me then
that she realized that the wall represented for her her old psychological "glass enclosure," in which she had protected her lonely
"grandiose self" as well as condensed projected elements from the
conflicts of her psychosexual development. Now she had a womanly
self-concept to protect. She recognized her aspiration to "super-
womanliness," and her desire to be an earth-mother involved in
rearing young living things, animals and children. The analysis of
this desire left her with a more realistic womanliness, one secure
enough to need no "walls," emotional or physical, for protection.
Suddenly, in the last week of her analysis, her desire for the walled
farmhouse—or any other—left her. The analysis was terminated as
planned. I have seen her by chance a few times during the five
years since then, and have talked with her briefly. She has two hand-
some children and, I think, a small dog. She lives in town on a lot
surrounded by a little picket fence which, I feel sure, is simply a
decorative feature. One can only conjecture whether or not it is
tinged with her desire to protect herself for psychological reasons,
but I believe (or at least I want to believe) that she could survive
happily without it.

The story of this analysand shows how psychological and physical walls can merge. In the previous chapter I spoke of the way Cypriot Turks and Cypriot Greeks maintain psychological distance between each other as members of different groups. Such distancing can be conceptualized as the raising of an invisible wall. Wherever actual dangers arose on Cyprus from the proximity of Greeks and Turks, concrete walls were built. Invested with emotion as these were, they also represented psychological walls impossible to break down. They stood until the recent division of the island into northern (Turkish) and southern (Greek) sectors, when borders were acknowledged though not yet legally established.

During the present Cyprus difficulties the walls in Nicosia and elsewhere on the island came to world attention far less than the Berlin Wall, because however significant they might be locally, they were not evidence of a struggle between two huge world powers. Now and then, however, when the Cyprus situation heated up, the term *green line* would flash around the world in news reports in reference to the wall in Nicosia so named, it is said, from a green crayon mark on a map of Nicosia that showed the division between Greek and Turkish sectors. The green line became a lasting phenomenon and a household word to people on the island. In 1955 and thereafter it became dangerous for Turks to enter the Greek sectors, and before the establishment of the Cyprus Republic in 1960, barbed-wire barriers appeared on the streets of Nicosia to separate the Turkish sections of the city from the Greek.

As open intracommunal hostilities broke out during Christmas 1963, the barbed-wire barriers returned and in time gave way to barricades, real walls, gun emplacements, minefields, and trenches. Cypriot Turks were imprisoned behind them in enclaves, and after the 1964 cease-fire the Cypriot Turks occupying whatever neighborhoods the Greeks had not seized were forbidden further movement. They were quickly surrounded by the peacekeeping forces of the United Nations, who were in turn surrounded by Greek troops.

Although the Turkish enclave in Nicosia was large enough to fill part of the city and to control part of the road leading to Kyrenia on the northern shore, smaller enclaves dotted Greek territory. One, for example, was simply a high school building that the Turks had defended and then lived in. The control of a stretch of the road out of Nicosia leading to the sea did not, however, give the Turks access to the sea itself since the road's northern part remained in Greek hands.

During the hostilities of 1963–64, 434 Cypriot Turks were killed and thousands wounded. The Cypriot Turks who fled for safety joined others of their group in their enclaves. Between 25,000 and 30,000 Turks became refugees, crowding into the already limited Turkish quarters. Since the island's Turkish population was only 120,000, it would appear that a fifth of those living in enclaves were refugees, survivors of overwhelming stress and change, victims of the massive psychic trauma of expulsion from their homes, the loss of many dear to them, and constant fear. Statistics verify the degree of uprooting and change they suffered.

Even before the present troubles in Cyprus, Turks had begun moving away from villages that were mixed. There were 230 mixed villages in 1911, and 85 occupied by Turks only. By 1921 there were only 221 mixed villages, and the trend away from them continued steadily but almost unnoticed. By 1946 there were only 192 mixed villages, and the number of Turkish villages had risen to 110. During the violence over Enosis before the establishment of the Republic of Cyprus, Turks were driven out of 33 of the remaining mixed villages. As a result of the Zurich and London Agreements of 1959 and the establishment of the Republic in 1960, some Turkish refugees had the courage to return to their ruined homes, which they had scarcely rebuilt before a struggle over Enosis resumed in 1963. The Turks were driven out of 103 villages, and between 25,000 and 30,000 were obliged to live in tents, caves, warehouses, etc., for at least five years. It was only after the beginning of the intercommunal talks in June 1968 that they were able to move into shabby refugee houses. When these talks began, the Greeks removed the outer ring of Greek soldiers from their encirclement of the enclaves, and some Turks could return to the villages they had left, although only 1,017 out of more than 25,000 did so. Fear and distrust of the Greeks led most Turks to remain refugees, even under what were in some cases subhuman conditions. Most of the 1,017 who ventured back did, indeed, face harassment and hardship.

The eleven-year history of the Turkish enclaves may be divided into two periods, during the first of which (1963–68) Turks were virtually imprisoned within them. During the second, between 1968 and the Turkish intervention of 1974, they were "free" to move out of them and to pass through Greek territory to visit, but the land they had fled in 1963–64 was not available to them for resettlement.

In the summer of 1968 I made my first visit to Cyprus since it had become a republic, a few weeks after the outer ring of Greeks had been removed from around the enclaves and the Turks within them allowed to go "freely" into the Greek sectors. My plane put down at the Nicosia International Airport, in the Greek sector. For most of the Turks who met me there—family members and friends—it was the first departure from their enclave in five years. Their excitement at seeing me for the first time since the beginning of the troubles years earlier was reflected in their gestures and the raising of their voices, but this was suddenly submerged in slow, cautious gestures and whispering communication. I saw that they were doubtful about actually being "free" in terrritory held by Greeks. One little girl brought to the airport was enchanted with her first close look at an airplane. Born in 1962, she had had no opportunity to see one at close range before, nor had she been able to see the sea only fifteen miles from her home.

My family and friends were silent as we drove back to the enclave in Nicosia through the Greek sector. It was only when we came to the entrance to the Turkish enclave where we were greeted by a soldier that they became animated again. The contrast between one side of the green line and the other was impressive. The Turkish side looked as though it were in ruins; the streets were pitted, and poverty was evident everywhere. I learned that the delivery of building material to the Turkish sector had been forbidden for a long time lest the Turks use it to fortify their enclaves, so nothing had been repaired.

When in the summer of 1968 the Greek soldiery withdrew from their encirclement of the Turkish enclaves, the Turks living in them did not rush through the newly opened gates of their "prisons." The wall around them had assumed psychological significance; not only did it protect them from outside danger, it enclosed them to form a cohesive living unit. Those who lived together inside developed a world of their own, one in which the reality of hope was tinged with magic and illusion. They felt safer in their familiar restraint than with freedom when it came. I will described later the life in the enclaves and indicate for what psychological processes the "walls" had provided a cover, but here I will give only my first impressions of what was taking place in the enclave of Nicosia.

Something about the people I saw going through the motions of everyday life in the coffee shops and on the street made them seem to me uncannily like robots living in a make-believe setting. How had they survived five years of this? I soon found one answer, although its significance escaped me at first. On our arrival at the house where we were to stay, we were immediately introduced to sixteen parakeets divided among three cages. I found it disconcerting to have my attention directed so insistently to the birds when I had been waiting eagerly for news about my relatives, but it was plain that my people thought it entirely natural that the birds had a high priority. In due time I will return to "the birds of Cyprus" with which I made this involuntary acquaintance and speak from the psychoanalytic point of view about their meaning.

It was immediately obvious to me that my relatives and their comrades in the enclave were all suffering from the need to adapt to severe stress arising from political pressures. Considerable psychiatric and psychoanalytic attention has been given to the effect of uprooting and loss on the group as well as on the individual. I propose to examine here the psychological processes of those Cypriot Turks who lived huddled together during such troubled times and to compare them with the manifestations of other groups that have experienced massive psychic injury because of extensive persecution or disaster. One dissimilarity to the situation of the Jews in Nazi concentration camps is, of course, immediately evident; the defensive-adaptive behavior of those awaiting certain death is not like that of persons who can still entertain the hope of survival or safety, no matter how long hope is deferred and how chronic it becomes.

Survivors and Interim Survivors Compared

The Cypriot Turks were survivors of the events of 1963–64, but they did not exhibit what is known as the *survivor syndrome* because their deliverance was incomplete and uncertain and they remained "prisoners." Although they awaited the next disaster, the occurrence or outcomes of which they were powerless to affect, they remained in a locale that was familiar to them and in which they could maintain the illusion of being safe. They were caught between a rescue from one danger and the threat of another. Their hope of real release from peril became chronic and vied with the dread of annihilation they felt for eleven years. The Turks in their enclaves were, in fact, *interim survivors,* with psychological processes that included both hope and hopelessness and were thus differentiated from the psychological processes of survivors who have outlived their danger. The classical survivor syndrome should be understood as a contrast to and background of the adaptation of those who had lived in the Turkish enclaves.

The survivors of World War II German concentration camps provided the psychiatrist and psychoanalyst with a hitherto unprecedented opportunity to study individual and mass reaction to overwhelming stress brought about by the politically motivated cruelty of man. Persecution in its other forms, i.e., the hunting down of people in hiding, emotional and intellectual erosion, and mass expulsion from a home, could also be studied in psychodynamic terms. It is interesting that when the Jews were rescued from the concentration camps, no one, "through an astonishing oversight" (Friedman, 1949), took into consideration the psychological plight of these victims. The naive notion that releasing the prisoners from their confinement would end their suffering seemed to prevail. Writing in 1949, Friedman noted how incredible it seemed in retrospect that when plans were first made for the rehabilitation of the Jewish survivors of the holocaust in Europe, no one considered how likely it was for them to have psychiatric difficulties; instead, everyone concentrated on the alleviation of their physical suffering. However, when the first survivors of the camps reached the United States, psychiatric help was provided for them, and an understanding of their situation in psychiatric terms began. Among those who grasped some of the psychological processes they underwent was the psychoanalyst Niederland (1961, 1964, 1968), who coined the term *survivor syndrome* to describe the constellation of symptoms brought about by their experience. He and other investigators (Bettelheim, 1960; Chodoff, 1963, 1970; de Wind, 1968; Eitinger, 1961, 1964; Fink, 1968; Hoppe, 1966, 1968; R. Jaffe, 1968; Lorenzer, 1968; Rappaport, 1968; Simenauer, 1968; Winnik, 1968) were among those who examined different aspects of the syndrome and its applications.

Psychoanalysis had provided us with the concepts of trauma and traumatic neurosis, but, as will be seen, the description of the latter was insufficient to cover the multitude and severity of the clinical manifestations of the survivor syndrome. Trauma occurs when a stimulus, usually one that is sudden and disruptive, arising from an external situation (or from an inner massive sexual or aggressive excitement), overwhelms the ego's capacity to mediate between the various forces making demands upon it and creates a state of helplessness. It is "a relative concept; factors of mental economy, dependent on constitution as well as on previous experiences and on the actual conditions before and during the trauma, determine what degree of excitation overtaxes the individual's capacity . . . the blocking of external motor activity increases the probability of a breakdown, and foxhole waiting is more dangerous than active warfare" (Fenichel, 1945, p. 117).

The trauma may be followed by traumatic neurosis, which is characterized by a block or reduction of various ego functions; spells of painful affects, especially anxiety or rage related to the traumatic experience; and sleep disturbances. The trauma is reexperienced in dreams, or its mental representation is repeated in the waking state, until mastery is achieved, often with the establishment of psychoneurotic symptoms. Although one can see elements of traumatic neurosis in the survivor syndrome, its uniformity and intensity, the specific scars it leaves on the victim's self-representation, and its persistence in the victim's children make it seem far from an average, typical traumatic neurosis. Massive psychic trauma such as was experienced by those in the Nazi camps takes precedence over issues of predisposition. The predispositions of the past are obliterated, and whatever pathology may have been present before the experience of such trauma plays little or no part in determining the outcome. Thus when the stress is sufficiently powerful it will produce the same psychological disturbance in virtually everyone who suffers it (Hocking, 1970; Koranyi, 1969; Lifton and Olson, 1976).

Rappaport (1968), viewing the situation of concentration camp survivors as being beyond traumatic neurosis, stated that "one can say that the regenerative powers of the ego are not limitless, that the human spirit can be broken beyond repair" (p. 730). The effects of incomprehensible psychic trauma do not disappear with time. Rangell (1976b) has written about how distant effects of such trauma may succeed the more immediate ones, and how the finite psychic space of a survivor is encroached upon by traumatic memories for an indefinite period, reducing the resources available for normal effective living. He explains this as follows:

There are subtle and far-reaching issues facing the survivors. In spite of the vastness of the unconscious, psychic space is limited. There is room and time in any individual psyche for only a limited amount of cognitive ideation and a finite number of memories, fantasies, and accompanying affects. The product of such space and time comprises the psychic life of an individual, the amount already spent and the amount still left. Mourning is a model of such an occupation of psychic space, a paradigm of how obsessive thoughts and memories related to psychic work that needs to be done crowd and consume psychic capacity. Traumatic memories of any kind encroach on this psychic time-space and reduce its available quantity; this is why psychic traumata age people. [p. 315]

The Proceedings of the Wayne State University Workshop on the Late Sequelae of Massive Psychic Trauma, which include studies of the survivors of the Nazi camps, were edited by Krystal in 1968 and published. In this volume, and in his other writings, Niederland reported that he had found many clinical manifestations among the 800 survivors of the Nazi camps that he examined and that they presented a clinical picture (under the classification of survivor syndrome) uniquely different from other forms of psychopathology. He (Niederland, 1968) itemized the following characteristics: (1)

anxiety, the most predominant complaint, associated with the fear of renowed persecution, with sleep disturbance in which "re-run" nightmares played a part, and with multiple phobias; (2) disturbance of cognition and memory, i.e., amnesia or hyperamnesia, and disorientation in which the present was not distinguished from the period of persecution; (3) chronic depressive states, covering the spectrum from masochistic character change to psychotic depression, correlated with what Niederland calls "survivor guilt," guilt at having survived a holocaust that swept away so many who deserved to live and with whom the survivors were often closely involved; (4) a tendency to seek isolation, to withdraw into brooding seclusion, with consequent injury to object relations; (5) the presence or appearance of psychosis, often seen in paranoid manifestations; (6) alterations in personal identity permitting the survivor to feel "I am now a different person" or even, in extreme cases, "No, I am not a person"; (7) chronic tension states, gastrointestinal or cardiovascular disturbances, and what Niederland calls the "typical 'survivor triad': headaches, persistent nightmares—chronic depression, and various other psychosomatic complaints" (p. 313); (8) a " 'walking' or 'shuffling corpse' appearance [that] gives the victim a macabre, shadowy, or ghost-like imprint, difficult to describe, but which seems to be in the nature of an all-pervasive psychological scar on the total personality" (p. 313).

To make their situation more tragic, it appears that the psychological difficulties of those who survived the horrors of persecution were passed on to their children. In 1968 de Wind wrote: "Today, for many of the ex-prisoners, the most serious problem is that they so often direct their aggression onto their children, thus fulfilling the Biblical saying that the sins of the fathers shall be visited upon the children unto the third and fourth generation" (p. 306). The survivor syndrome in the second generation represents the child's unconscious rage against a parent too emotionally crippled to offer security and confidence (Niederland, 1968). Other phenomena often seen in the children of those who survived the Nazi purge were discussed at a psychoanalytic workshop on the children of survivors, as reported by Sonnenberg (1974).

When Lifton (1968) studied the survivors of Hiroshima he found that in spite of the fact that the bomb came literally as a bolt from the sky and brought swift disaster rather than long months of incomprehensible stress, survivors in Japan had much in common with the survivors of the Nazi camps. The term *survivor syndrome* is nowadays more widely applied and refers today to what characterizes anyone who has undergone any devastating experience in which many people were involved and many perished. It is used of natural as well as of man-made horrors. A recent example is the Buffalo Creek disaster of February 1972, in which the collapse of a slag dam in the West Virginia mountains inundated sixteen towns and many coal camps in a seventeen-mile-long valley with millions of gallons of black water and sludge, killing 127. The dam had been formed of waste from coal-mining operations, and its sudden collapse caused waves of water as high as thirty feet. Lifton and Olson (1976) described the version of the survivor syndrome that manifested itself among the survivors of this tragedy. They found that, like those who lived through Hiroshima's holocaust, these people had a *death imprint*; their images of death and destruction were still vivid thirty months after the event. They also had death (survivor's) guilt, painfully condemning themselves for having lived while others perished. They felt psychologically numb to the extent that their ability to relate to others was impaired. Most of the survivors came to find comfort in ascribing an inner meaning to what had happened, declaring that it was the will of God.

K. T. Erikson (1976), a sociologist, described how much losing "the tissues of their community" affected the Buffalo Creek survivors. Rangell (1976), a psychoanalyst, was interested similarly in the disruption of the "ground" and "surround" of these victims. Nearly twenty years earlier he (Rangell, 1954) had described "attachment to ground" as a psychic prerequisite for the maintenance of the social state of poise. Referring to the Buffalo Creek disaster he wrote: "The opposite condition, a wavering hold on one's surrounding psychic ground, results in a basic anxiety with the threat of crumbling and even annihilation of the self" (p. 314).

While the "restricted" life awaits the survivor, he may make some adaptive attempts, as described in the literature. For example, Lifton (1968) talks about the art and literature that stemmed from

the Hiroshima tragedy. Williams and Parkes (1975) found an increase in the birthrate of the Welsh village of Aberfan for the five
years following the engulfment there of 116 children and 28 adults
by an avalanche of coal slurry. They attribute this rise mainly to
"a process of *biosocial regeneration* [italics added] by couples who
had not themselves lost a child" (p. 304). The Williams and Parkes
study holds interest for anyone attempting to understand the preoccupation of Cypriot Turks with the fertility of the birds they raised
as a hobby during their confinement.

The situation of the Cypriot Turks after the storms of 1963 and
1964 had passed is uniquely interesting. As noted, although they had
succeeded in outlasting great stress, they were always aware of
future danger; and although they were still alive, they were not
free but were confined in enclaves by the will of others. They were,
in fact, interim survivors who had withstood the terrible stress of
bloody days only to face dislocation, a reduced lifestyle, and the
loss of loved ones and property. They had become prisoners, in spite
of the fact that their "prisons" lay within the neighborhoods of
their own people in which it was possible to conduct some sem-
blance of normal life. They were free from survivor guilt since, although they still lived, they remained in danger, the pawns of a
situation entirely beyond their control. Since they were being
"punished" by an external agency, they were able to project any
inner guilt they might have had and were thus freed from painful
self-condemnation. They were like all other survivors, however, in
having experienced terrible hours that were relived daily in the
mind's eye. Memories of tragic events invaded the "psychic space"
needed for them to deal with impending danger and the unquench-
able hope of complete freedom and safety.

A close look at life within the enclaves will reveal the basic psychological issues with which the interim survivors were dealing.
Here I refer only to the first five years of life within the enclaves
before the gates were opened. The second phase of enclave living
will be described later.

Inasmuch as Turks are familiar with the extended family—if not
through personal experience, through the accounts of older relatives—the enforced crowding together did not introduce a life pat-

tern that was wholly new. The schools remained in operation, and the offices and stores stayed open, except for days on which a violent episode took place. At a superficial glance one would see life going on much as usual, but the Cypriot Turks were in touch with the outside world only through personnel of the United Nations who brought in money and food from Turkey. Many people were unemployed. Some, like schoolteachers, the management of whose schools had passed into enemy hands, continued working, but for much lower salaries than they had previously received. News of other enclaves was hard to come by. When as a concession Cypriot Turks were allowed to visit an enclave not their own they were harassed at all the checkpoints, whether their trip was under United Nations arrangements or not, and searched for concealed weapons. Moslem Turkish women felt particularly dishonored by such body searches.

As congestion within their living space led them to revert to the traditional extended family, the mechanism of externalization (see Chapter III) was increasingly employed, and ethnic group identity was exaggerated. Military training was mandatory for young people in the enclaves, and this reenforced the notion that the Greeks outside the walls were truly dangerous.

The physical walls, surrounded as they were with three rings of soldiery, were more and more invested with emotional symbolism and became an emotionally perceived protection that kept the "bad" enemy out and confined individual and group aggression within. In day-to-day living in the enclaves, aspects of aggressive drive derivatives could be seen as turned inward. Children's stories told by adults at bedtime had a special twist; the story would begin in the usual way with the trials and tribulations of a hero, but in these troubled times it would end with the hero's dismemberment or annihilation rather than with the classic triumphant happy ending. Moreover, accumulated aggressive drives evoked sadistic fantasies in which the Greeks would be made to suffer once help came from mainland Turkey. It was this accumulated aggression that kept the Turks from rushing out of their protective walls when they were at last allowed to do so. As long as one remained inside he need not face his id impulses. I will return later to consideration of this aggression, but it was the "bird phenomenon" that demonstrated most clearly the basic psychological processes of the interim survivor   the blending of his ego s chronic hopelessness with chronic hope.

The Birds and Pathological Group Narcissism

The parakeets in the house in which I stayed during the 1968 summer were being raised as an extended family. They were in three cages; the original pair—the "mother and father"—were pointed out to me, along with a "bride" who had just been moved into her new "home." One enormously fertile but crippled hen was a special pet; her fecundity more than made up for her imperfections. When I went out the day after my arrival, I found that the hobby of parakeet raising was not unique to our household but was enjoyed by all in the enclave. One saw parakeets in coffeehouses, markets, and other public places, as well as in homes, and I had to step over cages to make a purchase in the neighborhood grocery.

These birds were invariably regarded with great enthusiasm. They were always kept in cages, usually homemade, and several generations were likely to be in each cage. Their owners saw each one as an individual, were delighted when they were happy and fertile, and mourned any that died. There was particular regret over the death of one hen who seemed to have overtaxed her strength in laying a prodigious number of eggs. Avian pedigrees were worked out with great interest!

It would be impossible to pinpoint the origin of this curious hobby, which had, parhaps, simply spread as an extension of an interest of a few people. Parakeets are not native to Cyprus and must have been imported originally. What was striking about this preoccupation was that those caught up in it saw their fanaticism about parakeets as nothing out of the ordinary. The Greek communities on Cyprus had no such interest. It is curious that, according to Watmough (1954), a similar obsession with parakeets had appeared in England (where they were called budgerigars) during the widespread depression there before 1939. Watmough wrote: "In my lifelong experience . . . I had seen nothing comparable with this development, which was all the more remarkable because of the fact that it had occurred during one of the most depressing periods in the industrial history of our country" (p. 3).

Before suggestions about the psychological meaning of this mass hobby are formulated, the symbolic meaning of birds should be recognized. A review (Leach, 1949) of folklore and mythology concerned with birds shows a great variety of symbolic meaning connected with them. I will concern myself here only with birds as a symbol of freedom in the general sense, including psychic freedom. Psychic freedom is the goal of a child's struggle to achieve individuation. Thus I refer to the separation of the self-representation from the object representation; the integration of both; and the achievement of autonomy in behavior without the need to reactivate an internal image of the other for support in carrying out such behavior. Identification with the previously helpful object image is then completed, and the individual no longer need depend on such an image, which is now included in the self-concept.[1]

In the dreams of patients undergoing psychoanalysis or psychotherapy, birds not only may represent the penis, which can "go up" like a bird, but, in symbolism unrelated to body parts, may represent the ideational aspect of individuation and freedom. In treating schizophrenic and borderline patients who dreamed of themselves as birds, Corney and I (1968) recalled the myth of Icarus, who was advised by his father, Daedalus, not to soar too high nor swoop too low. The first admonition has long been understood in relation to the oedipal conflict. We dealt with the second, which represents the dilemma of separation-individuation. In our reporting of these dreams we noted that the patient saw himself as a bird, his

1. It should be remembered that in medieval times birds became an obsession. Like leaves and flowers, they were seen as discrete designs of nature and appeared in one of the earliest known medieval sketchbooks. The fourteenth-century cleric who embellished his manuscript with them would probably have explained that they represented souls because they could fly up to God. Clark (1969), in his studies of civilization as it is mirrored in art, makes the appropriate suggestion that the obsession with birds arose from identifying them with freedom. Feudal man was tied, along with his animals, to the land, living out his life within one small locality. Freedom to move about was given to few, but, as Clark notes, birds could escape confinement. Birds were cheerful, hopeful, impudent, and highly mobile—and their markings made them adaptable for the decorative heraldry of the Middle Ages.

flight representing efforts and failures in the achievement of individuation and intrapsychic separation from the symbiotic mother. Unresolved problems of separation-individuation (psychic freedom) are involved. Niederland (1971c) analyzed a patient with congenital torticollis who felt literally "entrapped in a cage" because of his serious deformity. He had many dreams in which he was a bird flying freely in the world.

I once analyzed a young man who had the habit of going to a park near Washington's National Airport to watch airplanes (big birds) take off. Under the phallic symbolism of airplanes in flight lay, as became evident in his analysis, pre-oedipal issues concerning the struggle of taking off from mother earth—or gaining individuation and psychic freedom.

Contemporary writings acknowledge the symbolism also. *The Birdman of Alcatraz* (Gaddis, 1955) tells of the prisoner who invested his birds with his desire for freedom. Reference to a prison as "a birdcage" is common; in fact, the inmates of a local prison near my office publish a newsletter they call *The Birdcage*. In a book for children (Sendak, 1970), being "free like a bird" is poetically and graphically illustrated. The old Peter Pan story (Barrie, 1928) has essentially the same symbolism. Maya Angelou (1970) calls her poignant account of black childhood and youth in an American community then wholly dominated by whites *I Know Why the Caged Bird Sings* and uses the symbol to express very much what the bird hobby meant to the Cypriot Turks. The old concept of a bird's nature is as familiar in Turkish expression as in the English phrase "free as a bird." Turks have an old custom of buying a caged bird and freeing it when a wish comes true or when they feel that they have been saved from some threatened personal disaster.[2]

2. The use of birds as symbols of freedom and the concept of caged birds as symbols of oppression must have universal appeal. A news item in *Time* for September 25, 1972, concerns the Cocos Islands, which lie in the Indian Ocean between Australia and Ceylon. The main island, which has a population of 500, has been ruled more or less benevolently as a feudal fiefdom for a century and a half by descendants of a Scottish sea captain named John Clunies-Ross. In 1955 Britain ceded its sovereignty over the islands to Australia, but the present ruler of the main Cocos island, a fifth-generation descendant of its original settler, forbade any representative of the Australian administration to set foot on it. Australia's

In view of such arguments for the symbolism of freedom invested in birds, we can suggest that the parakeets treasured by the Cypriot Turks during the first phase of their lives in enclaves represented to them parts of themselves. Their nurture in family groups represented the patterns of the traditional or modified extended family among human beings. Since the birds were confined in cages much as the Turks were confined within the "walls," the needy aspect of these virtually imprisoned Turks was externalized on the birds. As long as the little creatures sang, remained fertile, and had care they embodied the hope that the human population might also thrive, receive care, and achieve freedom. Anxiety initiated by sociopolitical stress was thus allayed by the actualization of the old concept of a bird's free nature. The sharing of the hobby of raising them provided a safety valve for mass anxiety. In their dilemma the Turks of Cyprus had become what could be described as helpless helpers; as long as they could help their birds to be happy and fruitful, they could entertain the hope that they themselves would receive help. They did not consciously think "we are like caged birds now, but we want to be free as birds on the wing," but their "needy parts" became the birds through the actualization of a simile.

Here we must turn our attention to the mechanism of regression. In schizophrenia, when regression is deep and firm ego boundaries are missing, the inability to distinguish between metaphorical and concrete meanings has been observed (Abse, 1971; Searles, 1962). The Cypriot Turks were regressed under stress. On the intellectual level they knew well enough that they were not birds, but their needy aspect was nonetheless projectively identified with them. The members of regressed groups abdicate some of the judgment they are accustomed to exercising as individuals, becoming more dependent on external authority than on responsible considerations

---

comfortable ignorance of the situation was jolted when a Malay headman on another island, Christmas Island, where the overpopulation of the Cocos had resettled after World War I, described for the Australians how their relatives and friends who remained on Cocos were "like birds in a cage," the symbolic phrase appearing in this context to sum up a complicated and oppressive situation.

of their own (Freud, 1921). Such a group is searching for an ideal model, a leader. Freud (1921) said: "Many equals, who can identify themselves with one another, and a single person superior to them all—that is the situation that we find realized in groups which are capable of subsisting" (p. 121).

The Cypriot Turks lacked a heroic figure to lead them during their life in enclaves. At the beginning of their siege they believed that Turkey would come to their aid. The bombing of Cyprus by Turkish aircraft in August 1964 put a stop to actual violence and battle and supported the notion of rescue at hand. Subsequent help from Turkey was largely limited to political activity, however, and the idealization of political leaders on the mainland could no longer be maintained. The Cypriot Turks were thus obliged to see external idealized authority vested in an abstraction of the expected "savior" from Turkey. They identified themselves with this "savior" as they so painstakingly cared for their parakeets. The stress under which the Cypriots were acting led them in a regressive way to unconscious identification with the birds *and* the savior as well, although without the schizophrenic delusion of conscious belief that they had become either (Volkan, 1972a).

Further meaning of the bird hobby will be illustrated by clinical findings in the narcissistic personality organization. An individual with such personality organization has a "grandiose self," to borrow a term from Kohut (1971). I (Volkan, 1976) see the formation of the grandiose self as Kernberg (1970, 1975) does—as a pathological formation in response to early conflicts of the oral-aggressive type. The person with narcissistic personality organization presents himself as a nonpareil who exists only to be adored by others. Kernberg tells how such people have a defensive organization strikingly like that of borderline personalities. He points out, however, that the former's reliance on such primitive mechanisms as primitive splitting, denial, projective identification, pathological idealization, and omnipotence differs in a particular way. Since the grandiose self of the narcissistic person is integrated although highly pathological,[3] he differs from the borderline individual in function-

3. The grandiose self reflects "pathological condensation of some aspects of the real self (the 'specialness' of the child reinforced by early experiences), the

ing rather well socially. Because of the persistence of primitive splitting, however, the felt characteristic of the grandiose self can coexist with feelings of inferiority. What is known about narcissistic personality in the individual can illuminate any group development of pathological narcissism (*group narcissism*).

The Cypriot Turks in the enclaves were suffering from severe narcissistic injury, especially during the first five years of their confinement; almost every aspect of their daily lives was under attack. I have spoken of the accumulation of their aggressive drive derivatives; reference to orality in this aggression can be seen in the oral ways it was dealt with. Minor tranquilizers were available without prescription, and among Cypriot Turks the habitual use of orally taken drugs was almost universal. The needy, "hungry" aspects of the self of each individual composing the group were primitively split and externalized, in a group response, onto pet birds. At the same time people held onto a grandiose group self, developing group narcissism, if you will. Like the grandiose self of a single individual, this group phenomenon stressed a conviction of innate superiority. Their culture encouraged all Turks to share the feeling of being destined to be heroic. The shared ideal-self (imagined superiority over the Greeks) and shared ideal-object (the fantasy of being saviors) were developed in an attempt to deal with narcissistic injuries that excited oral aggression.

When the birds were well fed and seemed happy, they became not only instruments of their owners' denial of their needy selves but also a means of maintaining their owners' belief in their grandiosity. When the birds sang, they were seen as joyously extolling their owners. The situation of the people confined in enclaves was far "freer" than that of the birds in their small cages, and the comparison enabled the former to feel less victimized by their dilemma. They lived in the psychological world of the interim survivor, their creation that surrounded and protected them. Freud (1921) de-

---

ideal self (the fantasies and self images of power, wealth, omniscience, and beauty which compensated the small child for the experience of severe oral frustration, rage and envy) and the ideal object (the fantasy of an ever-giving, ever-loving and accepting parent, in contrast to the child's experience in reality; a replacement of the devalued real parental object)" (Kernberg, 1975, pp. 265–266).

scribes the founding of groups on the basis of common need. Shared
unconscious fantasy can foster a particularly contagious form of
mutual identification. In the case of the Cypriot Turks, this identification strengthened their defensively formed group narcissism.

I supervise the psychoanalytic treatment of a narcissistic young
man whose mother's anticipatory grieving over her own early death
from cancer had made her inadequate in the mother role during
his childhood. He developed a pathological grandiose self, seeing
himself as a Robinson Crusoe of great self-reliance with no need for
a Man Friday. The repeating fantasies that enabled him to go to
sleep (transitional fantasies) (Volkan, 1973b) and protected his narcissistic personality organization placed him alone on an island,
self-sufficiently building himself a house, catching fish for food, etc.
Although he outwardly resisted help from others, he felt compelled
to save anyone he saw as needy, a representative of his inadequate,
grieving, and sick mother and his correspondingly deprived and
hungry self-image. The savior concept implanted in his narcissistic
organization led him to a search to repair the mother; but a deeper
wish was, of course, that when the mother was repaired, she would
in turn become a good mother to him. His compulsion to rescue and
repair others was also a defense against the aggression arising from
the frustration of having an inadequate mother.

This case also illuminates the compulsive mass reaction of Cypriot
Turks to become saviors, joy-givers, and caretakers of their birds.
They behaved like Robinson Crusoe without a Man Friday since
no mainland Turks came to their rescue. In their illusion they were
self-sufficient, and they saw the behavior of both the savior and the
saved as lying within their control. This illusion served its purpose
until the summer of 1968 when the Greeks allowed the Turks to
move out of the enclaves for the first time in years. Then the walls
of the Cypriot Turks' fantasy world collapsed, with resultant "group
depression."

The preoccupation with birds began to lessen a few months
after the enclaves were opened. Soon after this, I mentioned at a
conference attended by some Turkish intellectuals in Cyprus the
possibility that the caged birds I had seen and pondered over had
represented the imprisoned Turks. When my remark drew angry

protest, I realized that I had made the mistake of making an "imma-
ture interpretation," as it were. Within the year I heard from an
intelligent observer in Nicosia who wrote that the Turkish Cypriots
were at last able to move about and that they no longer had time
or inclination to raise parakeets. The birds disappeared. In 1973 as
I walked the streets of Nicosia I saw only one caged parakeet, and
that one was in a private house. None were to be seen in the coffeehouses, groceries, or other public places.

In 1974 I asked ten young Cypriot Turkish physicians and medical
students in Ankara whether they had any memory of the birds,
telling them that I was writing a book on Cyprus and wanted to
know what they remembered from their life in the enclaves before
1969. These young men had been in their mid- or late teens at the
time of the bird fad. None spontaneously referred to the birds, but
when I asked specifically about them they were able to recall them
with some difficulty, as if recalling a forgotten dream that had once
had emotional impact but no longer evoked any response. Two
actually used the analogy of a dream. The bird preoccupation had
once been in the service of an important psychic process that was
no longer active. One of the men thought I was making up a story
when I spoke of the birds and of how important they had been, for
he had no memory of them at all, but at a second interview on the
following day he confessed that logic was on my side; he did remember having once bought a parakeet for twenty shillings, but
for one he bought some time later the price was only three shillings.
It seemed clear to him that such a reduction in price meant that
the birds had become a glut on the market, but his actual memory
and emotions were no longer engaged in what his logical thinking
validated as an abstract proposition.

The Myth of the "Great Weapon"

Besides sharing the bird hobby during the first phase of their confinement in enclaves, the interim survivors of Cyprus also shared a
fantasy illustrated by the "great weapon" myth in which they
acknowledged danger and made a magical adaptation to it. A regressive resort to magic often appears at times of danger and is often

shared by a group under stress. Just as external dangers may be condensed with regressively reactivated internal ones, the magical defenses may include regressive reactivation of images of early nurturers and protectors.

Abraham (1913) declared that dreams are private myths, and that myths are collective dreams. Freud (1932b) observed that a study of myths resembles an analyst's reconstruction as he tries to understand his patient's dreams. Roheim (1950b) explored the possibilities of applying an analysis of mythology to the understanding of current psychological conflicts among members of a culturally homogeneous group. Arlow (1961) applied modern ego psychology to the study of myth and emphasized the difference between personal dreams and collective myth; dreams are meant to be forgotten, but myths are instruments of socialization. Emphasizing the adaptive uses of the latter, he said:

The myth is a particular kind of communal experience. It is a special form of shared fantasy, and it serves to bring the individual into relationship with members of his cultural group on the basis of certain common needs. Accordingly, the myth can be studied from the point of view of its function in psychic integration—how it plays a role in warding off feelings of guilt and anxiety, how it contributes a form of adaptation to reality and to the group in which the individual lives, and how it influences the crystallization of the individual identity and the formation of the superego. [p. 375]

In 1962 a psychoanalytic panel on mythology and ego psychology (Bergmann, 1966) used Arlow's paper as a point of departure. Panel members concerned themselves chiefly with the mythology of antiquity, but there emerged from their deliberations ideas that will help us to understand the establishment of the modern myth such as the myth of the great weapon to which I refer here. They gave general assent to Arlow's notion of the myth's adaptive function, and Kanzer pointed out: "Both the dream and the myth create symbols which expedite the transition between inner and outer reality. The dream symbol mobilizes memories which facilitate the transition to inner reality and autoplastic solutions; the myth is more of an intermediary toward outer reality and alloplastic solutions. External reality is accepted conditionally, provided there are still sufficient elements of denial admissible to safeguard the omnipotence of the ego and fulfill the wishes of the unconscious" (reported by Bergmann, 1966, p. 261). Stern, who was a member of the panel, went back to older psychoanalytic formulations, holding that myths originate in dreams, specifically from nightmares. He thus agreed with the views of Bergmann and Muensterberger. It was suggested that the myth arose at a time when dream and reality were not differentiated, the reference here being to the mythology of antiquity. Muensterberger spoke of primitive societies and the likelihood that the sharing of disturbing dreams within the clan made for the establishment of myths. What is interesting here is Stern's warning: "Myths . . . cannot be treated as phenomena isolated from the history of the group. To interpret a myth in isolation from its background should be comparable to interpreting a symptom or dream without considering the patient's personality, history, and the day residues conveyed by free association. In the study of myth, the material provided by patients in free association must be replaced by detailed knowledge of the group, of its social, economic and historic background" (reported by Bergmann, 1966, p. 262).

The emergence of modern myth under conditions of stress such as that of war is the subject of a number of psychoanalytic studies. Notable among them is the one by Bonaparte (1947), who collected the mythology born in different countries during the stressful period of World War II. She found, for example, that among the Germans, Hitler was a reincarnation of Siegfried. Odd mythic stories of striking likeness were circulated among people not in touch with one another. One, concerning a gypsy's clairvoyance, was elaborated differently in different lands, but it basically concerned a gypsy's being asked to guess the number of passengers on a train or bus, and then to guess when Hitler would die and when the war would end. She was to be paid if her guesses came true. Another mythic story told by both Germans and English concerned the powerlessness of the enemy. The English version had an Englishman traveling in an English automobile and being suddenly confronted by oncoming German tanks. When the car and the tanks collided, it was the tank, not the car, that was demolished. Naturally, the German version of this tale had the German car remain intact after demolishing the British tank. Each side thus reaffirmed through this shared story the denial of the danger posed by the other, and its belief in its own omnipotence.

The "secret weapon" appears in Bonaparte's list of war myths. This was variously described as a mysterious gas with which the Germans would put the English to sleep; a death ray; an English method for setting the sea on fire and burning the German enemy. Niederland (1971) told me in a personal communication that he found a myth of a secret or uniquely effective weapon among the concentration camp survivors he interviewed. I heard for the first time about the Cypriot Turks' "great weapon" when I visited the Nicosia enclave in the summer of 1968. It was half seriously and half jokingly mentioned by adults in moments of anxiety, and it appeared in the play of children. There was general agreement about where it was located—atop St. Hilarion's Castle, about ten miles from Nicosia, on the only peak of the island's northern mountains under Turkish control, one that marked the northernmost point of the Turkish enclave. Since the road from Nicosia to the northern shore held by Greeks ran nearby, this was a strategic site for any Turkish attempt to reach the sea. One of the first military tasks during the 1974 intervention in Cyprus was, in fact, the clearing of this road from enemy encroachment all the way to the shore. St. Hilarion's Castle has its own dramatic history and its own myths, one of which tells of a queen's jumping from one of its windows to die on the cliff below rather than surrender to the enemy. Cypriot children who have heard this tale regard the place with awe as a place for wars, courage, and sacrifice. As the site of a great weapon it is psychologically appropriate. The modern myth about it had a "kernel of truth" since it probably was a gun emplacement. Popular reference to the mystery on the mountain suggested the notion of a mighty phallus or an anal explosion that could be directed against the foe. There was also some suggestion in it of a maternal breast offered to the needy Turks. I became more aware of this maternal aspect in 1973 when the ring of Greeks around the enclaves had been gone for five years. The myth was still abroad, but it had faded. Conscious reference to the great weapon was infrequent, but it was evident that the mountaintop had become a symbol of Turkish omnipotence. A huge Turkish flag was hung on a steel cable stretching from the peak of St. Hilarion to another mountain-top nearby. It was so enormous that it could be seen as a red spot from many miles away. The great weapon had given way to a red spot, a benevolent nipple. Turkish Cypriots traveling out of their enclaves in Nicosia to the northern shore stayed in visual contact with this symbol as they moved among the Greeks. They looked for it and pointed it out. It was a nipple they shared, identifying Turks on the move to one another as children of this omnipotent spot. In Mahler's (1968) term, they were able to "refuel" at the mother's breast and control the anxiety excited by the move out of a pro-tected and familiar enclave.

Keeping Secrets after the Summer of 1968

The opening of the enclaves' "gates" into the Greek sectors began the second phase of life there. The inner world that the interim survivors had created within the walls was now exposed to reality testing. It now became necessary to weigh the belief on which their omnipotence had been based—that all inside the enclave were psychologically "all good" and those outside "all bad." Insofar as the Turks had been aware of what went on outside their walls during their confinement, especially the booming prosperity of the Greeks, they understood it only intellectually and missed much of its impact. I was an interested observer of their initial reactions to the outside world when I visited Cyprus in 1968. The first taste of freedom para-doxically evoked symptoms like those of depression. In a 1975 in-terview with me, Denktaş made the acute observation that freedom came as a shock to Cypriot Turks in 1968. He asked why they showed so little joy at being able to come and go and why they clung to their enclaves, always returning to "their shabby houses" at night when they ventured forth at all. A psychodynamic viewpoint provides an explanation. Cypriot Turks had become internally oriented to life in the enclaves, and when confinement was terminated, the "fit" of internal to external milieu was sufficiently disrupted to cause a psychological loss. Although they continued for the most part to live within the enclaves and to endure considerable cur-tailment of rights and shortages of goods, their adaptive-defensive illusions were no longer tenable. Their confinement had given them out of a situation of great discomfort and some danger a world shared with their compatriots in which the behavior of the needy and their mythic savior could be psychologically controlled. This world was now gone, and its inhabitants were faced with the humiliating recognition that a prosperous Greek life-style surrounded them on every hand.[4] Moreover, their aggression had built up over the years of confinement, leading them to fantasy that it would triumph once they confronted the Greeks. In reality, they were faced with an altogether different state of affairs, a large world dominated by the Greeks, one in which they had to be submissive and in which they had to realize the force of a new Greek object representation. Aggression was turned inward and directed against the self, and self-esteem was reduced. The minor tranquilizers and antidepressant drugs came into ever greater use as the populations felt this new stress.

It became necessary to make new adjustments to bolster the illusion that the Cypriot Turks enjoyed "power" and that the Cypriot Greeks had none. A policy of denying the Greeks admission to enclaves under absolute Turkish control offered some relief. Although it was dictated by military and political considerations, inasmuch as Cypriot Turks could enter Greek territory this nonreciprocal policy[5] gave the interim survivors the psychological means of handling their problem of low self-esteem and permitted them to retain a certain secrecy about their lives. Such secrecy could be seen as an anal retentive measure against the enemy in psychoanalytic terms, a situation that would make the enemy curious and make him fantasy in his frustration what it was that was being kept secret

4. See Markides (1977) for a description of an amazing and speedy development of the economy on the Greek side through the expansion of tourism, construction, and the exportation of agricultural produce after the establishment of the Republic of Cyprus.

5. Denktaş (1977) explained to me that the typical Turk who took advantage of the "freedom of travel" was in fact bowing as soon as he left his own area to the Cypriot Greek rule that his administration considered unconstitutional. When his administration offered the same "freedom" to Cypriot Greeks, they refused to avail themselves of it because of the unacceptability to them of submitting to "rebel rule" when in the Turkish enclaves.

from him. This control of their privacy gave the Cypriot Turks an illusion of power and contributed to the possibility of magical repair of their narcissistic injuries.

The analyst often sees secretive behavior in obsessional and narcissistic patients, and the way he works with the latter can shed light on the way Cypriot Turks used a political policy to ameliorate psychological hurt. One patient with a narcissistic personality (Volkan, 1976, chap. 9), having experienced a childhood he described as "unbelievably traumatic," had responded to his oral conflicts by the formation of a grandiose self. Although his mother and father fought bitterly and even abused one another physically, his grandfather gave him enough support over the years to make his grandiose self cohesive. When the old man was murdered by an unknown assailant, he sought psychoanalytic help. Still in his twenties, he was in a state of disorganization. He improved greatly after three years of psychoanalysis and was able to work efficiently and function well socially. A peculiar secretiveness persisted, however, in his analytic hours, and he seemed unable to "level with me" all the way. One day he made an indirect reference to a talisman he wore around his neck, and when I showed curiosity about it, we analyzed its meaning. It was his magical "secret" that allowed him to retain the illusion of omnipotence and grandiosity as long as he kept it, in spite of the ways in which his analysis was bringing him beneficial change. Its presence would in the end secretly defeat psychoanalytic efforts to disperse his grandiosity. Since it was a gold medallion, anal elements were condensed in it. Although he aways wore it I had never noticed it before because he wore it under his shirt.

I will limit my discussion of this talisman to its exemplification of the concept of something secret. My patient had purchased it a few months after his grandfather's death and associated the saint's head on it with his grandfather. This association suited his narcissistic attempt at glorification. The medal was a secret "linking object" (Volkan, 1972b, 1972c, 1976; Volkan, Cillufo, and Sarvay, 1976) used to connect the representation of the deceased with that of this pathological mourner. Since the mourner controls such a link, he has the illusion of being able to hold reunion with the dead—

or to "kill" him when his feelings, which alternate between a wish
to cling and a wish to separate, demand. My patient could contain
his rage as long as he kept the medal as a secret narcissistic defense
against the injurious loss of the man who had always confirmed his
belief in his grandiosity. As we analyzed the meaning of the talisman's support, he experienced a very primitive type of anxiety and
was for a short time disorganized before achieving reorganization.
He then no longer felt compelled to keep the medal around his neck.

Cypriot Turks were able to make a kind of magical talisman out
of their enclaves and used them to protect the cohesiveness of group
self-esteem and control over the discharge of rage. Their secretiveness about what went on inside the enclaves linked them to the old
"effective" enclosures they had once resented so bitterly but which
nevertheless protected them from intrusion.

At the time of which I speak, the shortest road connecting the
capital's Greek section with the northern shore ran for a few miles
through Turkish territory, and Greeks who wanted to use it had to
travel over it in caravans under United Nations escort. Even such
a minor demand for Greek submission helped the Turks to maintain
the illusion of their omnipotence. As the caravans of Greek cars
moved slowly behind the United Nations jeep, Turkish drivers took
joy in speeding past them. The shoe was now on the other foot, however briefly, and this daily ritualized "play" was engaged in over
and over for psychological reasons. But in spite of such bravado,
the low self-concept of the interim survivors surfaced again and
again from beneath the various adaptive measures by which they
clung to the illusion of power and chronic hope. Hypochondriacal
preoccupations were clearly present, along with a notion that
"within fifty years no Turk will be left on the island." One even
heard it said, "We'll all die off!"

Talks between Cypriot Greek and Cypriot Turkish leaders continued from time to time, as did talks between political leaders in
the two mother countries on the mainland, but such parley had become stale. Then came the events of 1974—the war and the establishment of Turkish control over the northern part of Cyprus. Once
again, both Cypriot Turks and Cypriot Greeks had to make adaptation to a new situation.

V "Why War?"

The Difficulty of Understanding War from a Purely Psychoanalytic Point of View

Before turning my attention to the events in Cyprus during the summer of 1974, I will briefly note the difficulties I face as a psychoanalyst writing about war. An exchange on this subject took place between Freud and Einstein in 1932; their communication became widely known under the title of "Why War?" Although Freud met Einstein in 1927 he had little to do with him until Einstein wrote to ask whether any of the insights of psychoanalysis could be profitably applied to the age-old search for a peaceful world. Einstein wrote:

> This is the problem: Is there any way of delivering mankind from the menace of war? It is common knowledge that, with the advance of modern science, the issue has come to mean a matter of life and death for civilization as we know it; nevertheless, for all the zeal displayed, every attempt at its solution has ended in a lamentable breakdown.
>
> There are certain psychological obstacles whose existence a layman in the mental sciences may dimly surmise, but whose interrelations and vagaries he is incompetent to fathom; you, I am convinced, will be able to suggest educative methods, lying more or less outside the scope of politics, which will eliminate those obstacles. [Freud, 1932, p. 199]

Freud wrote back to say that Einstein had taken him by surprise in posing the question of what can be done to protect mankind from the curse of war. "I was scared at first by the thought of my—I had almost written 'our'—incapacity for dealing with what seemed to be a practical problem, a concern for statesmen. . . . The result is not very fruitful when an unworldly theoretician is called in to advise on an urgent practical problem" (p. 203).

The guardedness of Freud's response arose from his feeling that there is no use trying to get rid of man's aggressive inclination. Conflicts among men are seldom settled without resort to violence. Certain psychical modifications accompany the process of civilization, and whatever fosters the growth of civilization opposes war at the same time; such modifications are the progressive displacement of instinctual aims and the attainment of successful control over instinctual impulses. Like Einstein, Freud favored the establishment of a central authority empowered to adjudicate all conflicts of interest. He was initially hopeful of what the League of Nations might accomplish, but he was subsequently disillusioned. We learn from Jones (1961) that Freud was dissatisfied with his exchange with Einstein and thought of it as sterile and boring.

Freud (1915) had spoken earlier of the disillusionment that war brings to men about the values of their civilization when it acquaints them with the barbarism they had supposedly outgrown in the process of becoming civilized, but which reappears unexpectedly in their behavior in wartime. He held to the ironic conclusion that man's fall back into barbarism is actually an illusion since he never has risen as far above it as he supposed. Its derivatives remain in the unconscious, and Freud's essay indicates that the same forces and psychic mechanisms that operate in the individual operate within national groups as well. That is not to say that he failed to be aware of the gap between individual motivation and social behavior; he acknowledged that psychological motivation for war is an obscure phenomenon. He was pessimistic about a possible role for psychoanalysis in the prevention of war or in the creation of communities effectively dedicated to peace. However, Arlow (1973) finds a certain optimism in his formulations, seeing in "Why War?" views considerably more sanguine than those expressed in The Future of an Illusion (Freud, 1927) and Civilization and Its Discontents (Freud, 1930).

Arlow refers to two of Freud's convictions. The first is that man has the capacity of mastering his instinctual life in the course of his individual development and of bringing it under the sway of reason, although Freud recognized that the realization of this possibility was a Utopian expectation. A second conviction that contributed to Freud's measured optimism concerned "the cultural process."

Arlow maintains that Freud, deeply influenced by Darwinian concepts, regarded the evolution of civilization as analogous to the development of the individual. Arlow states:

He [Freud] regarded these processes as organic, that is, biologically determined, sharing the most general characteristics of all life. Accordingly, as individual development tends toward reliable mastery by the ego over the instincts, so cultural evolution tends toward the strengthening of the intellect and the internalization of aggressive impulses. This transformation takes place under the influence of the communal superego. Thus the cultural development of the group and the cultural development of the individual are always interlocked. [pp. 195–196]

However, Arlow is quick to add insights gained from recent psychoanalytic formulations. He also states that history and clinical observation have yielded more than ample testimony that superego, individual or collective, has hardly served as a reliable ally in the quest for peace. Superego, as we know it today, far from being an integrated and consistently functioning mental structure, is full of contradictions—less so, perhaps, than the id, but definitely more so than the ego. It includes precursors in the prephallic phases, and thus residues of primitive modes of operation are retained even into adult years. This corresponds to instinctual fixation. Arlow adds: "Under conditions of stress and conflict, intrapsychic or international, superego functioning for the individual and the group is remarkably susceptible to regressive reinstinctualization" (p. 197). He goes on to note that the superego is unreliable since its demands may not correspond to the moral values of a culture but may reflect the ideals of a subculture, even a criminal one. Not only has the educational process often not been uncontaminated by some narcissistic or libidinal interest, but one need not look far to find how quick is the aggressive response to any attack on the moral idealism of an individual or a people.

Analysts who wrote about war as early as Freud shared his pessimism. For example, Jones (1915) suggested wryly that "a couple of centuries" of psychoanalytical research (p. 76) would be required before it could be hoped that wars would be impeded by psychoanalytic understanding. As Atkin (1971) emphasized, war is a "social institution," one into the innate psychological determinants of which psychoanalysis has thus far fallen short of providing satisfactorily clear-cut insights. Although we know that the locus of social action is ultimately the mind of the individual, group process, which has its own laws, involves many factors that lie outside the realm of individual psychology. Fenichel (1935) warned about this long ago in a paper never translated into English but extensively quoted by Mitscherlich (1971). Fenichel explored the pitfalls awaiting anyone who seeks to apply psychoanalytic methods to sociological issues. The first is the kind of unwarranted equating of individual and group evident in such phrases as "the nation's instinct for survival." A. Strachey's (1957) volume on the unconscious motives that lead to war discusses this issue from the standpoint of the individual's unconscious, failing to take into account all the complexities involved, and winding up with a suggestion she knew to be inapplicable—that psychoanalytic method be universally applied to selected persons whom it would be most profitable to analyze.

Another pitfall noted by Fenichel is the psychoanalyst's possible failure to see those cogent motivations for war that lie beyond the scope of psychoanalysis. For example, Glover (1933) does not find it necessary in writing on war even to wonder about the nature and genesis of a nation's war machine or its military potential. Fenichel suggests also that when the analyst investigates the phenomena of group psychology he tends to treat them as he would treat neurosis, although anything better classified as a national trait should not be considered a neurotic symptom (Eissler, 1965). In neurosis, reaction patterns are ritualized from childhood on; but in historically significant manifestations of mass psychology, these patterns fade into the background. The field is determined by the emotional reactions of the immediate present, such as the highly charged aggressive behavior of a great majority. The German people under the rule of the Nazis exemplify this; at that time the preshaped character structure and universal aggressive propaganda dovetailed into one another in a quite specific way to allow the unthinkable to become a reality (Mitscherlich, 1971).

In emphasizing the difference between individual and group process we need not, of course, lose sight of the fact that groups are composed of individuals, and that the collectivity of the constituent individuals' emotional life will determine the social emotional climate at any given time. The difficulty lies in studying the bridge—the jump, as it were—from the individual to the mass. We have been accustomed to looking at the individual's inner psychic processes from the structural point of view—that is, from the point of view of the interaction of one's id, ego, and superego and their relation with the outside world through the ego. Although we were aware that the superego as well as ego includes identification with objects that are realistic or fantasied and invested with libido or aggression, the structural point of view is essentially a highly individualized way of looking into a person. It offers a focus narrowed to the established inner structures of one individual. I believe, however, that the study of internalized object relations, in which there is increasing interest, provides a better means than we have previously had to explore the connection between the individual and the group to which he belongs. It permits us to study the internalization of interpersonal relations and to systematize how the self-concept develops from infancy on, with internalized object representations being based on the interaction the individual has with others, and how libidinal and aggressive drives express themselves in this exchange. The theory of internalized object relations that I follow here points to the bipolar development of self- and object images and representations prior to the ultimate integration of what was split. I suggest that in reality such integration may never be totally achieved, that certain "all bad" and "all good" constellations may persist and be externalized. Any group with a common history can bridge differences between the individual and the mass to which he belongs whenever all of the individuals share the "target" of their externalization. I gave examples of this in a previous chapter. Since I see it as quite possible that certain "targets" of externalization can be best explained by historical or sociological investigation, I agree with Mitscherlich (1971) that the psychoanalyst addressing himself to the psychological processes of large groups such as a display of collective aggression will need the collaboration of other specialists. Mitscherlich says: "Favourable instinctual development may counteract many unfavourable conditions of life within society; on the other hand, unfavourable social conditions may intensify the development of neurotic symptoms or characteristics . . . both aspects must be explored with equal subtlety: the vicissitudes of the individual life, as seen in the early object relations, and the vicissitudes of the social life, based on the objective conditions of a community. It follows that neither psychoanalytical nor psycho-social research can be pursued in isolation from each other" (p. 166).

Psychoanalytic writings on war—of which there are but few—usually consider war in a general way, regarding it as though it were a concept of neurosis or psychosis, in spite of the fact that our ideas about neurosis and psychosis have been derived from studies of the individual. Perhaps we should have something like case histories of different wars in order to understand how one is unlike another in respect to the group psychology manifest in them and the occasions for their eruption. After this introduction, I turn my attention to the 1974 war in Cyprus, hoping to understand some of its aspects.

Can a War Be "Ego-syntonic"?

War came to Cyprus with the first rays of the sun on July 20, 1974, five days after the coup against Makarios; so when the Turks landed, Greeks were killing other Greeks on the island, although they united in the face of the common enemy. First came the sound of Turkish aircraft passing over the Kyrenian range to drop paratroopers from mainland Turkey into the cloudless sky over the northern part of the Nicosia enclave. This was soon followed by the landing of Turkish infantrymen on the northern shore near Kyrenia in much the fashion of World War II invasions from the sea.

The Cypriot Turks were seized with frenzied excitement when they saw the paratroopers jumping. Only a few islanders had known with certainty that the military intervention was scheduled. Denktaş was of course aware of it, and had prepared a speech to go over the *Bayrak* radio, which was the voice of the Cypriot Turks in Nicosia. Denktaş (1977) later described for me how he had written this speech only four or five hours before the landing took place, and how he had had everyone in on the secret confined to his office almost up to the time of the landing lest the news get abroad prematurely. The technician who had taped the speech in advance to have it ready for broadcasting at the critical moment was sworn to secrecy and spent a sleepless night awaiting the liberation, which was met with general celebration when it came. People ran into the fields to welcome the paratroopers with food and drink. A fleet of cars, including ambulances as well as private cars, was hastily mobilized to transport the soldiers to the battlefront. Even a bread truck on its early rounds was pressed into service. The United Nations official assigned to Denktaş was caught up in the excitement also. Charged with being at Denktaş's side twenty-four hours a day after the Makarios coup and with reporting any activity of the Cypriot Turks to the United Nations headquarters in Cyprus, he found that telephone connections with the headquarters had been cut on the eve of the action while he slept. When the sound of aircraft told him what was going on, this very proper man, absolutely obsessional in his adherence to duty, was caught up by Turkish emotions; while watching the parachute drops with Denktaş, he saluted him in a moment of abandon and, seizing his hands in congratulation, cried, "You are truly saved!" (Denktaş, 1975).

Makarios had just escaped assassination by EOKA B, and had fled the island. The Cypriot Greeks who favored the junta acclaimed Sampson their president. Thus one Greek faction was opposed to another in murderous action, and the Cypriot Turks feared lest they be massacred in the general bloodbath. Once the Greeks stopped fighting among themselves, it became clear that the downfall of pro-Makarios support would follow, with an attempt to gain Enosis, and that the Akritas plan, or a modified version of it, would be put into operation. The information about this plan that I gleaned from Turkish sources (Denktaş, 1974) concerned a secret document supposedly prepared by the Greeks in 1963 to bypass all of the obstacles against Enosis. It had been published on April 21, 1966, in the local Greek newspaper *Patris,* with the avowed purpose of exposing the mishandling by Makarios of the national cause of Cypriot Greeks. Alarmed by this publication, Cypriot Turks translated it into English, and the authenticity of the translation, which was distributed to influence world opinion, was supposedly never disputed. I lack a historian's knowledge as to whether this document was the result of serious and sinister plans, but what is important here is that the Cypriot Turkish administration as well as the Cypriot Turk in the street believed what it said.[1] What really worried them was the statement that when time for the declaration of Enosis should arrive and it met resistance from the Turks, Cypriot Turks would be rapidly and forcefully put down. The speed with which this step was to be taken—its completion within a day or two was expected—was designed to make outside intervention impossible. Although one section of this document asserted: "We do not intend to engage, without provocation, in massacre or attack against the Turks" (Denktaş, 1974, p. 48), the Turks believed that their resistance to the Enosis movement would bring about their massacre,[2] and their dread of this led to the establishment of a hopeless emotional climate. The Turkish government on the mainland was propelled into action by concern for the Turkish Cypriots, added to any other motive it may have had.

Cyprus was fertile ground for fear of mass destruction and the dread of annihilation. It had long been the scene of violence and terrorism. It could be said that the entire life of any Cypriot native now of middle age had been intertwined throughout its course with mass aggression. The presence of unconcealed danger around him was as natural to him as the air he breathed or the bread he ate. He

1. Denktaş's (1977) view on the Akritas plan held that it had been prepared before 1963 and that the Bloody Christmas of December 1963 (see Chapter I) was part of it. According to Denktaş, the "secret armies" of the Greeks referred to in the plan had been mobilized 18 months earlier. At a meeting with Denktaş in February 1977, Makarios told him that he had approved the formation of these secret armies because his minister of the interior had told him that the Turks were preparing also. Denktaş wrote to me further that Glafcos Clerides, his Cypriot Greek counterpart in intercommunal negotiations, had acknowledged the existence of the Akritas plan, which he called a "contingency plan." Inasmuch as Turks felt that the plan had been put into effect as early as December 1963, it would appear that it would never be hard for the Greeks to identify a "contingency" that would justify putting the plan into operation.

2. Denktaş (1977), responding to my inquiry about massacres, told me that as far as the Turks were concerned, the massacre of Cypriot Turks by Cypriot Greeks did occur in 1963, 1964, 1967, and during the Turkish military operation of 1974. He claimed that in 1964, 203 Cypriot Turks had been randomly rounded up from the streets and put to death.

would remember from his childhood the bombing forays of Germans and Italians in World War II, during which the island had been British territory. Although this bombing had brought little devastation, it did bring fear and familiarity with the screaming of sirens and the ominous look of bomb shelters. Soldiers from every corner of the British Empire walked the streets clad in a great variety of uniforms. People were fitted to gas masks and introduced to black austerity bread. The fear of invasion mounted after the Germans occupied Crete. Just as castration anxiety has little to do with actual castration—in my twenty years of psychiatric practice I have yet to know of a father who actually castrated his son—the islanders' fear of invasion persisted in spite of the fact that from year to year no invasion actually took place. It is often not the occurrence of a disaster but the persistent threat of its occurrence that causes symptom formation. The world seemed to be a dangerous place, and its internalization was dangerous accordingly.

After the Second World War, Cyprus was faced with the violence and threat of the movement for Enosis, which had Cypriot Greeks killing Cypriot Greeks and British alike and Cypriot Turks and Cypriot Greeks slaughtering one another. Even before the outbreak of actual war in 1974 the Greeks on the side of Makarios fought against those who favored the government in Athens. The Island of Aphrodite had no lasting peace in this century, and those born there to turbulence knew no other way of life. It is no wonder that when Sampson became president and signaled the beginning of the actualizing of Enosis, the Turks felt that a war was required.

I have spoken about how aggression accumulated within the Turkish enclaves. Mitscherlich (1971), referring to Fenichel's (1935) ideas, concluded that the phenomenon of warfare, the aggressive behavior of a community, must not be taken merely as the expression of an accumulated surplus of aggressive drive in the individuals involved in it. No individual declares war by himself because he has been unable to sublimate his aggressive drive, and the aggressive drive by itself would not require war under another set of circumstances. Mitscherlich does suggest, however, that "it would be one-sided" to disregard the existence of the aggressive excitement of the individual or to underestimate its contribution to the conduct of war. It remains a question, he says, whether in any given case this aggressive excitement triggers a chain reaction in which violence finally affects the whole community. "It seems that in the present day the subjective sense of being exposed to enemy aggression is an indispensable prerequisite for going to war. Hence those groups within the body of a nation actually interested that there be war will work to create such a feeling" (p. 165). There had been "war readiness"—to borrow a term from Glover (1933) and Atkin (1971)—among both island and mainland Turks and their Greek counterparts for many years. Atkin describes this readiness as being purely psychological rather than the actual preparedness for war that is the function of any society's "war institution." It was an only partly conscious state of mind genetically antecedent to the social and psychological behavior involved in a defense establishment. When the Turkish military actually took control of northern Cyprus, mainland Turks were supported by a psychological readiness that went back to far earlier plans to divide the island. Similarly, the Greeks had been psychologically ready to defend "their" island. There had been a lethal weapon of some sort under almost every rock for years, and a corresponding war mentality existed in either group.

The average Turk on the streets of Cyprus had wanted very much for a long time to be saved by Turkey but had so given up hope as to be skeptical in assessing what was taking place. I learned later that the average Greek also denied the possibility of Turkey's taking military action; so when it came at last it was a shock to both sides in spite of a general war readiness, and not until some time after the paratroopers landed were the first shots fired. Once engaged, however, the struggle was vicious. Its first round took three days, Turkish troops gaining a stronghold between Nicosia and Kyrenia with the help of Cypriot Turkish soldiers. Negotiations in Geneva followed. The Turks proposed that the Turkish Cypriots living in enclaves scattered among the Greek majority should be given land of their own, preferably the top third of the island, although the possibility of establishing cantons in the Swiss manner was suggested. Failing to get what they wanted from the negotiations, the Turks took action again for the second time in twenty-seven days, their jets crowding the air over the island.[3] Reenforced Turkish troops took over about 37 percent of northern Cyprus within sixty hours. They had no intention of seizing the whole island but wanted only what they called their "fair share." The Greeks naturally saw nothing fair about it.

Glover (1933) held that civilized nations are at a disadvantage in war because they are without the ritualistic control of killing that characterizes primitive man. Moreover, the civilized are able to use sophisticated rationalizations to conceal their unconscious motivation for going to war—Glover's concern here was largely the sadistic and masochistic impulses that are expressed in armed conflict—and are not like primitive people who do not hesitate to declare that they want to make war in order to punish their enemies. The psychoanalyst knows that insanity includes elements of psychic reconstruction, and Glover, calling war "a mass insanity," wrote that "insanity is simply a dramatic attempt to deal with individual conflict, a *curative process* initiated in the hope of preventing disruption, but *ending in hopeless disintegration*" (p. 31). By implication, then, the mass insanity of war represents the attempt of a group to cure itself, but it nonetheless results in destruction. Fornari (1966) also saw war as a kind of "cure."[4]

3. This second military operation was a necessity for the Turks since there were many Cypriot Turks, most of them in enclaves, remaining in territory held by the Greeks. The Greek threat of exterminating them unless Turkey withdrew was taken seriously. This military action liberated many more Turkish enclaves (Denktaş, 1977).

4. Like Money-Kyrle (1937, 1951), Fornari depended on Kleinian theories in explaining war's psychology: "war could be seen as *an attempt at therapy* [italics added], carried out by a social institution which, precisely by institutionalizing war, increases to gigantic proportions what is initially an elementary defense mechanism of the ego in the schizoid-paranoid phase. In clinical paranoia . . . the Terrifier is projected into a reality of the external world which is usually only imagined to be dangerous. In war, however, the Terrifier is projected into a really dangerous enemy, who may really kill and be really killed. From this point of view, war would not seem to be a mental illness, but rather an attempt to control the fear of an absolute destruction, such as that expressed by the Terrifier, through a system which, ritualizing and relativizing the destroying and the being destroyed, would appear to constitute a costly and tragic system of security, involving an intricate interplay between the inner and the outer world, between illusion and reality" (pp. xvii–xviii).

Still another view of war as "therapy" was voiced by Mitscher-lich (1971), following Freud's notion that by decreasing the innate aggression of the group it becomes a condition of internal peace. He held that World War II significantly depleted the surplus of aggressive instinct among the national communities of Europe and that it was thus impossible after such ghastly bloodletting to involve them further in any major international conflict and that even internal political tensions were kept within bounds.

Atkin (1971) speaks of the "war institution" as being ego-syntonic and acceptable in most cases to individual concepts of morality. "For most, patriotism (the exaltation of the group) is a legitimate, acceptable, rationalized displacement of the individual's narcissism. The same legitimacy can be applied to the projected hate component of ambivalence, the most repressed and the most sacrificed to the civilizing group process. The war institution can thus be seen as a manifestation of the nation's will to survive and to maintain its character. The national self-consciousness and the self-esteem of the citizenry serve to integrate and strengthen the nation" (p. 562). Atkin notes that the shining flame of patriotic glory, as a virtue and a goal, has only recently been dimmed, and even now only among some of the intelligentsia. He refers to the way in which Freud pondered whether the pacifism he shared with Einstein was a "*constitutional* intolerance, an idiosyncracy" (Freud, 1932, p. 215). Stating that psychoanalysis has never flinched from seeing the human condition as it is, Atkin asks, "Can we expect man to live above his 'emotional income'?" (p. 562).

It was my observation that the war in Cyprus was "ego-syntonic" for the Turkish Cypriot population. It relieved the low self-esteem that lay beneath a pathologically grandiose group self. The Turks who came as invaders from the mainland were responding to the frustration of having been unable for years to save their brothers and sisters on the island by becoming at last their "saviors." The narcissistic hurts they had suffered at the hands of the Greeks were repaired. Rochlin (1973) has written extensively about how aggression, whether in the individual or in the group, provides a means by which to gain a sense of worth, and how aggression may be in the service of defense of the self. Adaptive function of the use of aggression has been observed (Hartmann, 1939; Hartmann, Kris, and Loewenstein, 1949; Solnit, 1966), but we must not forget its basically destructive nature.

When I visited Turkey soon after the war, I could see the pleasure it gave the people there to share aggressive feelings toward a common enemy. They experienced a political and social unity that lasted for many months, although this was not an achievement easily realized in view of the political fragmentation of Turkey at the time. It has been said that political leaders know instinctively how to provoke war against another nation in order to avert civil war or civil disorders. Although it was the bitter enmity between two Greek elements on Cyprus that triggered the war there, the war benefited the Turks by giving them inner peace and a new self-esteem. The prime minister, Ecevit, was temporarily elevated to the role of a second Atatürk, and the Turks on the island joined those on the mainland in identifying themselves as his followers.

Rochlin (1973) states that although a similarity can be seen in many respects between the psychology of the group and that of the individual, there are important distinctions between them that are all too often overlooked. He notes that one essential difference is nowhere more clearly illustrated than by the readiness of a group to invest its interests in a leader, a cause, or a purpose far more quickly than any individual ever falls in love or becomes devoted to a goal in work. In other words, the narcissism of the group quickly attaches itself to a choice, or as quickly withdraws from one.

Their discovery of a new hero in Ecevit increased the cohesiveness of the Turks as a group. Ecevit became a symbol to them. Unfortunately, he was the head of a peculiar coalition government that included extreme rightist elements, and within a year, when he attempted to cash in on his popularity by resigning and dissolving his government in an attempt to push Turkey toward a new election, he lost when the other parties formed a coalition of their own and blocked new elections. He became Turkey's prime minister again for a short time after the June 1977 elections and again in January 1978.

He is known as a peace-loving man. He is a poet who can speak eloquently in English as well as in Turkish. Turkey was fortunate to have him at the helm during those critical times. An Ecevit phenomenon developed in Cyprus—his photograph hung in houses and shop windows, replacing, one might imagine, the once ubiquitous birds of Cyprus that had been the needy selves of the Cypriot Turks. Ecevit's pictures became the shared idealized object, something that glued together a newly developed group self-concept. In clinical terms, the expression of this group self-concept resembled the kind of mania one sees in individuals. For many months after the war it was usual for Cypriot Turkish parents to name their sons after Ecevit and their daughters after his wife. I know of no better illustration of Freud's (1921) formulation of how group members identify with the image of the leader and, secondarily, with each other.

The Other Side of the Coin

Although the liberated Cypriot Turks found the war "ego-syntonic" and a lift for their group concept, the personal tragedies that always attend the destructive acts of man swept across the island like rolling thunder. The Turkish army in its initial move and in the second action that followed it put to flight the Cypriot Greeks who had been living in the North. It is estimated that 150,000 of them became refugees in the South and 65,000 Cypriot Turks fled to the North. Although I was unable to visit Greek refugee camps to interview those huddled within them, I can imagine the incredible hardships they underwent. The Turkish army divided the island by what was called the Attila line, a replacement for the old green line that had divided Turkish enclaves from Greek territory. The name was picked up by the Greeks to symbolize Turkish aggression they considered barbaric and by the Turks to recall the ruthless conqueror from Central Asia, the Turks' original home. They identified themselves with him since their archaic group aggression was not only in the service of terrorizing the enemy but, what was perhaps more important, a means by which to preserve the cohesion of their group self. Approximately 20,000 Cypriot Greeks who could not move quickly into the South remained in the territory held by the Turks.[5] My report on their situation appears in the following chapter.

The Turks were in a position of great danger as war began. In its first move the Turkish army occupied only a small triangular area that opened the enclave in Nicosia to the Kyrenian shore. The enclaves elsewhere were at once surrounded or captured by the Greeks. Eleven thousand Turks were trapped in the Famagusta enclave that lay in the shadow of Othello's Tower and behind the walls of the ageless city that once again protected its occupants from capture. The situation was different in the southern port city of Limassol, where in the absence of any natural or man-made barrier the Turks were quickly overrun. Those who survived were confined for months in a football stadium nearby. In its second thrust the Turkish army liberated the Cypriot Turks who had been confined in two big enclaves at Famagusta and Serdarlı, which is midway between Nicosia and Famagusta, and the occupants of smaller enclaves in the North, but tens of thousands of Turks remained scattered throughout the territory held by the Greeks in the South. These tried to escape to the North, most of them traveling on foot in the hope of going undetected. Their flight to safety required the abandonment of everything they had, as well as the surrender of their land. Many of these refugees were killed and others were wounded. A new "business" came into existence in southern Cyprus; Greeks aiding the Turks in the South to escape charged as much as $200 a person. When I interviewed some of these "escapees" I learned of the imaginative and dangerous ways people were smuggled through the lines. A baby would be hidden in a tin container of the kind used to ship cheese, and the container would be picked up by Turks according to plan after the baby had been smuggled through the checkpoint in it. A special backseat was installed in some cars in order to hide adults, who were obliged to breathe through tubes while in confinement there. The clandestine northern flight of these Turks continued until the fall of 1975, when an agreement was drawn up to permit open travel to the North. By the summer of 1977 the official count of the Cypriot Turkish administration showed only about 100 Cypriot Turks remaining in territory held by the Greeks.

5. In the summer of 1977 Denktaş gave the number of Cypriot Greeks still in the North as 1,800; after the death of Makarios most of these began applying for permission to move South.

The voluntary northward migration of almost all of the 65,000 Turks initially trapped in the South resulted in a de facto division of the population.

In spite of the suffering of the migrating Turks of the South, those in the North continued to celebrate their liberation for months. Before the Cypriot Turkish administration could bring the situation under control, the people looted houses, factories, and villages that had belonged to the Greeks. The impoverishment of the Turkish refugees and the enrichment of many lower-class Turks in the North by looting overturned the social scene. For example, it was said that the erstwhile employers of a middle-aged Turkish woman who had been a maidservant were paying social calls on her in view of her overnight prosperity, based on her vast store of loot hidden away. So widespread was the looting that a euphemistic new word was coined for it, *buluntu*, which means "something found." At social events there was considerable chatter about the "found things" in the house of one or another of the group. As the old moral strictures on the individual and on society were shaken, people felt that they had the right to own the "found things" and even stole such "found" items from one another.

The general preoccupation with *buluntu* was still evident when I visited northern Cyprus six months after the war, but it ended soon thereafter, perhaps because of steps taken by the administration or, possibly, because there was nothing more to be "found" readily by individuals. The government put what remained in warehouses and offered for sale the television sets, clothing, canned goods, and other supplies left behind by the Greeks. Other steps taken by the administration to dispose of Greek belongings will be noted in the next chapter.

Such preoccupation with material things had psychological usefulness, I believe, inasmuch as it permitted a group that had for a long time nursed a severe narcissistic hurt to acquire narcissistic supplies in some abundance without guilt. One sometimes heard the situation actually put into words in such remarks as, "See—we were deprived of all luxury for eleven years, and now it is our right to have them!" However, it is of greater significance that this concern over the material helped the people to ignore their psychological difficulties. They were all faced with immense change, in which loss in some degree was inevitably present, and it was necessary to go through the pain of mourning the losses in order to accept the change. Even "victors"—if victors there be after such extensive human destruction—must mourn.

VI   Mourning and Adaptation after a War

The Burning of the Blankets

The agency of the Cypriot Turkish administration responsible for resettling Turkish refugees from the South tried to place them in situations as much like those they had left behind as possible. Since there were more vacated villages in the North than had been left behind by migrating Turks in the South, suitable matching, such as the placement of mountain villagers in mountainous terrain, usually was possible. A guide called the *kılavuz* was assigned to each community newly settled by Turkish refugees. Most often a young man with some college education, the kılavuz in a sense represented the settlement agency in Nicosia, the capital city. He was given a house for his own use and put in charge of a building suitable for a warehouse, in which were stored usable items such as beds, sewing machines, food, and television sets that the Cypriot Greeks had left behind in their flight. The immigrants were assigned to houses comparable to those they had formerly had.

I was given permission to study these new "Turkish" villages on my Cyprus visit six months after the war was over. As luck would have it, I was in the office of the agency in the office complex belonging to Denktaş when a message came from one of the villages reporting trouble. One of the new settlers had burned the blankets given him by his kılavuz. I was told that complaints like this from the field were common (Savalaş, 1975) and that the people in the agency were often puzzled at the stubbornness and apparent ingratitude of immigrants who refused to accept the provision made by a kılavuz. The first interpretation of the blanket-burning was that the recipient was a greedy man who wanted something finer than he had been given, and the same rationale seemed to apply to the case of a man who had broken all the windows of the house assigned to him. No one seemed satisfied with his lot, although I was told that all of the settlers in this village were considerably better off than they had been in their old homes, and that they recognized this. Most of them were farmers who could not but acknowledge the superior promise of their current holdings; but although time was passing, few seemed to have taken appropriate steps toward plough-ing and planting their fields. A troubleshooter was being sent into the village where the blankets were burned. I went with him and noted that he was a man well able to handle psychological group processes. The site of my first fieldwork, a village chosen entirely by my chance presence in the agency office when the blanket-burning was reported, was about fifteen miles from Nicosia, near the main road between that city and Famagusta. Turkish tanks had traveled this road six months earlier. Greek villagers had fled before the arrival of the enemy, and the buildings of the village proper had not been destroyed although walls close to the road were pocked by bullet holes and the only service station was burned. The village was a modest one with but one church and one school; it had two coffeehouses, but no more than ten modern buildings, most being made of mud-and-hay bricks in the usual Cypriot fashion.

Fifty-three Turkish families settled there by spring 1975. One of these had come from Central Anatolia,[1] but the others had all fled from the same small farming community in the South. They had left in great fear and with grave risk since such migration was forbidden by the Greeks before the autumn of 1975. Their *mukhtar* (head man) retained his role in the new location, as did their school-teacher. Except for the family from Anatolia, the only stranger

1. Soon after the war, permission was given those in the military forces of the mainland who had fought on Cyprus to settle there with their families if they wished. The families of military men who died in the war were also allowed to settle in northern Cyprus and given free houses in which to live. Later, the Turkish government encouraged even more settlers to come from Anatolia. It is estimated that at least 10,000 Turks from the mainland—mostly those of Cypriot origin—went to live in the Turkish section of Cyprus to increase the Turkish strength there and to promote the economy. Although in this move no one was forced to migrate, this process resembled the earlier "exile" method of sys-tematic emigration and settlement described in Chapter III. It could thus be said that the historical process of Turks emigrating to Cyprus, begun in 1572, still continues.

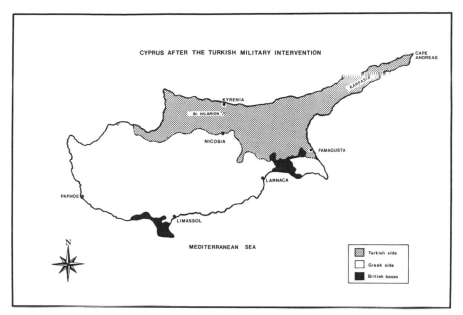

Map 2. Cyprus after the Turkish military intervention

among these people was the official kılavuz. Some houses remained empty; a dozen more refugee families might have been accommodated. Each building bore a crudely scrawled code number required by the central Cypriot Turkish administration as a means of inventory and control. Somehow these ugly scrawls depressed me, reminding me of the tattoos used in concentration camps. They certainly detracted from any homelike aspect these houses might have had, and they served to remind the villagers that their houses were not their very own.

I found that thirty-eight of the fifty-three family heads were given to complaints that were sometimes just vague expressions of discontent. Sixteen of these men were asked to gather in a coffeehouse, the usual place for men to socialize, and the mukhtar joined them there in a three-hour discussion with the troubleshooter. I observed the group processes at work and interviewed some of the participants individually in a method that proved so successful in the collection of data that I used it later in other villages. All of the sixteen men admitted when they were prodded that they and their families were better off than they had been in the past, or at least during the eleven years in which their lives had been full of discomfort and fear. They declared, in fact, that they would rather die than return to the South. They were elated over the Turkish victory and were full of nationalistic pride, but on one level they continued to give vent to a generalized charge of hostility by constant complaining.

One complaint concerned the name of the village. The authorities in Nicosia charged with providing Turkish names for the hitherto Greek communities offered names that were nationalistic, like "The Village of the Brave Soldiers," or names with reference to the environment, like "Olive Grove," but the settlers wanted to use the names of the villages from which they had fled, modifying them slightly as American settlers called their cities after the homes they remembered in such names as New Rochelle and New Glarus. The coffeehouse bore a sign announcing that it was a "Refugees' Coffeehouse," and this disturbed the troubleshooter, who thought it was time that the new settlers stopped thinking of themselves as refugees and saw themselves as the possessors of free Turkish land. Although the villagers saw the force of his argument, they did nothing to alter the sign.

When the discussion got around to the reason why one of these men had burned his blankets, I began to see what psychological process was at work. It became clear that the settlers saw the blankets as being unacceptably contaminated by a Greek aura. After the war ended, the Cypriot Turkish administration had too little new bedding to meet the need; so an order went out to make quilts from whatever suitable fabric the Greeks had left behind. Some of the material made into quilts came from garments; so, by extrapolation so to speak, all of the bedding issued suggested to the settlers body contact with Greeks in the past. The blankets were thus perceived as links between the Turks and the Greeks, and the villagers sought to "prove" by burning them that there was no more contact with the Greeks, that separation had taken place. It was a question of burning one's bridges.

It was, however, a symptomatic act inasmuch as the villagers were in the midst of a process of mourning and real psychological separation from the Greeks had not yet become possible. The man who had smashed the windows of his new house was also involved in an attempt to create an illusion of psychological separation from the Greeks who had lived in it, who were unknown to him and whose appearance he could only dimly imagine. During my interview with

him, this man expressed his uneasiness at living in a Greek house
which he was expected to make his home in spite of the telltale
numbers daubed on the wall. Since Greekness and Turkishness
met in this house, it was necessary to make a separation; so he
smashed the windows. As I listened to him, I became aware that
he was not only attacking the Greek aspect of the house—and he
perceived what was Greek as bad and dangerous because he had
so recently escaped with his family from the annihilation he expected at Greek hands—but was also expressing his feelings of
guilt over occupying the home of someone expelled from it. Such
feelings, which resembled those of survivor guilt, made his abode
an uncomfortable one, however adequate it may have been physically (Volkan, 1977).

Mourning and Adaptation

The psychological processes of those newly settled in the villages
of the North can be best understood after reviewing the process of
mourning that precedes adaptation to loss and change. Since the
prototype of mourning is the response of grief occasioned by a death,
it will be useful to examine what this involves.

In spite of certain semantic difficulties, those who have investi-
gated the subject agree about a sequence of reactions to be expected
whenever an adult deals with the death of someone of importance
to him (Bowlby, 1961; Freud, 1917; Parkes, 1970, 1972; Pollock,
1961; Volkan, 1972c, 1974). Such a loss is initially denied. Then the
bereaved feels anger and "a yearning to recover the dead" (Bowlby
and Parkes, 1970). Disorganization gives way to reorganization in
which the loss is accepted as an irreversible event and the preoccupation with the image of the dead person is no longer intense
and unrealistic. Although a normal progression from one phase to
the next can be seen, the forward movement is not without some
back-and-forth fluctuation.

Freud (1917) held that grief is not a pathological condition but
a psychological process that runs its course over an interval of time.
He suggested that any interference with normal grief or mourning
is potentially harmful. As the work of mourning goes on, memories
and expectations connected with the one who has died are brought,

one by one, into the mind of the mourner. When they are closely examined, it becomes possible to detach the libido that had been invested in the deceased; and when the mourning is completed, the mourner's ego becomes "free and uninhibited again" (Freud, 1917, p. 245). Pollock (1961, 1977) stressed the adaptational aspect of the mourning process. Freud's original work demonstrated how the loss of a loved object—or even of an ideal—is transformed into ego loss which, as Pollock showed, uses the adaptational process of mourning to heal itself.[2]

My research on mourners (Volkan, 1966b, 1970, 1971, 1972b, 1972c, 1976; Volkan, Cilluffo, and Sarvay, 1975; Volkan and Showalter, 1968) shows that mourning can become complicated (pathological), with the mourner fixated at one of the normally sequential but often overlapping phases; such a development may relate to the mourner's level of maturity, the suddenness of the loss, or its nature. I have found the fixation most likely to occur at the phase in which the mourner yearns to recover the lost object. Such yearning appears simultaneously or alternately with dread of recovering the dead. These polar responses reflect the ambivalence with which the mourner had regarded the dead person before he died. The mourner so fixated keeps a part-object representation of the deceased as an "inner presence" (Schafer, 1968)[3] with which he continues to have a relationship. "Although this relationship is of necessity conducted internally, it involves—as the patient perceives it—interaction that, to all intents and purposes, is between two persons (or their representative parts such as face, head, etc.) on an ambivalent plane" (Volkan, 1976, p. 70).

Our research also showed that such a mourner invests certain inanimate objects with magical powers that connect him with what he has lost. These I term "linking objects." They are chosen from among the belongings of the dead, something he wore, like a watch; something he used as an extension of his senses, like a camera—an extension of seeing; symbolic or realistic representations of him

2. "Mourning processing, like working through, is internal work to restore psychic balance" (Pollock, 1977, p. 16).

3. "Inner presence": an introject the pathological mourner feels to be as if it were a foreign body that does not melt into his own self-representation by the process of identification.

such as a photograph; or something that was at hand when the news of the death was received or when the mourner saw the body. The latter are last-minute objects since they recall the last moment during which the full impact of the living personality of the other was available. Linking objects provide an external locus in which part of the mourner's projected ambivalent object relationship (Jaffe, 1968) is "frozen" rather than being renounced.

The wish to annihilate the deceased along with a simultaneous longing for him is condensed in the linking object, which provides in addition an external reference for the painful and unresolved work of mourning. In order to understand the meaning of the blanket-burning episode better, the principle of the linking object being dealt with by a pathological mourner should be applied. One young patient kept as a linking object a photograph of his dead father that he kept out of sight in a folder. In his fantasy the folder represented his father's coffin and he was afraid to open it. At his father's funeral he had entertained the fantasy that the coffin did not contain his father's body; this was a reflection of his wish that his parent still lived. "Quite by accident" he placed the folder beneath a dripping water pipe; this act represented his wish to "kill" his father (to complete grieving), and it was appropriate since his father had been snorkeling in the sea just before he died and this activity was supposed to have contributed to his death. Further associations to the act indicated that the dripping water also represented the tears of the bereaved son that he had been unable to shed. The act put the work of mourning "out there," so to speak (Volkan, 1971).

Although I have been speaking about the mourning that follows someone's death, the same principles apply to mourning occasioned by other losses as well. Any change significant to the ego is mourned. "To be able to mourn is to be able to change. To be unable to mourn, to deny changes, carries great risk to the individual and to the organization" (Pollock, 1977, p. 29). And it seems to me that groups exhibit a response to loss or change that reflects what we have seen in the mourning of an individual; the pattern seems basically the same.

Mourning among the Cypriot Turks

After the war I was able to observe in Cyprus three overlapping
types of mourning: the reaction to the death of loved ones; the reaction to a change of location; and the reaction to having lost interaction with an enemy. I will discuss the latter two here and return
to the death of loved ones later. During the first postwar year natural
progress in these kinds of mourning could be discerned, but there
were also elements suggestive of complication (pathology).

Fixation in the initial phase of grieving over the death of an
individual, during which the mourner denies that death has occurred, is, of course, immediately evident to others, and psychiatric
help is sought for those seen to be "out of touch with reality," so
the chronicity of this state is usually prevented. Six months after
the war in Cyprus was over, I noticed aspects of a parallel phenomenon of fixation in the initial phase of mourning among the
Cypriot Turks.

One small Turkish village in the northern mountains was near
two villages formerly occupied by Greeks, and only a few miles
from a large Greek town. This village had been attacked from
three sides when war broke out, and some villagers died in the
struggle. Surrender was prevented only by the last-minute arrival
of Turkish aircraft, which bombed the enemy. After the war, the
nearby Greek town, now vacated, was taken over by Turkish refugees from the South. The survivors of the beleaguered village reacted
strangely toward the new occupants of the town the Greeks had
left, finding all sorts of excuses not to go near them. By failing to
face up to the change that had taken place—which included a new
immunity from harassment—they were able to deny its occurrence.
Because of their geographical location and isolation from other
Turkish settlements, they had been accustomed to little exchange
with others for eleven years, and they now referred to the Turks
newly settled nearby as "strangers." The Greeks who had been
ousted had been, of course, considered "bad" and dangerous by the
villagers, but their presence, in which the villagers had made a
heavy psychic investment, particularly with their aggressive drive,
had been oddly reassuring simply by being familiar over time. It
would appear that the process of mourning may become compli-

cated not only through an excessive libidinal investment in the object that is lost but also through the excessive investment in it of aggression. The disappearance of anything in which considerable aggression is invested may usher in a period of safety, but it may also evoke shock and disbelief. As time wore on, the inhabitants of the old village still found it difficult to visit the settlers' town; they could not tolerate *not* seeing Greeks there since the illusion of enemy ghosts, so to speak, was necessary in the bargaining for psychological separation. At last, however, reality prevailed.

The village of the burned blankets was also engaged in a mourning process. The occupants shared the diffuse anger so typical in the second phase of mourning. It surfaced in their complaints. The new settlers had gained better homes and fields by moving, but it had cost them their "attachment to the ground" (Rangell, 1976b). They stubbornly clung to their identity as transients, as the coffeehouse sign attested, and demanded that their new holdings be connected with their old habitat by the use of a related name. The dwellings they remembered had become an introject (an inner presence) in the bosom, internally regarded as an element in the process of mourning. As they tried to establish links between their new surroundings and those of the past, internally or externally, they could not help finding links between themselves and the Greeks they had replaced, and between their self-concept as it was based in one place and their self-concept as it was placed in another. In the linking objects that kept the association with the Greeks alive there was considerable guilt. The burning of the blankets and the smashing of windows had become necessary to the gaining of an illusion that mourning was over.

The most common link to the Greeks was the rubbish left behind as they fled. Great heaps of it lay about. All that was valuable had been taken from the heaps still to be seen in empty houses or in the fields. In some places such rubbish had been gathered in a pile near the center of the village. I was present when an official from the Turkish administration in Nicosia begged the village fathers to burn the rubbish in their village, emphasizing the fact that it was unsanitary and might spread disease. "All it will take," he pointed out, "is a match and a can of gasoline to rid yourself of this ugly presence." The villagers agreed with everything he said but continued to point out to me items in the pile such as broken toys or children's books written in Greek. I was moved at feeling that in their recalcitrance in hanging onto this rubbish there was a hidden cry. They were too angry to cry openly, to complete their mourning, but the guilt they felt at replacing the Greeks who had owned these simple family belongings, now rubbish, accounted for their resistance, however strongly the rubbish represented the "bad" aspects of the enemy as well as their humanity.

The island's appearance changed greatly between my first visit there six months after the war and my return six months later. It was still possible to see bullet holes in the walls of buildings, some collapsed buildings had not been repaired, and the skeletons of burned tanks still stood about; but burned-out forests were being replanted, and it was clear that life was coming back to the place of death. Most of the rubbish heaps had disappeared. Mourning was taking its course and giving way to adaptation to the new life, although one could still stumble on situations that were poignant and find individual Turks who had been unable to grieve and leave their mourning behind.

At the time of the first anniversary of the war I met by chance a Cypriot Turk who was operating a beautiful casino at the seaside. He had at one time owned a modest restaurant not far from the casino but had lost it during the troubles of 1964. For eleven years he had lived as a refugee, longing for life by the sea. After 1974 the Turkish administration gave him the casino to replace the restaurant he had lost, which had long ago been demolished. Although he had never known the Greek proprietor of the establishment that was now his, he kept looking for traces of him. When he found a passport he decided was his predecessor's, the photograph of the owner was missing. Its absence gave his imagination full play; he fantasied how the man had lived and what his feelings had been on the trips his passport indicated he had taken to Iceland and Spain. The Cypriot regarded the passport as a talisman and carried it in his pocket while he worked. It was a linking object between him and the original Greek owner of the casino, and he clung to it as though he were trying to bargain with the unknown Greek and to identify with his introject.

I was told (Fehmi, 1975) a most unusual story that concerned not a linking object according to my description but an object that became an emotional bond between a newly arrived Turkish refugee and the Greek whose home in the North he now occupied. The Greek owner had departed in great haste, leaving behind almost all of his belongings. On entering his new home the Turk was amazed to find *his own photograph* on the mantelpiece. It had been taken in 1936 during the annual sports festival of the Larnaca American Academy, which was attended by both Cypriot Greek and Cypriot Turkish students. The two students in the photograph were shown receiving trophies they had won in an athletic contest; one was the former Greek owner of the house, and the other was the Turk who supplanted him there. It seems unlikely that there were more than two copies of the picture in existence. The Turk had had one but had left it behind in his old home, and the other greeted him on his arrival in the house assigned to him. The two people in the picture had not communicated with each other since 1936.

Cypriot Greeks under Turkish Rule

I am sure that there are countless tragic stories about the Greek refugees. One can imagine the horror, shock, and helplessness that was their lot. Although I had no way of going into the territory held by the Greeks and interviewing people there,[4] I was able to study the conditions of some of the 20,000 who had been trapped in Turkish territory in 1974. Most of them were on the Karpasia Peninsula, which I visited about a year after the war. To venture there I had to obtain permission not only from the Cypriot Turkish administration but also from the Turkish military authorities who were stationed there. I went with the troubleshooter who had accompanied me to the new Turkish settlements and an interpreter, since my Greek is now not adequate for even simple conversation.

4. There is one sociopsychological study on the Cypriot Greek refugees (Evdokas et al., 1976) in which a Cypriot Greek psychiatrist, along with psychologists and other social scientists, prepared a questionnaire of eight mimeographed pages which was given to a sample of refugees. This questionnaire gathered information given on a conscious level by Cypriot Greek refugees concerning their living conditions, economic conditions, social problems, etc., and the research group "interpreted" their answers.

As we passed the military post that guards the entrance to the peninsula, I was emotionally influenced by the absence of any other vehicles on the road we traveled. Their ābsence gave us the feeling of entering a ghostly place. The Greek town we visited had originally contained some 2,500 people, but some of these had escaped. Others, accepted by the Greek authorities in the South, had been permitted to leave, but the Greek authorities for political reasons favored leaving some of the Cypriot Greeks "trapped" in the North. The population had been reduced to 1,900 at the time of our visit. The appearance of the people did nothing to remove my impression of being in a ghost town for they were silent and slow-moving. The town seemed clean and sterile, probably because the walls had been freshly painted throughout its length to erase nationalistic slogans written in Greek that praised the struggle for Enosis, etc. The Cypriot Greeks were further humiliated by being obliged to hang posters supporting Turkish nationalistic pride in the windows of their coffeehouses and on the walls.

Three policemen and a doctor, all Turkish, had been assigned to the town. There were no physical signs of destruction, since the war had bypassed this area. When I tried to use the same interviewing method I had used in the Turkish sections, I could reach no understanding of the emotional situation of those with whom I spoke, although they seemed interested, and treated us to soft drinks. They were all wary, and I felt that all of those in the coffeehouse were depressed. Although they were at liberty to carry out their daily routine in the town and to work in the nearby fields, there seemed to be little interest in working. They were not under undue pressure to work since the Red Cross gave each four English pounds a month, but I felt that depression kept them detached from the notion of work in any case. No weddings or entertainments had taken place there during the postinvasion year.

These people were also victims of what I call the "television war" on Cyprus. At the time of the establishment of the Republic of Cyprus, the island boasted only one television station, which broadcast in English, Greek, and Turkish in a prescribed manner; but after the 1963–64 events, Cypriot Greeks gained control over the station, and the Greek language was used chiefly except for some films in English. The Greek television and radio facilities were used energetically in a sort of cold war. After the failure of the mainland Turks to come to the rescue of their brothers on the island, the Cypriot Greeks used almost as a theme song for any broadcast in Turkish the lamentation of a Turkish song that began "I waited, but you never came!" This was rubbing salt into the narcissistic wounds of the island Turks. Interestingly, after the war the Cypriot Greek television began a nightly Turkish newscast to acquaint the Cypriot Turks with the Greek stand on the island. The government of mainland Turkey then built a strong station on the southern mountains of Anatolia and began beaming Turkish television to the island. By the time we visited the Greek village, the antenna for reception had been set to pick up the mainland Turkish broadcast and the Greeks could hear programs broadcast in their own language only with difficulty.

On our visit to this Greek town I was interested to see whether group processes paralleling those at work in the Turkish enclaves (see Chapter IV) might have become evident within the postwar year. A Cypriot Greek doctor who worked with the Turkish physician assigned to the town provided me with some clues when I visited him at the local hospital. Since he was suspected of being an EOKA B adherent, he had been harassed by a group of Cypriot Turks soon after the military operation. I appreciated his dedication to helping the townspeople in spite of his own personal feelings of hurt and anxiety. He reported that the chief complaint since the war had been something referred to as difficulty in breathing, and he had a good appreciation of its obvious meaning. It was usually accompanied by stomach trouble and sleep disorders. He also mentioned a statistical increase in the number of cases of hypertension. Another symptom reported by some patients was hallucination in which the patron saint of the monastery of Cape Andreas, which is at the tip of the Karpasia Peninsula, appeared.

The First Year after the War

It was clear during the first year after the war that although the Turkish army had succeeded in dividing the island in two geographically, psychological acceptance of such division was not accomplished as quickly, even by Cypriot Turks. It took time to adapt to it, and the sequential steps of the mourning process had to be taken before the new realities on the island could be accepted. The mourning process was complicated in a time during which the political stituation remained explosive and the settlement of serious differences was far from complete. Nicosia's old green line was not substantially altered, for not only did the Turkish military not cross it into the Greek side of the capital, but it was guarded on either side by members of the opposing forces.

On my visit there in 1975 there were many nights when I slept no more than a block away from the border, and I sometimes heard gunfire. People paid little attention to this and went on with whatever they were doing, saying that there was no problem as long as the fire was not returned. The soldiers on guard on either side had a ritual of abuse. As soon as night fell they would call out their scorn of the other side and curse their enemies, stopping to permit similar imprecations to be hurled back at them from the other side. One thought of an invisible orchestra leader coordinating the antiphony. This curious performance seemed to give a feeling of security to those living on the border; as long as the soldiers expressed themselves so freely, there seemed no cause for alarm. Nevertheless, the border psychology was not without fear. Those living in the Turkish houses on the green line (now called the Attila line) in the capital city could see the Greek houses on the other side across a vista that included some empty buildings, barricades, and military encampments. One Turkish neighborhood penetrated Greek territory in a sort of cul-de-sac; the additional exposure of this position led to more anxiety that was usual elsewhere, and this was heightened at night. Stray bullets were not uncommon, and since a child had been killed by one, people avoided sitting in their windows or on their balconies. Someone took steps to relieve the feeling of anxiety by erecting a flagpole in the cul-de-sac where it faced the Greek community, standing higher than the flag displayed by the Greeks. Since it was illuminated at night, the Turkish flag thus loomed over the Greek banner twenty-four hours a day. Magical gestures soothe anxiety when people are regressed!

My observations on the Turkish side showed the establishment

of a "postwar culture" during the year after the war. Aside from the
initial looting and its material and psychological effects, other
aspects of the recent experience left their mark. Suddenly the shell
cases that had so recently meant death became collectors' items
greatly valued for home decoration. Polished, painted, or reshaped
in arty ways, they became umbrella stands or vases. It was usual
for a host to display his collection of them to visitors. People unlucky
enough not to find shell cases bought them to keep in style. This was
basically a counterphobic adaptation hidden beneath the nationalistic pride of survivors. People put off repairing the holes made by
firearms in their houses, and when children came visiting they were
encouraged to engage in something like an Easter egg hunt, being
given a knife or screwdriver to probe the holes for bullets. A host
took pride in pointing out bullet holes in his furniture, as though
he gained distinction from having survived an attack so immediate
and so savage. At the same time it seemed as though being so close
to evidence of fire made fire seem less dangerous, and the people
gave careful attention to the different kinds of bullets, their source
(they were American, perhaps, or Czechoslovakian), the weapons
that had fired them, and whether they had been fired by the Greek
assailants or the Turkish rescuers. Places where people gathered
remained scarred by war. In Serdarlı I watched men play *tavla*
(backgammon), a popular pastime, in the yard of a coffeehouse
one wall of which had been ruined by shells and in the shadow of
a damaged minaret left in disarray; this was a full year after the
war's end. Small found bullets were used for necklaces, perforated
and hung on a cord. Bent bullets were those that had been fired,
and these were particularly prized; they represented a defused
explosive, a defanged attacker. Young Turkish men were especially
fond of necklaces made from them.

The Itching Phenomenon

Mourning over those killed in battle can be complicated, for a
number of different reasons. For example, A. Mitscherlich and M.
Mitscherlich (1975), using psychoanalytic methodology, pointed
out that the people of Germany could not effectively come to grips

with the process of mourning for their dead because they had been a sacrifice to Hitler, and to mourn them would be to acknowledge an alliance with Hitler and all he represented. They would thus be in contact with their own guilt because of an implicit association with Nazi crimes.

The Cypriot Turks seemed unable to mourn their war dead, for an entirely different reason. Those who died in the Cyprus struggle died for the freedom of their people rather than to support an evil leader. They were, in fact, idealized, but it is difficult to "kill" idealized ghosts, who are seen as still alive—somewhere—in glory. It was an evidence of unfinished mourning when, on the first anniversary of the war and on those that followed, mourners had local newspapers publish the names and photographs of the war dead, accompanied by expressions of love and reassurance that they would live forever in the hearts of those they left behind.

The adaptation of the Turkish Cypriots to their losses and all of the changes on the island was not without its painful elements such as guilt, and these had to be hidden *under the skin,* as it were. Unconscious feelings of guilt are of "no small moment in the 'climate' of a society [and] under certain circumstances these processes will provoke violent frustrations, and aggressive reactions" (Mitscherlich, 1971, p. 164). The assimilation of guilt feelings within a community after a war may be an important factor in the promotion of renewed war, as Wangh (1968) suggested. It is possible that on Cyprus such unconscious collective feelings of guilt play a part in the failure of any negotiations seeking a peaceful solution for its problems, since guilt dictates the perpetuation of suffering.

In the beginning of summer in 1975 I learned, from the chance remarks of one Turk to another here and there in Ankara, about a general belief that the waters of the Cyprus beaches were contaminated by some organism that caused itching. The story of this came first from islanders who visited Turkey. When I went to Cyprus a little later I found the rumor about the itch widespread, although there was an inconsistency about it inasmuch as no one stayed out of the water for fear of contamination. Such an inconsistency raised doubt about its truth. I asked a number of physicians if they had seen evidence of the itch among patients who used the bathing beaches, and had negative replies from all. Psychoanalytic investigation (Musaph, 1968; Musaph and Prakken, 1964) has shown that itching can be a sign of repressed anxiety, repressed rage, or repressed sexual excitement. Accordingly, I tried to formulate what went on in unconscious fantasy beneath the skin of Cypriot Turks.

The start of the Turkish military operation of the summer of 1974 had been made on the northern beaches of the island at the peak of the swimming season, when Cypriot Greeks and tourists swarmed there. Cypriot Turks were tolerated, but it humiliated them to use a beach of which not one inch belonged to their group. Military action in the summer of 1974 saw this playground strewn with the dead, and the stains of the quicklime scattered over them as a hygienic measure remained as late as mid-spring of the following year. The Turkish army marked the spot with a statue honoring those of their number who fell there on the first day of the war, and the place was thus hallowed by death and suffering as well as triumph. On a field trip to this spot six months after the war ended, I could see the personal effects of soldiers long gone and of civilians who had fled in haste; piles of Greek military shirts, boots, etc., still cluttered the place, with quicklime scattered around them. Parents warned their children to pick up nothing lest they come to harm (suffer with *itching*) because of the residual quicklime or the bacteria of bodily decay.[5]

Although the rumor about the itch may have been first connected with the northern beaches near Kyrenia, where quicklime had actually been used, it may very well have spread psychological contamination to other beaches that fell under Turkish control after the war. After the northern beaches were cleaned and the Turks resumed swimming and sunning there, notices were posted

5. Turkish folkways connect quicklime with punishment. In Baybars's (1970) account of his childhood in Cyprus during World War II, he tells of the shooting down of a German plane over the island; its occupants were captured after they parachuted to safety. He recalls asking the women what the fate of these captives would be. One woman said:

"They're already in Satan's flames. They were all taken to a pit filled with quicklime and thrown into it."

"What is quicklime, mother? Mother said: Shush, shush. Carry on with your coloured papers, there's a good boy. Yes, the woman said. Yes, yes. Quicklime burns you up. That's what these Germans deserve" (pp. 90-91).

warning of the need to report the finding of any suspicious objects. Although the piles of personal effects and stains of quicklime were gone, they must have left a memory trace. And it was not unusual to find in the water bits of green plastic associated with the body bags used to carry corpses after the military operation. When wet plastic pieces adhered to a bather's skin he quickly tore them off. Signs of shot and shell in the walls of hotels and other buildings reminded one of the tragedy of a year earlier even as one heard the joyous laughter of the bathers. Although the scene was one of careless outdoor fun, as in any other seaside resort in the summer, an investigator sprung from these people could easily pick up hidden meanings in the jokes and apparently trivial remarks they made. One common joke concerned the fact that small fish bit the bathers. One swimmer would say to another, "They're so used to eating human flesh (meaning the dead that had floated there) that they're trying to eat us up!" Nervous laughter would follow such a remark (Volkan, 1977).

After my return to the United States in the autumn of 1975 I saw the film *Jaws* and heard remarks about it from my patients on the couch. The uneasiness of the Cypriot Turkish bathers could be compared to the quickened fear of sharks that a bather anywhere might have after seeing the film, and his secret dread that what seemed nothing but a submerged rock might turn out to be something vastly more malign. The uneasiness pointed to guilt about enjoying oneself in a place of death. As survivors, the bathers felt guilty. The biting fish were punishing them, but the sharp prick of their jaws at least reminded them that they were alive.

Their feelings about bathing in a place of death surfaced usually quite subtly in remarks bathers made as they quit the water; something was sure to be said expressing surprise that they had survived their dips, and—by implication—surprise that they had not joined the legions of those who met death there. Anxiety stemming from the superego's demand that one refrain from enjoyment in a tragic place appeared over and over in such supposedly offhand comments. Moreover, I observed this survivor guilt being condensed with the guilt they felt over enjoying themselves in places from which the Greeks had been expelled. Their feeling of being now "owners" of the beach would take some time to be assimilated. The story that follows shows this condensed second kind of guilt.

In the summer of 1975 a moving poem written by a little Cypriot Greek girl now living in the southern part of the island appeared in the *Cyprus Mail*. The *Mail* was published in English and distributed to the Greek neighborhoods, from which it found its way into Turkish hands. She had lived near the northern beach before the war, and she grieved over the loss of her home there and was sad to be called a refugee. After reading this poem, a group of Turkish bathers took notice of the nearby houses, beautiful buildings built only a few years earlier by Greeks but now occupied by Turks. The Greek expulsion was part of a cycle; the land on which these houses stood had been Turkish until eleven years before the war, and the Turks had been run off by the Greeks. If we accept as free association of a sort the typical Turkish response to this poem, we must assume that the Turks felt guilt, guilt that they tried to modify by the intellectual rationalization, rooted in reality, that the expulsion of the Greeks was justified by their earlier expulsion of the Turks from the same territory.

A brief formulation can be offered. The itching phenomenon seems to have been rooted in the real circumstance that quicklime of the sort that had been strewn over the bodies does cause itching and burning. Even after the lime was gone, the itch continued to be a symbolic connection with the dead; it represented not only the guilty feelings of the survivors who had expelled enemies from their homes (now the quicklime burned *their own* skins) but a proof that the survivors were indeed alive, as skin sensations made clear. The fish bites and the clinging bits of green plastic helped to perpetuate the belief in the "itch."

The Third Year after the War

I returned to the northern part of Cyprus around the third anniversary of the war, flying from Istanbul on a plane marked "Cyprus Turkish Airlines." It was rented from a firm based in Europe, and its pilot and hostesses spoke British English. Near the old airport the British had used during World War II, now rebuilt by Cypriot

Turks, I saw a new modern air terminal soon to be officially opened, one vastly more impressive than any in Turkey. I was coming to a "new" country, the Turkish Federated State of Cyprus. Although not officially recognized by any country other than Turkey, it was well on its way to becoming a cohesive democratic state full of the excitement and pain of being newly fledged.

The political scene was competitive. An opposition party challenged the Denktaş government, and postal workers and some teachers were out on strike. In view of the rising cost of living there was much discussion of economic issues. Nevertheless, there was confidence in the future and an expectation that the new state would before long be generally recognized. It was expected that even before recognition came, the island's "new reality" would so impress other nations that trade would pick up and prosperity would come. The Turks were learning, though slowly, to care for the formerly Greek orange groves, and were beginning to export the fruit. There was even talk of an undersea pipeline to bring water from the Toros Mountains in southern Turkey to maximize production in the already fertile fields of northern Cyprus. Dreams, realities, and frustrations mingled.

Logic told me that there would be no Turkish Federated State of Cyprus without the continued presence of Turkish soldiers and that northern Cyprus had become in effect an extension of mainland Turkey. One saw no Cypriot currency—Turkish money was in use everywhere. Many tourists began coming to northern Cyprus from Turkey; Cypriot Turks who had been living elsewhere, mostly in England, flocked back for visits; and many Turkish scientific conventions were being scheduled in the old Greek hotels in Cyprus that now had Turkish names. I learned that American, German, and British tourists, of whom only a very few were to be seen in the North, were swarming into the southern ("legal") part of the island, access to the Turkish Federated State being available only by boat or plane out of Turkey.

Some Turks from the mainland have already settled on the island, and the foreign press spoke of friction between the native Cypriot Turks and such newcomers. The Greeks exploited such news items for propaganda. Obviously, the newcomers, especially those from

Anatolia, which is less westernized than Cyprus, brought a life-style that differed from the island's, and among themselves Cypriot Turks did indeed talk about their peasant dress and provincial notions. Relations with the Turkish soldiers made for some dis-comfort also, as their roistering on the beaches made these places less attractive for family outings. It would be a grave mistake, how-ever, to think of the Cypriot Turks as in any way denying their blood brotherhood with other Turks, wherever they might come from.

The people by now have repressed their affect concerning their war memories, which have become duly "memorialized." The physical evidences of war on the northern shore and such psycho-logical aftermaths as the itching phenomenon have given way to an imposing memorial which marks the site of conflict. Blasted Greek tanks which previously were scattered around northern Cyprus are now lined up near the war memorial, and people passing by on their way to the popular beaches sometimes stop to look at them, but the profound emotional response such sights evoked three years ago is no longer there.

Makarios died a few days after my arrival, on August 3, 1977. There were headlines about his death in the newspapers on the Turkish side, but they evoked neither joy nor sorrow there. The news was greeted with general indifference, and the few comments about it that I heard were disparaging. Only the politicians wondered what Makarios's disappearance from the scene might mean for the future. It rained on the day of his funeral. Rain being highly unusual in Cyprus during the month of August, an official of the Cypriot Turkish government, believing (correctly) that the Greeks would capitalize on the downpour by calling it the tears of heaven, announced that it was an old Turkish belief that rain attends the burial of a sinner to wash away his sins! The salute of guns given in the Greek section of Nicosia at the time of the funeral awakened fear in the Turkish section lest the Greeks were beginning to fight one another again and stray bullets might again be a threat. Cypriot Turks watched the funeral of Makarios on the Cypriot Greek tele-vision as if they wanted to make certain that the man whose name they associated with devilish deeds was indeed gone. Only by their close attention to the television did they betray the concern that underlay their surface indifference, which reappeared, undisturbed, when the event was over.

I returned to the village of the blanket-burning, accompanied by the same troubleshooter with whom I had gone there earlier. The service station at the outskirts of the village was now busy, and its walls bore a huge sign with the name of an American oil company instead of the scars of battle. The sign turned out to be one that the owner had found and used, along with another advertising sign that featured a bikini-clad girl, purely for decorative purposes, since the gasoline he sold came from mainland Turkey. When we drove to the coffeeshop that had formerly borne the sign saying "Refugees' Coffeeshop" we found the sign gone and a Turkish flag painted in its place on the newly painted white wall. Some of the dozen or so people gathered there recognized the troubleshooter. They all seemed to know that he had become the director of the prime minister's office complex, and talk turned to their getting their share of water, there being some current dispute over the distribution of water from a spring some miles away. Whereas three years earlier these people clung to their psychic investment in the places they had left and over which they still grieved, they now seemed heavily invested in the land on which they now lived. Their indifference to tilling the northern fields was gone, and now they had a keen interest in working them and in obtaining additional water to make them more fruitful. There were five men there who seemed to be in their thirties, and I sensed that one belonged to an opposition party. Our arrival did nothing to distract them from the game of cards in which they were engrossed, but when it was time for news on the radio they gathered excitedly around it to hear more particulars about the death of Elvis Presley, and after this they joined with the rest of us in the room.

The "linking objects" that connected the Cypriot Turks with the Cypriot Greeks were no longer obvious, although they surfaced now and then; on occasion someone in whose home I was visiting would bring me the picture of the Greek who had formerly occupied his house and speak about him, but the interest in these poignant mementos was no longer obsessive.

VII "Living Statues"

My First Encounter with a "Living Statue"

Many years ago when I was in charge of the psychiatric service for adult inpatients at the University of Virginia Hospital, I came to know a bright twenty-seven-year-old Jewish graduate student who had been admitted to the hospital after a suicide attempt. During my interviews with him I noticed an unusual symptom; he wept in silence although he was crying passionately, with tears coursing down his cheeks, an expression of great sadness on his face, and sobs convulsing him. No matter how exaggeratedly he threw himself into his spells of weeping, it was always with this eerie soundlessness. Moreover, his crying would come to an abrupt stop and he would resume his conversation with me as though no interruption had occurred. When I called his attention to the abrupt way in which he stopped his violent, if silent, display of emotion, he said that when he wept he had a sensation of having an iron hand tight around his neck, and that it was pressure from this hand that halted his crying.

He had been born in 1943 in Nazi-occupied Belgium to parents in hiding. Although his parents were legally married, his mother, by denying that she was Jewish, managed to emerge from hiding and bear her infant in a hospital, even though this move labeled the child as illegitimate. There were Jews employed in the hospital, and the mother asked that her child be circumcised. This request was probably a daring move for a Jewess to take in her determination to cling to her son's Jewish identity as well as her own, since it involved considerable danger under the circumstances. When she left the hospital she joined her husband in hiding, taking the baby with her. The infant's first seventeen months were spent in hiding. He slept in a chest of drawers.

Both parents had originally come from Poland, which they had left before the Nazi invasion. The father was once caught by the Nazis before going into hiding, but he had escaped by jumping from the train on which he was being taken along with other Jews to a concentration camp. When the war was over and the couple and their child were living in safety, they sought word of relatives left behind in Poland. They could learn nothing of their fate and concluded that they had been victims of the Nazi persecution.

Five years after their liberation, when the child was seven, the family went to New York, where the father, a tailor, hoped to prosper at his trade. He died when his son was thirteen, however, after having exhibited classical signs of the survivor syndrome (see Chapter IV) and suffering from psychosomatic illnesses. His death was caused by multiple sclerosis. When I saw the son as a patient years later, he told me that his mother remained in the apartment in which they had lived together as a family and that she was determined to stay there although the neighborhood had deteriorated and she had twice been mugged and beaten by marauding teenagers. It could be said that her tenacious adherence to the old neighborhood in the absence of any financial need to stay there indicated that psychologically she had never left the hiding place and continued to live in a physical and emotional prison.

Soon after her husband died this woman appeared on a television show with an account of her family's terrible ordeal designed to attract sympathy and financial aid, and she encouraged a similar beseeching attitude in her son although he resented seeing it in himself when he came to recognize it. The boy was sent each summer "to camp" in order that he might "breathe fresh air."[1] In this insistence the wish for freedom was condensed with survival guilt in reference to those relatives and friends who had not escaped the concentration *camps*. Shortly after the father died, the mother abruptly terminated the Jewish mourning rites she had instituted and took her son into the country "for fresh air." As one might expect, the boy was as unable to grieve over his father's death as anyone contaminated with survivor's guilt. He needed to defend himself

1. The preceding chapter notes how Cypriot Greeks trapped in an area occupied by Turks had a similar preoccupation with breathing.

against dependency and the possibility of abandonment. While he was in the country he caught a snake, which he put in a bottle of acid to watch its skin disintegrate. This was an attempt to "kill" his father—to terminate the process of mourning—but since he identified with his father he developed dermatological problems himself for which he required lengthy treatment. He kept his father's broken camera, equipped with a "time delayer," as a linking object (see Chapter VI). The "time delayer" helped to postpone the grieving process, and its resemblance to a syringe reminded him of the injections he had learned to give his dying parent. He had had fantasies of "killing" him with these injections. Only much later, when he married a "Zionist" woman, was he able to "breathe comfortably." He anticipated that she would protect him against the world and enable him to direct his aggression outwardly, and when he began to fear that he would lose her he attempted suicide.

This young man's description of his early years in hiding was of great interest. He would recall how "my mother salvaged strings of spinach from the garbage and made soup out of them" or "we needed to bathe but there was no water and no soap." As he went on with particulars of their plight, he likened their experiences to those of Anne Frank. His memories were so lively that I had to keep reminding myself that this man had been but an infant during the time of hiding and could not possibly remember the events he described to me. It was evident that the parents had conveyed their memories to him. The child had been made a living repository of a tragic history so that it would never be forgotten. His identity as a human being was secondary to his identity as a living memento of Nazi persecution.

We uncovered the meaning of his unusual silent sobbing and his abrupt way of stopping his weeping under the pressure of an "iron hand" around his neck. It appeared that when the family was in hiding the owner of the house made a practice of frightening the two Jewish families sheltered in it by telling them that the Gestapo had arrived. This was a dodge to obtain belongings from the Jews to sell, and only once did the Gestapo really come to the door. The dog barked a warning. The infant who was to become my patient was crying loudly and those in hiding felt that he would give them away with his wailing and should be strangled for the safety of the group. His father set about choking him,[2] but desisted when it was clear that the Gestapo had moved on, and let his child breathe again. It is difficult to imagine the complexity of the father's feelings as he found himself in this tragic situation. Family stories later stressed how the father had striven to rid himself of the guilt attached to this episode by repeatedly assuring his child that he would never have been surrendered alive to the merciless Nazis. The unfinished psychological business between father and son, and the latter's inability to cry, contributed to his inability to mourn the death of his father when it came. External events involving aggression had shattered the life pattern of this family. They could do little about these events except to create a special child as a memorial to their experiences and to the historical tragedy in which they had been caught up.

I supervised the psychoanalytic psychotherapy of this patient, which was conducted by one of my assistants over a period of three years. The patient's outlook on life improved, his domestic problems lessened, and he was able to graduate from the university. But his basic mission in life—to be a living repository of historical tragedy—remained and resisted all attempts in his treatment to alter it. Characteristics of what analysts call "negative therapeutic reactions" (Freud, 1923) appeared. In analysis the condition of some patients worsens after a period of effective therapeutic management; in other words, the patient gets worse just when he might be expected to improve. It was not surprising that this was true of the patient in question here in view of one of his symptoms—whenever he was in a theater he would be overtaken by hysterical blindness that made it impossible for him to see the exit signs. There was no exit for this man from his emotional hiding place, nor any escape from the illness that was his character.[3]

2. This pattern of strangling and choking a child to prevent him from crying out and betraying those in hiding to the Gestapo has been observed by Niederland (1961) also.

3. Olinick's (1964) review of negative therapeutic reactors shows that one factor is that defenses are directed against expected inner loss and helpless re-

My assistant presented this patient's case at a psychiatric meeting held at the University of Virginia and spoke of his frustration in attempting a cure. The audience was, not surprisingly, moved by the story of this patient, of which I have provided only a summary here. As the discussion of technical aspects of the psychoanalytic psychotherapy of this patient took place, several Jewish psychiatrists made an emotional plea that we not attempt to "cure" this man since any cure was likely to erase living testimony to history. I am indebted to Seymour Rabinowitz (1973) for the term of "a living statue" with which he referred to this patient. At the time I did not know that I would meet other "living statues" in Cyprus.

The first I encountered in Cyprus had similarly been made by his parents the repository of tragic historical events. Another is an older man singled out by others in authority to be, as victim, a living statue. I must emphasize that while in Cyprus I knew such people only on the Turkish side, and that in describing them it is necessary to recognize the incredible aggression exhibited by the Greeks toward the Turks. It is equally necessary, however, to recognize that all peoples around the world have aggression, and that had I had the opportunity of studying Greek living statues in Cyprus, I no doubt would have been struck by the aggression of the Turkish group also. One must acknowledge, too, that it is when the "collective reduction" of the superego occurs that human aggression finds its utmost potential of destructiveness. The collective aggression of the group is considerably more dangerous than the aggression of the individual (Mitscherlich, 1971).

By now actual monuments have been erected on the Turkish side of Cyprus to commemorate those who died in the war. The

gression to the primary identification with the depressed mother. My patient's mother may not have had the classical symptoms of clinical depression, but there is no doubt that she was rendered "helpless" in a dangerous external world. The following description of negative therapeutic reactions describes my patient very well. "Inevitably the mother's resentful helplessness and overcompensatory, possessive demands, and the infant's or child's impotent aggressiveness will reinforce each other, with the result that the child grows up to be a welter of contradictions: demanding, but so fearful of disappointment as to be spuriously independent and rejecting; apprehensive of intrusion, yet fearful of isolation; wanting love, but able only to command or buy its counterfeit, dependence on and from the partner" (Olinick, 1964, pp. 544-545).

emotional impact of what had taken place did not, however, really hit home for me until I saw flesh-and-blood memorials who symbolized the recent struggle. It will be clear in the two examples I report here that a convergence of special circumstances accounts for the fact that these two individuals became "living statues."

I saw many people who had been beaten during their escape to the North, and who repeated their trauma in nightmares a year later. I saw the relatives of a young man who had been obliged helplessly to watch him slowly die over a period of several days because he had been wounded in a contested strip of land from which it was impossible to rescue him. In Serdarlı I interviewed a family of man, wife, teenage daughter, and prepubertal son for two hours to learn their reactions to the war. They had been in a town surrounded by Greek Cypriots after the Turks invaded Kyrenia, and for weeks they faced what seemed like certain death until their liberation by Turkish tank forces during the second move of the Turkish army. As he recalled those days six months afterward, the family's young son lapsed into such an emotional state that he began shaking all over as though the terror were still present. Out of consideration for his anxiety I terminated my interview.

I treated a medical student in Ankara in 1974 who had been in Limassol confined in the stadium with other Turks (see Chapter V) for ninety-seven days before a prisoner exchange was effected. After being exchanged he returned to Ankara to continue his education, but he was unable to escape the feeling of extreme guilt occasioned by the fact that his relatives and friends were trapped in Limassol while he went free. He had repeating nightmares of being killed by a firing squad; his captors had indeed kept the group in the stadium terrorized by pretending to shoot them. He took pleasure in nothing, and on one occasion when he attended a movie and found himself beginning to enjoy it, he left the theater. His symptoms disappeared after six months, however, especially after his parents were freed. I believe that he benefited from his brief psychotherapy.

I observed the Turkish children playing "war" in Nicosia during the first postwar year.[4] They were absorbed in such play and had

4. Children were no longer playing "war" in the summer of 1977.

replicas of dugouts and gun emplacements in their backyards. They had special code messages and talked to one another with walkie-talkies. While playing they were in a different world. I knew that they had a need to repeat in play what had once been a dangerous reality in order to master the harsh experience. I knew also that their adaptation to life would be warped because of what they had undergone. There were countless examples of this. The psychic life of children and adults alike could not escape being scarred by the Cyprus conflict. Their conscious and unconscious memories would keep what had happened alive. However, it took a special twist of fate to make the living statue different from the many who suffered the war, and he had a sense of special destiny and behaved accordingly.

A Boy Named "War"

In the spring of 1975, six months after the Turkish military intervention, I was asked to see professionally a bright eleven-year-old boy whom I liked on sight. I had been asked to suggest treatment for his obsessive-compulsive behavior. His name was Savaş, which means "war." Since I cannot conceal his identity altogether if I am to tell his story, I am not at liberty to give details of his personal life nor the story of his family, but must limit myself to what is publicly known about him. I have permission from him and from his father to report his story.

His opening remark to me on our first meeting was that books are usually written only about famous people, like Atatürk, who are no longer alive, but that one had already been written about him. I felt that he was referring to himself as having been immortalized. He is the son of a famous Turkish poet and novelist whose work is widely read on the island, his home, as well as on mainland Turkey. The father used to serve in the Cypriot Turkish Parliament, representing the party that opposes Denktaş. On December 25, 1963, during the so-called Bloody Christmas (see Chapter I), his wife and mother were captured by the Cypriot Greeks, as were most of the other Turks living in their mixed village near Nicosia. The poet escaped capture himself because on the day of the seizure he had gone to the city. On the first night of his wife's captivity she gave birth to a son in the Nicosia General Hospital, which was then under Greek control. The newborn child was left in a crib with other Turkish infants who happened to be there at the time, and the room in which they were placed was used as a morgue for Turkish casualties. A British nurse, shocked at this situation, managed to separate the living infants from the dead Turks. The poet did not know for some time if his wife and his mother had survived their capture, but they were reunited on January 10, along with the newborn child, who was named "War" because of the circumstances of his birth.

Between January 13 and March 10 the poet wrote a series of poems addressed to his son. They were published under the title *Letters to My Son Savaş* (Yaşın, 1965). Along with the poet's previously published two volumes (Yaşın, 1958, 1964), these letters constitute a poetic history of the Cyprus struggle seen from the viewpoint of a Cypriot Turk. *Letters* begins with a description of the events taking place at the time when the infant "was opening his eyes on the world," and the verse conveys a sense that this child was an immortal—or at least a very special—being.

> With a bullet from a lowly person
> You could have died, Savaş,
> Before you were born:
> You would die in your mother's belly
> Without getting to know
> The miracle called life
> Thanks to which you were saved.
> You were born . . .
> You might not have been born. [p. 18]

Each of the poems, most of which start with a salutation like "Listen well, my son Savaş," clearly indicates that this is a child of destiny, a child who drew in the stink of death with his first breath, etc. The volume concludes with a poem about "Those who returned and those who did not." It is a father's account to his son of what happened on that March day when the Red Cross returned the captive Turks to the Turkish section. (The Makarios government then permitted the Turks captured during the Bloody Christmas to be released.) Those who had not been seized sought frantically among the returnees to learn whether their loved ones had been restored or were gone forever. It is a moving poem, written from the viewpoint of the poet waiting in the crowd for the arrival of the Red Cross vehicles, sharing the anguish of those whose lost ones failed to reappear. The poet is helpless and hopeless as he waits. The poem ends by his turning to the statue of Atatürk on the square where the crowd had gathered. In his poet's mind he sees "tears" in the eyes of this statue, and with his poet's ears he hears it say:

> If I were alive, my children,
> I would expunge your trouble. [p. 171]

It was clear that the parental perception of Savaş as the symbol of Bloody Christmas was later included in the boy's self-representation. The poet's anguish, hope, and despair, along with his wish to be saved, were deposited in his son's self-concept. The child felt himself to be the symbol of the Turkish struggle on the island and also identified himself with the statue of Atatürk. One of his presenting symptoms was an odd sensation in the skin of his face; it felt dry, and he thought that if he scratched it, parts of his countenance would chip off as though it were the face of a stone statue.

Although he had carried the burden of being a special symbol of the Cyprus struggle for as long as he could remember, the boy became symptomatic during the Turkish military operation when a stray bullet passed over his head as he sat in his room. This event reactivated in him the self-concept of being close to death and being saved by a "miracle." This narrow escape promoted his identification with Atatürk (or the statue of Atatürk that is the savior in his father's poem), since during the Gallipoli campaign this national hero had a similar narrow escape that is celebrated in Turkish tradition. A bit of shrapnel striking him in the chest shattered the watch in his breast pocket without injuring him.

After the war the family was given a Greek house in a town where a battle had been bitterly fought. When they took occupancy they discovered dead bodies still lying in the beautiful orange grove nearby, and the child learned the stink of death. This experience reactivated in his mind the lines his father had written about his

being an infant whose first breath of life bore the taint of the de-
caying dead around him. Once again his idea of being a symbol of
the struggle dominated his self-concept. As a symbol it was necessary for him to be perfect in order to meet the expectations of his
father and of those his father reached with his stirring poetry. This
need led him to be obsessively perfectionistic in a thousand little
ways, avoiding the cracks on sidewalks, insisting that when he
turned on a water faucet the stream be precisely centered, etc.[5]

In 1975 Savaş followed me to Ankara when I returned there from
Cyprus and received help from a child psychiatrist. He wrote to
me after my return to the United States, and in his letters I could
see the identification with his father's tongue expressing itself.
Savaş is becoming quite a poet himself. During my visit to Cyprus
in the summer of 1977 he excitedly sought me out and shared with
me some of his short stories. I was delighted to find him without
symptoms, although it is clear he still regards himself as destiny's
child.

To Kill Oneself or to Become a Living Statue

I first met my other living statue at a propaganda exhibit in Kyrenia
at which the progress of the Turkish intervention appeared in a
photographic display. My eye was caught by a face in one of the
pictures that expressed something beyond human pain. The picture
showed the man with the anguished face seated by a mass grave
from which bodies were being exhumed. I learned that two days
after Turkish troops landed near Kyrenia some EOKA B fanatics
attacked two Turkish villages near Famagusta, killing almost all of

---

5. As a psychoanalyst I am, of course, aware that Savaş's psychoneurosis centered around the mental conflict between his drives and the ego-superego forces
that strove to control these drives and limit their expression. As might have been
expected, he had memory traces and fantasies relating to oedipal danger and
regression to the anal phase of expression against which he defended, etc., but
the inclusion in his self-concept of a conviction that he was a unique memorial
to the Cyprus struggle was unmistakably cogent in his clinical situation and demanded that he be perfect. The awed attention of his parents caused his ego to
mature more rapidly than his drives; this inequality paves the way for obsessional
neurosis (A. Freud, 1966).

the inhabitants and burying them in two mass graves. The second phase of the Turkish onslaught brought the region back into Turkish hands, and a few survivors who had hidden successfully during the EOKA B attack were able to show the Turkish authorities where the victims were buried. The man whose face was so striking had been taken to the site to learn if his relatives were among those buried there, and the unforgettable photograph showed him just as he recognized their mutilated bodies. The Turkish government used the pictures of this horrible scene in propaganda publications to show the savagery of the Greeks. (I have seen publications put out by the Cypriot Greeks in which the bodies of Greeks killed by Turkish bombing of a hotel were pictured and shown as evidence of the savagery of the Turks. Each side tried to outdo the other in its propaganda effort.) I saw the tragic face of the man I learned was Mr. T. over and over, so it lost some of its fascination for me and I became rather numb toward it, but I was surprised to be faced with Mr. T. in person in the doorway of the house in which I was staying, on a day during the first anniversary of the war. I recognized him at once. He was apparently in his early sixties, with thick curly gray hair, expressionless eyes, and a monotonous voice. He carried under his arm the framed enlargement of a child's photograph. It turned out that my host had taught the child, who was Mr. T.'s youngest and a victim of the EOKA B massacre. The photograph was to be given to my host to hang in the school the boy had attended. I learned that the stricken father gave similar photographs to all who had known the boy well.

I saw him often after that, steering his bicycle with one arm, riding like a zombie, his other arm folded over one of the pictures he was delivering. Everyone seemed to know him and to be tolerant toward him, with a kind of courtesy that seemed to contain the wish to share his anguish but the fear of doing so, and a sense of obligation no doubt based on guilt or a sense of duty; he seemed to belong to everyone.

He readily agreed to have a series of interviews with me. He spoke of having seen a psychiatrist who gave him sleeping pills; and I sensed that although he really expected little help from me, he was ready to talk because he felt that the story belonged to the world and I was entitled to hear it. He had taken his thirty-six-year-old wife and their two sons, one ten and the other six, on a holiday from Nicosia on July 15, going to the village of Maratha, near Famagusta, where his wife's parents lived. Five days later the Turkish troops landed on Cyprus, and the day after their landing the EOKA B men seized the village and took the villagers away in buses to a nearby Greek community. The women and children were later returned to Maratha and the men taken elsewhere, where they were ordered to dig their own graves although they were not butchered outright but were beaten with barbed wire and forced to sleep naked on the ground. There were seven men in Mr. T.'s group. After three days of torture they were turned over to United Nations soldiers, who returned them to their villages, but the EOKA B came back and began taking the male villagers away one by one. Everyone knew that they were being led away to their death, and Mr. T. knew that his turn would come. When the United Nations Peace Force visited the village, Mr. T. was said to be very ill; he told me during our interview that he had pretended to be gravely ill, too ill to open his eyes, but I gathered that, in view of the beatings with barbed wire he had undergone and the burning of his body with lighted cigarettes, he had truly been in bad shape. I believe that his guilt over being saved from the common fate made him recall his illness as pretense, but it is possible that he was histrionic about his condition out of fear for his life. In any case, although the United Nations personnel were without authority to intervene to the point of removing the villagers to a safe place, they were authorized to take the sick to a hospital. Thus Mr. T. and a ninety-year-old man who had had a stroke were removed from the village and taken to a Red Cross center from which they were sent to a hospital and safety in an area under Turkish control. When the village was recovered by the Turks, Mr. T. heard about the mass graves, which ultimately yielded eighty-eight bodies. While he watched the exhumation, as the photograph showed, he was able to recognize seven bodies that belonged to his family—those of his wife, his two sons, his seventy-two-year-old father-in-law, fifty-five-year-old mother-in-law, and twenty-two-year-old sister-in-law, and her ten-year-old son.

As Mr. T. described the exhumation for me, his hitherto expressionless face altered. He rose and moved about. I felt that he was alone at the site of the exhumation and that I was to all intents and purposes no longer with him. Uttering inhuman grunts and cries, he spoke of the bullet hole in the head of his ten-year-old child and of the decapitation of his younger son. "I know you," he cried out. "I'd know you anywhere—I recognize your shoes!" His wife's legs had been cut off below the knees. "Why not cut straight? Why was the cutting zigzag?" His wife's body should have stayed in one piece, he felt, but not only were her legs gone but when it was moved with a shovel the mutilated body fell apart at the waist. As he reached this point in his narration, Mr. T. whispered to me, "That is all; that is all," and he again became a zombie. I could not utter a single word. I was moved beyond speech. Quietly Mr. T. left me.

In our next interview, on the following day, I learned that Mr. T.'s murdered wife had been his second wife. Mr. T. was the son of a poor man who eked out a living by raising and selling chickens at home; he was brutal and had kicked his son when the boy was thirteen. The boy became an apprentice to a carpenter, a relative of whom he married while he was still very young. The couple had six children before her death in 1963. At the time of our interviews the youngest of these was fifteen, the eldest thirty-five. It was the two sons of a second marriage who perished in the massacre.

Further particulars about this man would be irrelevant. The merciless blow dealt him by fate overrode the resources of any kind of personality organization; but I made the formulation that he had a harsh superego that demanded adaptation by obsessional means. When he contemplated suicide after the tragedy, he consulted a religious advisor who acted as an external superego, forbidding him to commit suicide in spite of his wish to die.

I wanted to know how anyone could adapt to tragedy like his. I was able in ensuing interviews to gather data about him, but I must admit that his story had such a powerful effect on me that it was difficult to maintain a professional attitude toward him. I expected him to have linking objects (see Chapter VI). His main focus was on the lost younger son; and over the eleven months since he had found the boy's body, he had collected everything that had belonged to the child and placed it in a makeshift museum. One of the daughters of his first marriage was the mother of two sons, aged 4½ and 1½ respectively, and their bereaved grandfather caused them to have a legal change of name to become the namesakes of the boys he had lost. Thus the two youngsters became for him living linking objects.

One of Mr. T.'s most noticeable symptoms was his poor memory. Although the victims of a tragic event often block out its memory while retaining trivia unconnected with it, Mr. T. forgot routine affairs of everyday life while remembering every painful detail of his tragedy. He had to carry a paper and pencil in his pocket with which to list daily tasks and obligations.[6]

It happened that the bodies from the massacre were finally buried in rows, in the first of which all of Mr. T.'s family members except the beloved youngest son were buried side by side. The child had been buried at the end of the row, with other bodies separating his from those of his family. Mr. T. felt that the child was thus "alone," and wanted to have the body exhumed again, to lie next to the other family members. I learned that he had gone to the authorities with the request that the body be moved, but that when they seemed to be about to grant his request he would shy away from carrying the matter to a conclusion and actually moving the body. I realized that to have his son no longer "alone" was now the greatest mission of his life—and that if this mission were completed he would no longer have anything to live for. Thus it was not surprising that

6. Rangell's (1976) notion that psychic space is limited and that in severe traumatic neurosis thoughts and memories related to the trauma preempt most of it is certainly applicable here. Schlesinger (1970), who reviewed the Freudian concept of forgetting, states his views of the matter in a paradox. First of all, "repression is as much a form of memory as it is a form of forgetting" (p. 358). Second, forgetting, apart from repression, may be the normal result of the organizing process of memeory, and thus an aspect of adaptation rather than the enemy of memory. In the case of Mr. T., memory concerned with everyday activity was simply not central to the schema currently dominant. He was engrossed in his tragedy, and issues related to it filled his nighttime dreams as well as his thoughts by day.

although he concentrated fiercely on this goal, he never consummated his wish

Mr. T. identified with his little boy, who supposedly had greatly resembled him. He spoke spontaneously of taking the child on the handlebars of his bicycle to ride past the statue of Atatürk in Nicosia. He told how the child had imitated the attitude of the statue by folding his arms across his chest. Like Savaş, he spoke spontaneously of this famous statue. It was clear to me that this man had two choices; he could kill himself, or he could live with his memories of the dead, treating those he had lost as though they were still alive—for example, regarding the dead and buried son as being too much "alone"—and assume a new identity, that of being a memorial for the tragic events in Cyprus; the authorities seemed to accept him in this role readily enough.

Three years after my series of interviews with Mr. T., I arranged another meeting with him, in the summer of 1977. He seemed grateful for a moment that I remembered him and sought him out; I thought I caught a fleeting expression of pleasure on his face. But that was all. My last interview showed me that no essential change had occurred within him—or for him. I heard that he had been given a new home by the Cypriot Turkish government, but that he would complain to Denktaş (1977), saying "How can you give me a house with but one bathroom? Don't you know that I have children—they need bathrooms, too!" Then he would recover himself in a return to reality, only to repeat his demands for arrangements pleasing to the family members he was keeping "alive."

My last glimpse of this man came as he rode away from me on his bicycle. He left me feeling that I must offer him an apology for what had been meted out to him by the human race to which I belong. But I felt that he was beyond hearing any apology; he was already a national monument rather than a man.

VIII Pilgrimage

Returning to the Dream of Seven Layers of Oriental Rugs

As I reached the halfway point in writing this book, I began to wonder why the first thing that came to mind when I began it was the dream I had had during my analysis—why had I chosen to open my first chapter with the report of a dream of a small and frightened representation of myself caught within *seven*[1] layers of Oriental rugs? The dream apparently came about because in analysis I had regressed to the point where the fragmentation and splitting of my self- and object representations was revealed; as I went forward from there, armed with a new grasp of my old self-concept and concepts of others, I could integrate more firmly than before my sense of identity and my internalized object world. During the months after I wrote about this dream and watched my book take shape, the dream kept coming to mind, along with a feeling of curiosity about it and an urgency that it be understood in terms of my present state of psychological being. I then began to understand the hold it had on me; it had come at a turning point in my personal analysis, when disorganization of the regressed psychic structure was being followed by a new organization. By association I recalled a remark made about Erich Lindemann some years ago by a friend who declared that the psychiatrist so well known for his 1944 paper on grief had been a "classical analyst" until he studied the victims of the Cocoanut Grove fire. His professional involvement with this tragedy had changed him and given his life a new direction. Since I never met Lindemann, I have no way of knowing whether my friend's statement was true, but the sense of his assessment came to mind when I was in Cyprus six months after the war, interviewing

1. In my associations to the dream the reader will note the condensed reference to the number seven.

those who had escaped from the South after facing extreme hardship and torture. I was aware that I would not be the same after going through the Cyprus experience.

The island Turks put on a celebration of the Turkish military intervention on its first anniversary, with all the usual speeches and parades. As I watched one parade in Nicosia hand-in-hand with my little American-born son who, in a sense, represents my life in the United States, I began to cry as I saw old men marching. I regretted bitterly that my father, who had died a few years earlier, was not alive to taste the new freedom, and I felt him near me. I felt myself to be a link between him and the grandson he had never seen. The birth of a free Turkish sector in northern Cyprus was accompanied by the birth of a new ego in me; I seemed to feel the establishment of a firmer generational continuity within myself. I understand now that the reappearance of the rug dream in my awareness indicates that my activities on the island were in the service of integrative functions of my ego, and that the writing of this book organized for me by means of the secondary process a new identity with a firm tie to my heritage. This development enriches, I believe, my total identity in the country of my adoption.

Garza-Guerrero (1974) likens the formation of a new identity after moving to a new country to the process of mourning. Initially there is "culture shock," which G. Ticho (1971) described as a result of a sudden change from an "average expectable environment," in Hartmann's (1939) term, to a strange and unpredictable one. I agree with Garza-Guerrero that in this phase the newcomer reactivates in fantasy those "good" self- and object units, along with their gratifying affective links, that were in the past a source of all that is now lacking and missed. The immigrant has a growing feeling of discontinuity; but if things are not too complicated, he goes through a mourning process that is necessary for human adaptation (Pollock, 1961). Garza-Guerrero states that once the immigrant works through the mourning for what he has abandoned, he can form a new identity that is neither total surrender to the new culture nor the sum of bicultural endowment. The new identity will reflect in a remodeled ego identity those selective identifications with the new culture that were harmoniously integrated or that proved congruent with the cultural heritage of the past.

Although the United States recently celebrated its Bicentennial Year, it may still be considered a land of immigrants. However strong the sense of American nationality may be among the population, many still have ties with an "old country" and recognize a unique ethnic heritage of their own. If the processes Garza-Guerrero described are not undergone smoothly and if there are complications, difficulties in psychological adaptation, of which the denial of the heritage left behind is but one, may appear. Alongside such denial may exist a split-off unconscious longing for total immersion in the old country. When the children of immigrants identify themselves with parents who have such split-off longing, they are likely to receive from them unconscious conflicts about generational continuity; the immigrant's difficulty in psychological adaptation and identity formation in a new country may be passed on to his children.

Garza-Guerrero speaks of the "complicated culture shock" the immigrant experiences when he is a refugee from sociopolitical upheaval in his homeland. The mourning process required for a smooth adaptation to the new culture cannot progress smoothly when certain circumstances attended one's departure from his native land; an emigrant may have been too frightened, too angry, or too guilty at the time he fled to foreign shores to be psychologically prepared either for the separation or for assimilation in the new culture.

I came to the United States *seven* months after my graduation, in the early part of 1957 when the EOKA tension was felt throughout Cyprus. Soon after I began my internship in a Chicago hospital, I received a newspaper clipping from my father about the brutal death of Erol, my roommate during my days in medical school in Ankara; he had been murdered by EOKA terrorists. He had been the nearest thing to a brother I ever had. He came from Cyprus as I did, and was younger than I and thus in a lower class in medical school. We had shared a small apartment in Ankara for almost two years. It seemed that soon after I left for the United States, Erol left

Turkey to visit his ailing mother in a mixed village on Cyprus, and while buying medicine for her from a Greek in the local pharmacy he had been gunned down so savagely that *seven* bullet holes were found in his body. The newspaper clipping told how his murder had shocked the Turkish community on the island, and how crowds had attended his funeral. The seven bullets that riddled the body of my slain friend were another important association to the number seven in my dream. Until I began to write this book I had not fully realized the strength of my "survivor's guilt," and how I had failed to complete my mourning over Erol's death. I see now that my initial efforts to adapt to a new culture had been accompanied by complicated mourning and the guilt I felt at outliving the young companion to whom I had been so devoted. Although in my personal analysis I had revisited my childhood, as it were, in the customary analytic regression, some unfinished business of my psyche related to my identity continuity remained as I embarked on my transformation into an American.

A "Second Look" and a Pilgrimage

Under the general title of *The Second Look*, S. Novey (1968) specu- lated as to why some patients in psychoanalysis or psychoanalytic psychotherapy have an urge to explore old diaries and papers and to return to the physical settings and persons important to them in an earlier phase of their lives. Novey is aware that such behavior may in some instances constitute "acting out," but "in many more they constitute behaviors in the interest of furthering the collection of affectively charged data and thus helping the treatment process" (p. 87). Poland (1977) has written about travels taken to places im- portant in the individual's history, not made in the course of an analysis, but made against inner resistance with the goal of master- ing internal conflicts, including generational conflicts acquired by identification. In a sense I see the visit I made to Cyprus in 1968, soon after finishing my personal analysis, like the one described by Novey; and my 1974–75 trip to Turkey and Cyprus seems like the ones Poland describes, however difficult it might be to differentiate these journeys one from another in respect to the concept of their purpose.

Poland refers to the kind of journey he describes as a pilgrimage. A pilgrimage is a difficult journey that demands sacrifice, and it usually involves considerable distance. It often has a religious meaning and represents an act of devotion and a search for the forgiveness of sins. Poland suggests that such journeys are connected with a person's change to a new level of integrity.[2] He is aware that such trips are often made defensively as a magical gesture to conceal anxiety and to obviate the need for difficult emotional work—as flights from the confrontation of interpsychic conflict—but when the traveler has the capacity for introspection and a strong observing eye, his journey can be utilized in the service of the ego's integrative functions. Thus such actions can prove adaptive in the promotion of psychic change just as they may promote change in an analysis (Wheelis, 1950).

The plans for the sabbatical leave that took me to my homeland were made rather impulsively, and they demanded sacrifice. They were made, of course, without any advance knowledge of the great upheaval that would take place in the summer of 1974. My purpose in going was ostensibly to spend a year as a visiting professor in Ankara, to visit Cyprus while in the region, and to work on a psychohistorical study of Atatürk (Volkan, 1978a), the founder of modern Turkey; but my intellectual interest in the project implied an emotional need to understand the Turkish experience and the nature of my own Turkishness which had been established according to the guidelines of Atatürk. My later self-analysis made it clear that I was also trying to mend the image of my dead father, who had been a schoolteacher under British rule in Cyprus. During my childhood he had been under some constraint to depreciate his Turkishness, although it was not something he had to deny; in spite of this, my image of him was that of a fiercely Turkish man. The British frowned on the designation of Turkish schools as Turkish, and called

---

2. The journey's outcome is a shift in the sense of one's self, at times in relation to unassimilated introjects and at times in the strengthened relation of the ego to the superego.

them Moslem; his affiliation with such schools caused my father
conflict inasmuch as he was an adherent of Atatürk's antireligious
views, which prevailed among most intellectuals in mainland
Turkey at the time.

According to family myth, my father had "bravely" identified
himself with Atatürk before my birth, on the occasion of the leader's
dramatic rejection of the fez. Atatürk went calculatedly to the most
conservative of Anatolian communities wearing a European sort of
hat instead of the customary Turkish headgear. As he stepped down
from the train, he moved among the people gathered at the station
and pointed at his hat, announcing: "The name of this is *hat*." This
act caused the Turkish men to remove their traditional headgear
and rush off to obtain hats (homemade) for themselves. The story
goes that my father, wearing a hat in imitation of Atatürk, walked
into a coffeehouse in a traditional Cypriot Turkish village and
stepped up on a chair to demonstrate his conversion and to convert
the villagers, whereupon he was threatened by some of them who
were armed.

Atatürk was part of my idealized self, as he had been part of my
parent's idealized self. It was necessary that I bring him down to
human size if I were to understand him, and to resolve the conflicts of my father and to appreciate the courage he had displayed in
the Cyprus that was British at the time. This required alteration of
my own self-concept, and such an undertaking was in itself enough
to make my journey to Turkey a pilgrimage as Poland understood
such journeying. Moreover, at the outset of our travels I found myself and my family crossing Europe toward Turkey in August 1974
without news of how the war in Cyprus was faring and without any
assurance that my relatives and friends were still alive. I sensed a
recathexis toward my Turkishness as I passed from south of Vienna,
a city attacked by the "terrible Turks" centuries ago, and moved
through Austria, Yugoslavia, and Bulgaria into European Turkey,
searching for the remnants of the Ottoman Empire. Once I arrived
in Turkey, the project of writing this book took place alongside
the project of my Atatürk study. I visited those places in Turkey
where Atatürk had fought and created, but I also visited the sites
of the recent battles in Cyprus. At the same time I developed a

keen interest in archeological settings, historical buildings, and the whole panoply of the past. The seven layers of smothering rugs were now in some sort of order, as it were, and my fearful representation in the dream had been sigificantly altered by my new psychological awareness of my identity in the perspective of history itself.

References
Name Index
Subject Index

References

Abraham, K. 1913. *Dreams and Myths*. Nervous and Mental Diseases Monograph 15. New York: Jeliffe & White.

Abse, D. W. 1971. *Speech and Reason*. Charlottesville: University Press of Virginia.

Adams, T. W. 1966. The first Republic of Cyprus: A review of an unworkable constitution. *Western Political* 2. 19:475–490.

———. 1971. *AKEL: The Communist Party of Cyprus*. Stanford, Calif.: Hoover Institution Press.

Alastos, D. 1960. *Cyprus Guerilla: Grivas, Makarios, and the British*. London: Heinemann.

Angelou, M. 1970. *I Know Why the Caged Bird Sings*. New York: Random House.

Arlow, J. A. 1961. Ego psychology and the study of mythology. *J. Am. Psychoanal. Assoc.* 9:371–393.

———. 1973. Motivations for peace. In *Psychological Bases of War*, ed. H. Z. Winnik, R. Moses, and M. Ostow, pp. 193–204. Jerusalem: Jerusalem Academic Press.

Armstrong, C. P., and Gregor, A. J. 1964. Integrated schools and Negro character. *Psychiatry* 27:69–72.

Atkin, S. 1971. Notes on motivations for war, toward a psychoanalytic social psychology. *Psychoanal. Q.* 40:549–583.

Banfield, E. C. 1958. *The Moral Basis of a Backward Society*. Glencoe, Ill.: Free Press.

Barker, D. 1959. *Grivas: Portrait of a Terrorist*. London: Gresset.

Barrie, J. M. 1928. *Peter Pan, or The Boy Who Would Not Grow Up*. New York: Charles Scribner.

Bateson, M. D. 1972. *Our Own Metaphor: A Personal Account of a Conference on the Effects of Conscious Purpose on Human Adaptation*. New York: Alfred A. Knopf.

Baybars, T. 1970. *Plucked in a Far-Off Land: Images in Self Biography*. London: Victor Golancz.

Bedevi, V. 1965. *Kıbrıs Tarihi* [*The History of Cyprus*]. Nicosia: Kıbrıs Türk Tarih Kurumu Yayınlarından.

Benedict, R. 1959. Child rearing in certain European countries. In *An Anthropologist at Work*, ed. M. Mead, pp. 449–458. Boston: Houghton Mifflin.

Berger, M. 1951. Understanding national character and war. *Commentary* 11:375–386.

Bergmann, M. D. 1966. The impact of ego psychology on the study of the myth. *Am. Imago* 23:257–264.

Berkowitz, D. A., Shapiro, R. L., Zinner, J., and Shapiro, E. R. 1974. Concurrent family treatment of narcissistic disorders in adolescence. *Int. J. Psychoanal. Psychother.* 3:379–396.

Bettelheim, B. 1960. *The Informed Heart*. Glencoe, Ill.: Free Press of Glencoe.

Blos, P. 1967. The second individuation process of adolescence. *Psychoanal. Study Child* 22:162–186.

———. 1968. Character formation in adolescence. *Psychoanal. Study Child* 23:245–263.

Bogardus, E. 1928. *Immigration and Race Attitudes*. Boston: Heath.

Bonaparte, M. 1947. *Myths of War*. London: Imago.

Bowlby, J. 1961. Process of mourning. *Int. J. Psycho-Anal.* 42:317–340.

Bowlby, J., and Parkes, C. M. 1970. Separation and loss within the family. In *The Child in His Family*, vol. 1, ed. E. S. Anthony and C. Koupirnik, pp. 197–216. New York: Wiley Interscience.

Brody, E. B. 1961. Social conflict and schizophrenic behavior in young adult Negro males. *Psychiatry.* 24:337–346.

———. 1963. Color and identity conflict in young boys. *Psychiatry.* 26:188–201.

Cahen, C. 1968. *Pre-Ottoman Turkey*, tr. from the French by J. Jones-Williams. New York: Taplinger.

Cambor, C. G. 1969. Preoedipal factors in superego development: The influence of multiple mothers. *Psychoanal. Q.* 38:81–96.

Cansever, G. 1965. Psychological effects of circumcision. *Brit. J. Med. Psychol.* 38: 321–331.

Cantril, H. 1965. *The Pattern of Human Concerns*. New Brunswick, N.J.: Rutgers University Press.

Chodoff, P. 1963. Late effects of the concentration camp syndrome. *Arch. Gen. Psychiatry* 8:323–333.

———. 1970. The German concentration camp as a psychological stress. *Arch. Gen. Psychiatry* 22:78–87.

Clark, K. 1969. *Civilisation.* New York: Harper & Row.

Coles, R. 1967. *Children of Crisis.* New York: Harcourt, Brace.

Couloumbis, T. A., and Georgiades, E. P. 1973. Cyprus: A treasure house for social scientists. *Midwest Q.* 14: 121–132.

Davidson, W. D. 1968. Proposal to the American Psychiatric Association for the establishment of a Task Force on Psychiatry and Foreign Affairs, Sept. 28.

Demirel, S. 1975. Personal communication.

Denktaş, R. R. 1974. *The Cyprus Problem.* Nicosia: Turkish Cypriot Administration.

———. 1975. Personal communication.

———. 1977. Personal communication.

De Wind, E. 1968. The confrontation with death. *Int. J. Psycho-Anal.* 49:302–305.

Eissler, K. R. 1965. *Medical Orthodoxy and the Future of Psychoanalysis.* New York: International Universities Press.

Eitinger, L. 1961. Pathology of the concentration camp syndrome. *Arch. Gen. Psychiatry* 5:371–379.

———. 1964. *Concentration Camp Survivors in Norway and Israel.* London: Allen & Unwin.

Erdentuğ, N. 1959. *A Study of the Social Structure of a Turkish Village.* Ankara: Ayyıldız Matbaası.

Erikson, E. H. 1963. *Childhood and Society.* New York: W. W. Norton.

Erikson, K. T. 1976. Loss of communality at Buffalo Creek. *Am. J. Psychiatry* 133:302–325.

Evdokas, T., Mylona, L., Paschalis, C., Olympios, C., Chimona, S., Kavala, E., Theodorou, N., and Demetriadu, E. 1976. *Refugees of Cyprus.* Nicosia: Theopress.

Eyüboğlu, I. Z. 1974. *Bütün Yönleri ile Anadolu inançları* [*All Aspects of Anatolian Beliefs*]. Istanbul: Koza Yayınlari.

Falk, A. 1974. Border symbolism. *Psychoanal. Q.* 43:650–660.

Favazza, A. R. 1974. A critical review of studies of national character: A psychiatric-anthropological interface. *Operational Psychiatry* 6:3–30.

Fehmi, H. 1975. Personal communication.

Fenichel, O. 1935. Über Psychoanalyse, Krieg und Frieden. *Int. arztl. Bull.* 2:30–40.

———. 1945. *The Psychoanalytic Theory of Neurosis.* New York: W. W. Norton.

Ferenczi, S. 1921. The symbolism of the bridge. In *Further Contributions to the Theory and Technique of Psychoanalysis,* pp. 352–355. London: Hogarth Press.

———. 1922. Bridge symbolism and the Don Juan legend. In *Further Contributions to the Theory and Technique of Psychoanalysis*, pp. 356–358. London: Hogarth Press.

Fink, F. H. 1968. Developmental arrest as a result of Nazi persecution during adolescence. *Int. J. Psycho-Anal.* 49:327–329.

Fornari, F. 1966. *The Psychoanalysis of War*, tr. from the Italian by A. Pfeifer. Bloomington, Ind.: Indiana University Press, 1975.

Foster, G. M. 1965. Peasant society and the image of limited good. *Am. Anthropologist* 67:293–315.

Frank, J. D. 1967. *Sanity and Survival: Psychological Aspects of War and Peace*. New York: Vintage Books.

———. 1969. Psychologic aspects of international negotiations. *Am. J. Psychother.* 23:572–583.

Freud, A. 1966. Obsessional neurosis: A summary of psychoanalytic views. In *The Writings of Anna Freud*, pp. 242–261. New York: International Universities Press, 1969.

Freud, S. 1895. Draft H. Paranoia. In *The Standard Edition of the Complete Psychological Works of Sigmund Freud*, 1: 206–212. London: Hogarth Press, 1953.

———. 1915. Thoughts for the times on war and death. In *The Standard Edition of the Complete Works of Sigmund Freud*, 14:273–301. London: Hogarth Press, 1957.

———. 1917. Mourning and melancholia. In *The Standard Edition of the Complete Psychological Works of Sigmund Freud*, 14:243–258. London: Hogarth Press, 1957.

———. 1921. Group psychology and the analysis of the ego. In *The Standard Edition of the Complete Works of Sigmund Freud*, 18:65–143. London: Hogarth Press, 1955.

———. 1923. The ego and the id. In *The Standard Edition of the Complete Psychological Works of Sigmund Freud*, 19:49–66. London: Hogarth Press, 1961.

———. 1927. The future of an illusion. In *The Standard Edition of the Complete Works of Sigmund Freud*, 21:5–56. London: Hogarth Press, 1961.

———. 1930. Civilization and its discontents. In *The Standard Edition of the Complete Psychological Works of Sigmund Freud*, 21:59–145. London: Hogarth Press, 1961.

———. 1932a. Why war? In *The Standard Edition of the Complete Psychological Works of Sigmund Freud*, 22:197–215. London: Hogarth Press, 1961.

_____. 1932b. The acquisition and control of fire. In *The Standard Edition of the Complete Works of Sigmund Freud*, 22:187–193. London: Hogarth Press, 1961.

Friedman, P. 1949. Some aspects of concentration camp psychology. *Am. J. Psychiat.* 105:601–605.

Gaddis, T. E. 1955. *The Birdman of Alcatraz.* New York: Random House.

Garza-Guerrero, A. C. 1974. Culture shock: Its mourning and vicissitudes of identity. *J. Am. Psychoanal. Assoc.* 22:408–429.

Geertz, C. 1973. *The Interpretation of Cultures.* New York: Basic Books.

Gerst, M. S., and Tenzel, J. S. 1972. The psychological attitudes of Greek and Turkish Cypriots toward one another. Paper read at the 125th Annual Meeting of the American Psychiatric Association, Dallas, Texas, May 1.

Gibb, H. A. R. 1949. *Mohammedanism—An Historical Survey.* London: Oxford University Press.

Giovacchini, P. L. 1967. Frustration and externalization. *Psychoanal. Q.* 36:571–583.

Gitelson, M. 1948. Character synthesis: The psychotherapeutic problem of adolescence. *Am. J. Orthopsychiatry* 18:422–431.

Glover, E. 1933. *War, Sadism, and Pacifism.* London: Allen & Unwin.

Goodman, M. E. 1952. *Race Awareness in Young Children.* Cambridge: Addison Wesley Press.

Gough, H., and Heildrun, A. 1965. *The Adjective Checklist Manual.* Palo Alto, Calif.: Consulting Psychologist Press.

Grivas, G. 1961. *The Memoirs of General Grivas,* tr. C. Foley. New York: Praeger.

_____. 1964 *Guerilla Warfare and EOKA's Struggle: A Political-Military Study,* tr. A. A. Pallis. London: Longmans, Green.

Group for the Advancement of Psychiatry. 1958. *Psychiatric Aspects of the Prevention of Nuclear War.* GAP Report No. 57. New York: Group for the Advancement of Psychiatry.

Guntrip, H. 1968. *Schizoid Phenomena, Object Relations, and the Self.* New York: International Universities Press.

Halberstam, D. 1972. *The Best and the Brightest.* New York: Random House.

Hamilton, J. W. 1966. Some dynamics of anti-Negro prejudice. *Psychoanal. Rev.* 53: 5–15.

Hartmann, H. 1939. *Ego Psychology and the Problem of Adaptation.* New York: International Universities Press.

Hartmann, H., Kris, E., and Loewenstein, R. M. 1949. Notes on the theory of aggression. *Psychoanal. Study Child* 3/4: 9–36.

Hasluck, F. W. 1929. *Christianity and Islam under the Sultans*, vols. 1 and 2. Oxford: Clarendon Press.

Hill, G. 1940–42. *The History of Cyprus*, 4 vols. Cambridge, Eng.: Cambridge University Press, 1952.

Hocking, F. 1970. Psychiatric aspects of extreme environmental stress. *Dis. Nerv. Syst.* 31:542–545.

Hoppe, K. D. 1966. The psychodynamics of concentration camp victims. *Psychoanal. Forum* 1:75–80.

———. 1968. Re-somatization of affects in survivors of persecution. *Int. J. Psycho-Anal.* 49:324–326.

İnalcık, H. 1964. Kıbrıs Fethinin tarihi manası [The historical meaning of conquering Cyprus]. In *Kıbrıs ve Türkler* [Cyprus and Turks], pp. 21–26. Ankara: Türk kültürünü Araştırma Enstitüsü.

Itzkowitz, N. 1972. *Ottoman Empire and Islamic Tradition*. New York: Alfred A. Knopf.

Jacobson, E. 1964. *The Self and the Object World*. New York: International Universities Press.

Jaffe, D. S. 1968. The mechanism of projection: Its dual role in object relations. *Int. J. Psycho-Anal.* 49:662–677.

Jaffe, R. 1968. Dissociative phenomena in former concentration camp inmates. *Int. J. Psycho-Anal.* 49:310–312.

Jones, E. 1915. War and individual psychology. In *Essays in Applied Psychoanalysis*, 1:55–76. New York: International Unversities Press.

———. 1949. *Papers on Psycho-Analysis*, p. 87. London: Hogarth Press.

———. 1961. *The Life and Work of Sigmund Freud*, vol. 2. New York: Basic Books.

Keefe, E. K., Cover, W. W., Giloane, W., Moore, J. M., Teleki, S., and White, E. T. 1971. *Area Handbook for Cyprus*. Washington: Government Printing Office.

Keniston, K. 1965. *The Uncommitted*. New York: Harcourt, Brace.

———. 1968. *Young Radicals*. Boston: Atlantic–Little Brown.

Kennedy, J. A. 1952. Problems posed by the analysis of Negro patients. *Psychiatry* 15: 313–327.

Kernberg, O. F. 1966. Structural derivatives of object relationship. *Int. J. Psycho-Anal.* 47: 236–253.

———. 1967. Borderline personality organization. *J. Am. Psychoanal. Assoc.* 15: 641–685.

———. 1970. Factors in the psychoanalytic treatment of narcissistic personalities. *J. Am. Psychoanal. Assoc.* 18: 51–85.

———. 1972. Early ego integration and object relations. In *Patterns of Integration from Biochemical to Behavioral Processes*, ed. G. G. Haydu. *Ann. N.Y. Acad. Sci.* 193: 233–247.

———. 1975. *Borderline Conditions and Pathological Narcissism*. New York: Jason Aronson.

———. 1976. *Object Relations Theory and Clinical Psychoanalysis*. New York: Jason Aronson.

Kinross, L., 1965. *Ataturk: A Biography of Mustafa Kemal, Father of Modern Turkey*. New York: William Morrow.

Klein, M. 1946. Notes on some schizoid mechanisms. *Int. J. Psycho-Anal.* 27:99–110.

———. 1955. On identification. In *Our Adult World and Other Essays*, pp. 55–98. New York: Basic Books.

Kohut, H. 1971. *The Analysis of the Self: A Systematic Approach to the Psychoanalytic Treatment of Narcissistic Personality Disorders*. New York: International Universities Press.

Koranyi, E. K. 1969. Psychodynamic theories of the "survivor syndrome." *Canad. Psychiat. Assn. J.* 14:165–174.

Krystal, H., ed. 1968. *Massive Psychic Trauma*. New York: International Universities Press.

Kubie, L. S. 1965. The ontogeny of racial prejudice. *J. Nerv. Ment. Dis.* 141: 265–273.

Lampl-de Groot, J. 1962. Ego ideal and superego. *Psychoanal. Study Child* 17:94–106.

Langer, W. L. 1971. Foreword. In *The Psychoanalytic Interpretation of History*, ed. B. B. Wolman, pp. vii–x. New York: Basic Books.

Leach, M., ed. 1949. *Standard Dictionary of Folklore, Mythology, and Legend*, vol. A-I: 142–144. New York: Fund & Wagnalls.

Lerner, D. 1962. *The Passing of Traditional Society*. Cambridge, Mass.: The Free Press of Glencoe.

Lewis, R. 1971. *Everyday Life in Ottoman Turkey*. London: B. T. Batsford.

Lifton, R. J. 1961. *Thought Reform and the Psychology of Totalism*. New York: W. W. Norton.

———. 1968. *Death in Life: Survivors of Hiroshima*. New York: Random House.

———. 1970. *History and Human Survival*. New York: Random House.

———. 1972. On psychohistory. In *Psychoanalysis and Contemporary Science*, vol. 1, ed. R. R. Holt and E. Peterfreund, pp. 355–372. New York: Macmillan.

Lifton, R. J., and Olson, E. 1976. The human meaning of total disaster: The Buffalo Creek experience. *Psychiatry* 39:1–18.

Lind, J. R. 1914a. The dream as a simple wish-fulfillment in the Negro. *Psychoanal. Rev.* 1:295–300.

————. 1914b. The color complex in the Negro. *Psychoanal. Rev.* 1:404–414.

Lindemann, E. 1944. Symptomatology and management of acute grief. *Am. J. Psychiatry* 101:141–148.

Loizos, P. 1976. Notes on future anthropological research on Cyprus. In *Regional Variation in Modern Greece and Cyprus: Toward a Perspective on the Ethnography of Greece,* ed M. Dimen and E. Friedl. *Ann. N.Y. Acad. Sci.* 268:355–362.

Lorenzer, A. 1968. Some observations on the latency of symptoms in patients suffering from persecution sequelae. *Int. J. Psycho-Anal.* 49:316–318.

Lustman, S. L. 1962. Defense, symptom, and character. *Psychoanal. Study Child* 17:216–244.

McNall, S. G. 1974. Value systems that inhibit modernization: The case of Greece. *Studies in Comparative International Development* 9:46–63.

————. 1976. Barriers to development and modernization in Greece. In *Regional Variation in Modern Greece and Cyprus: Toward a Perspective on the Ethnography of Greece,* ed. M. Dimen and E. Friedl. *Ann. N.Y. Acad. Sci.* 268:28–42.

Mahler, M. D. 1963. Thoughts about development and individuation. *Psychoanal. Study Child* 18:307–324.

————. 1968. *On Human Symbiosis and the Vicissitudes of Individuation.* New York: International Universities Press.

Mahler, M. D., and Furer, M. 1963. Certain aspects of the separation-individuation phase. *Psychoanal. Q.* 32:1–14.

Markides, K. C. 1977. *The Rise and Fall of the Cyprus Republic.* New Haven: Yale University Press.

Mayes, S. 1960. *Cyprus and Makarios.* London: Putnam.

Mitscherlich, A. 1971. Psychoanalysis and the aggression of large groups. *Int. J. Psycho-Anal.* 52:161–167.

Mitscherlich, A., and Mitscherlich, M. 1975. *The Inability to Mourn: Principles of Collective Behavior.* New York: Grove Press.

Modell, A. 1968. *Object Love and Reality.* New York: International Universities Press.

————. 1976. "The holding environment" and the therapeutic action of psychoanalysis. *J. Am. Psychoanal. Assoc.* 24:285–307.

Money-Kyrle, R. E. 1937. Development of war: Psychological approach. *Brit. J. Med. Psychol.* 16:219–236.

———. 1951. *Psychoanalysis and Politics: A Contribution to the Psychology of Politics and Morals.* New York: W. W. Norton.

Muller, H. J. 1961. *The Loom of History.* New York: American Library. A Mentor Book.

Musaph, H. 1968. Psychodynamics in itching states. *Int. J. Psycho-Anal.* 49:336–339.

Musaph, H., and Prakken, J. R. 1964. *Itching and Scratching.* Basle: Karger.

Myers, H. J., and Yochelson, L. 1948. Color denial in the Negro. *Psychiatry* 11:30–46.

Niederland, W. C. 1956. River symbolism, Part I. *Psychoanal Q.* 25:469–504.

———. 1957. River symbolism, Part II. *Psychoanal Q.* 26:50–75.

———. 1959. Further remarks on river symbolism. *J. Hillside Hospital* 8:109–114.

———. 1961. The problem of the survivor. *J. Hillside Hospital* 10: 233–247.

———. 1964. Psychiatric disorders among persecution victims. *J. Nerv. Ment. Dis.* 139:458–474.

———. 1968. Clinical observations on the "survivor syndrome." *Int. J. Psycho-Anal.* 49:313–315.

———. 1971a. The naming of America. In *The Unconscious Today: Essays in Honor of Max Schur,* ed. M. Kanzer. New York: International Universities Press.

———. 1971b. The history and meaning of California. A psychoanalytic inquiry. *Psychoanal. Q.* 40:485–490.

———. 1971c. Personal communication.

———. 1977. Personal communication.

Novey, S. 1968. *The Second Look: The Reconstruction of Personal History in Psychiatry and Psychoanalysis.* Baltimore: Johns Hopkins Press.

Novick, J., and Kelly, K. 1970. Projection and externalization. *Psychoanal. Study Child* 25:69–95.

Olinick, S. L. 1964. The negative therapeutic reaction. *Int. J. Psycho-Anal.* 45:540–548.

Osgood, C., Suci, G., and Tannenbaum, P. 1957. *The Measurement of Meaning.* Urbana, Ill.: University of Illinois Press.

Özbek, A., and Volkan, V. D. 1976. Psychiatric problems within the satellite extended families of Turkey. *Am. J. Psychother.* 30:576–582.

Öztürk, O. M. 1963. Psychological effects of circumcision as practiced in Turkey: A preliminary report. *Turkish Journal of Pediatrics* 7:126–130.

———. 1966. Folk interpretation of illness in Turkey and its psychological significance. *Turkish Journal of Pediatrics* 7:165–179.

———. 1973. Ritual circumcision and castration anxiety. *Psychiatry* 36:49–60.

Öztürk, O. M., and Volkan, V. D. 1971. The theory and practice of psychiatry in Turkey. *Am. J. Psychother.* 25:240–271.

Parkes, C. M. 1970. Seeking and finding a lost object: Evidence from recent studies of the reaction to bereavement. *Soc. Sci. and Med.* 4:187–201.

———. 1972. *Bereavement: Studies of Grief in Adult Life.* New York: International Universities Press.

Peristiany, J. G. 1976. Anthropological, sociological, and geographical fieldwork in Cyprus. In *Regional Variation in Modern Greece and Cyprus: Toward a Perspective on the Ethnography of Greece*, ed. M. Dimen and E. Friedl. *Ann. N.Y. Acad. Sci.* 268:345–354.

Poland, W. S. 1977. Pilgrimage: Action and tradition in self-analysis. *J. Am. Psychoanal. Assoc.* 25: 319–416.

Pollock, G. H. 1961. Mourning and adaptation. *Int. J. Psycho-Anal.* 42: 341–361.

———. 1977. The mourning process and creative organization. *J. Am. Psychoanal. Assoc.* 25:3–34.

Rabinowitz, S. 1973. Personal communication.

Rangell, L. 1954. The psychology of poise—with a special elaboration on the psychic significance of the snout or perioral region. *Int. J. Psycho-Anal.* 35:313–333.

———. 1974. A psychoanalytic perspective leading currently to the syndrome of the compromise of integrity. *Int. J. Psycho-Anal.* 55:3–12.

———. 1976a. Lessons from Watergate: A derivative for psychoanalysis. *Psychoanal. Q.* 45:37–61.

———. 1976b. Discussion of the Buffalo Creek disaster: The course of psychic trauma. *Am. J. Psychiatry* 133:313–316.

Rapaport, D. 1952. Projective techniques and the theory of thinking. In *The Collected Papers of David Rapaport*, ed. M. M. Gill, pp. 461–469. New York: Basic Books, 1967.

Rappaport, E. P. 1968. Beyond traumatic neurosis. *Int. J. Psycho-Anal.* 49: 719–731.

Reich, A. 1953. Narcissistic object choice in women. In *Annie Reich: Psychoanalytic Contributions*, pp. 179–208. New York: International Universities Press.

Rochlin, G. 1973. *Man's Aggression: The Defense of the Self.* Boston: Gambit.

Roheim, G. 1950a. *Psychoanalysis and Anthropology.* New York: International Universities Press.

———. 1950b. The oedipus complex, magic, and culture. In *Psychoanalysis and the Social Sciences*, 2:173–228. New York: International Universities Press.

Sağlamer, K. 1974. *Ecevit olayı, bir başbakanın, doğumu* [*The Ecevit Incident and the Making of a Prime Minister*], 2 vols. Istanbul: Belge Yayınları.

Sâlışık, S. 1968. *Türk-Yunan ilişkileri tarihi ve etnik'i eterya* [*The History of Turkish-Greek Relations*]. Istanbul: Kitaş.

Savalaş, A. 1975. Personal communication.

Schafer, R. 1968. *Aspects of Internalization.* New York: International Universities Press.

Schlesinger, H. J. 1970. The place of forgetting in memory functioning. *J. Am. Psychoanal. Assoc.* 18:358–371.

Searles, H. F. 1960. *The Nonhuman Environment in Normal Development and in Schizophrenia.* New York: International Universities Press.

———. 1961. Anxiety concerning change, as seen in the psychotherapy of schizophrenic patients—with particular reference to the sense of personal identity. *Int. J. Psycho-Anal.* 42:74–85.

———. 1962. The differentiation between concrete and metaphorical thinking in the recovering schizophrenic patient. *J. Am. Psychoanal. Assoc.* 10:22–49.

———. 1963. The place of neutral therapist-responses in psychotherapy with the schizophrenic patient. *Int. J. Psycho-Anal.* 44:42–56.

———. 1965. *Collected Papers on Schizophrenia and Related Subjects*, pp. 19–38. New York: International Universities Press.

Selçuk, A. 1974. *Üçüncü adam olayı ve neden Ecevit* [*The Third Man Incident and Why Ecevit*]. Istanbul: Sel-Kan Yayınları.

Sendak, M. 1970. *In the Night Kitchen.* New York: Harper and Row.

Sezgin, S. 1975. Personal communication.

Shapiro, E. R., Shapiro, R. L., Zinner, J., and Berkowitz, D. A. 1977. The borderline ego and the working alliance: Indications for family and individual treatment in adolescence. *Int. J. Psycho-Anal.* 58:77–87.

Shapiro, E. R., Zinner, J., Shapiro, R. L., and Berkowitz, D. A. 1975. The influence of family experience on borderline personality development. *Int. Rev. Psychoanal.* 2:399–411.

Shils, E. 1957. Primordial, personal, sacred, and civil ties. *Brit. J. Sociology* 8:130–145.

Simenauer, E. 1968. Late psychic sequelae of man-made disasters. *Int. J. Psycho-Anal.* 49:307–309.

Sinofsky, F., Fitzpatrick, J. J., Potts, L. W., and de Mause, L. 1975. A bibliography of psychohistory. *History of Childhood Quarterly* 2:517–562.

Skinner, J. D. 1966. Symptoms and defense in contemporary Greece—A cross-cultural inquiry. *J. Nerv. Ment. Dis.* 141:478–489.

Smith, L. 1949. *Killers of the Dream.* New York: W. W. Norton.

Solnit, A. J. 1966. Some adaptive functions of aggressive behaviour. In *Psychoanalysis—a General Psychology: Essays in Honor of Heinz Hartmann,* ed. R. M. Loewenstein, L. M. Newman, M. Schur, and A. J. Solnit, pp. 169–189. New York: International Universities Press.

Sonnenberg, S. M. 1974. Children of survivors. *J. Am. Psychoanal. Assoc.* 22:200–204.

Spitz, R. A. 1965. *The First Year of Life.* New York: International Universities Press.

Stanton, A. H. 1958. A comparison of individual and group psychology. *J. Am. Psychol. Assoc.* 6:121–130.

Stephens, R. 1966. *Cyprus, a Place of Arms.* London: Pall Mall Press.

Sterba, R. F. 1965. Remarks on Conrad's "Heart of Darkness." *J. Am. Psychoanal. Assoc.* 13:570–583.

Stern, L. 1977. *The Wrong Horse.* New York: New York Times Books.

Strachey, A. 1957. *The Unconscious Motives of War: A Psychoanalytic Contribution.* New York: International Universities Press.

Sümer, E. A. 1970. Changing dynamic aspects of the Turkish culture and its significance for child training. In *The Child and His Family,* ed. E. J. Anthony and C. Koupernik, pp. 413–428. New York: Wiley Interscience.

Teicher, J. D. 1968. Some observations on identity problems in children of Negro-white marriages. *J. Nerv. Ment. Dis.* 146:249–256.

Tenzel, J. H. 1971. Problem in cross-cultural communication: Cyprus, a case study. Presented at the Fifth World Congress of Psychiatry, Mexico City, Nov. 28–Dec. 4.

Tenzel, J. H., and Gerst, M. S. 1972. The psychology of cross-cultural conflict: A case study. Presented at the 125th Annual Meeting of the American Psychiatric Association, Dallas, Texas, May 1.

Thass-Thienemann, T. 1968. *Symbolic Behaviour,* p. 30. New York: Washington Square Press.

Ticho, G. 1971. Cultural aspects of transference and countertransference. *Bull. Menninger Clin.* 35:313-334

Van der Waals, H. G. 1952. Discussion of the mutual influences in the development of ego and id. *Psychoanalytic Study of the Child* 7:66-68.

Vassiliou, G., and Vassiliou, V. G. 1970. On aspects of child rearing in Greece. In *The Child and His Family*, vol. 1, ed. E. J. Anthony and C. Koupernik, pp. 429-444. New York: Wiley Interscience.

Vassiliou, V. G., and Vassiliou, G. 1974. Variations of the group process across cultures. *J. Group Psychotherapy* 24:55-56.

Vitols, M. M. 1961. The significance of the higher incidence of schizophrenia in the Negro race in North Carolina. *N.C. Med. J.* 22:147-158.

Vitols, M. M., Walter, H. G., and Keeler, M. H. 1963. Hallucinations and delusions in white and Negro schizophrenics. *Am. J. Psychiatry* 120:472-476.

Volkan, V. D. 1963. Five poems by Negro youngsters who faced a sudden desegregation. *Psychiat. Q.* 37: 607-617.

———. 1966a. Some observations of the psychodynamic processes of two Negroes with leukodermia. *Psychiat. Q.* 40:34-42.

———. 1966b. Normal and pathological grief reactions—A guide for the family physician. *Va. Med.* 93:651-656.

———. 1970. Typical findings in pathological grief. *Psychiat. Q.* 44:231-250.

———. 1971. A study of a patient's "re-grief work" through dreams, psychological tests, and psychoanalysis. *Psychiat. Q.* 45:255-273.

———. 1972a. The birds of Cyprus: A psychopolitical observation. *Am. J. Psychother.* 26:378-383.

———. 1972b. The linking objects of pathological mourners. *Arch. Gen. Psychiatry* 27:215-221.

———. 1972c. The recognition and prevention of pathological grief. *Va. Med.* 99:535-540.

———. 1973a. Externalization among Cypriot Turks. *World J. Psychosynthesis* 5:24-30.

———. 1973b. Transitional fantasies in the analysis of a narcissistic personality. *J. Am. Psychoanal. Assoc.* 21:351-376.

———. 1974. Death, divorce, and the physician. In *Marital and Sexual Counseling in Medical Practice*, ed. E. Nash, D. W. Abse, and M. R. Louden, pp. 446-461. Hagerstown, Md.: Harper and Row.

———. 1975a. Cosmic laughter: A study of primitive splitting. In *Tactics and Techniques in Psychoanalytic Therapy*, vol. 2, ed. P. L. Giovacchini, pp. 427-440. New York: Jason Aronson.

_____ .1975b. Turkey. In *World History of Psychiatry,* ed. J. G. Howells, pp. 383–399. New York: Brunner/Mazel.

_____ . 1976. *Primitive Internalized Object Relations.* New York: International Universities Press.

_____ . 1977. Mourning and adaptation after a war. *Am. J. Psychother.* 31: 561–569.

_____ . 1978a. Immortal Atatürk: Narcissism and creativity in a revolutionary leader. *The Psychoanalytic Study of Society,* 9: (in press).

_____ . 1978b. The "glass bubble" of the narcissistic patient. In *Stable Instability, Modern Approaches to the Borderline Syndrome,* ed. J. LeBoit and A. Capponi. New York: Jason Aronson. (In press).

Volkan, V. D., Cillufo, A. F., and Sarvay, T. L. 1976. Re-grief therapy and the function of the linking object as a key to stimulate emotionality. In *Emotional Flooding,* ed. P. Olsen, pp. 179–224. New York: Human Sciences Press.

Volkan, V. D., and Corney, R. T. 1968. Some considerations of satellite states and satellite dreams. *Brit. J. Med. Psychol.* 41:283–290.

Volkan, V. D., and Showalter, C. R. 1968. Known object loss, disturbance in reality testing, and "re-grief work" as a method of brief psychotherapy. *Psychiat. Q.* 42:358–374.

Waelder, R. 1971. Psychoanalysis and history: Application of psychoanalysis to historiography. In *The Psychoanalytic Interpretation of History,* ed. B. B. Wolman, pp. 3–32. New York: Basic Books.

Wangh, M. 1968. A psychogenetic factor in the recurrence of war. *Int. J. Psycho-Anal.* 49:319–335.

Watmough, F. Z. S. 1954. *The Cult of the Budgerigar.* London: Dorset House.

Wedge, B. 1968. Training for a psychiatry of international relations. *Am. J. Psychiatry* 125:731–736.

Werner, H. 1948. *Comparative Psychology of Mental Development.* New York: International Universities Press.

West, L. J. 1967. The psychobiology of racial violence. *Arch. Gen. Psychiatry* 16:645–651.

Wheelis, A. 1950. The place of action in personality change. *Psychiatry* 13:135–148.

Williams, R. M., and Parkes, C. M. 1975. Psychosocial effects of disaster: Birth rate in Aberfan. *Brit. Med. J.* 2:303–304.

Winnicott, D. 1963. Psychiatric disorders in terms of infantile maturational process. In *The Maturational Process and the Facilitating Environment,* pp. 230–241. New York: International Universities Press.

Winnik, H. Z. 1968. Contribution to symposium on psychic traumatization through social catastrophe. *Int. J. Psycho-Anal.* 49:298–305.

Yaşın, O. 1958. *Kıbrıs Mektubu [The Cyprus Letter]*. Istanbul: Varlık Yayınevi.

_____. 1964. *Kanlı Kıbrıs [Bloody Cyprus]*. Istanbul: Varlık Yayınevi.

_____. 1965. *Oğlum Savaş' a Mektuplar [Letters to My Son Savaş]*. Nicosia: Çevre Yayınları.

Yurdanur, S. M. 1974. *Dün Atatürk, bu gün Ecevit [Yesterday Atatürk, Today Ecevit]*. Istanbul: Gül Yayınları.

Xydis, S. G. 1973. *Cyprus: Reluctant Republic*. The Hague: Mouton.

Zinner, J., and Shapiro, R. 1972. Projective identification as a mode of perception and behavior in families of adolescents. *Int. J. Psycho-Anal.* 53:527–530.

Name Index

Subject Index